Whaddaya Mean I Gotta Be Lean?

Building the bridge from job satisfaction to corporate profit

Jeff Hajek

Velaction Continuous Improvement, LLC

Whaddaya Mean I Gotta Be Lean?
Building the bridge from job satisfaction to corporate profit by Jeff Hajek

ATTENTION: QUANTITY DISCOUNTS ARE AVAILABLE TO YOUR ORGANIZATION. For more information, please contact the publisher.

Velaction Continuous Improvement™, LLC
P.O. Box 14700
Mill Creek, WA 98082
Orders@Velaction.com
www.Velaction.com
1-800-670-5805

ISBN 978-1-60628-001-0
Printed and bound in the United States of America.

Publisher's Cataloging-in-Publication
Hajek, Jeff
Whaddaya mean I gotta be lean? : Building the bridge from job satisfaction to corporate profit/ Jeff Hajek.
p. cm.
Includes bibliographical references and index.
LCCN 2008927376
ISBN-13: 978-1-60628-001-0
ISBN-10: 1-60628-001-5
1. Job satisfaction. 2. Total quality management.
I. Title. II. Title: Whaddaya mean I gotta be lean?
HF5549.5.J63H35 2009 650.1
QBI08-600142

Contents

DISCLAIMER

The purpose of this book is to provide information on Lean and job satisfaction. The information is not intended to provide advice about any legal, financial, accounting, engineering, tax, psychological, or other professional services. If legal or other expert assistance is necessary, the services of a competent professional should be sought.

This book is designed to educate and entertain. It includes information gathered from multiple sources, including many personal experiences. The reader should use this book as a general guide and not as the ultimate source of information. It is not the purpose of this manual to include every possible bit of information regarding this subject, but rather to complement and supplement other resources available to the reader. You are urged to read as much available material as you can find and to learn as much as possible about Lean and job satisfaction; you are then encouraged to tailor the information to your individual needs. The suggestions offered may not be suitable for every situation. Likewise, the examples provided within are not meant to imply that the reader will achieve the exact same results. Each instance will vary.

The author has made every effort to make sure that the information contained in this book is reliable and accurate based on information available as of the publication date. However, it is difficult to ensure that all information provided is entirely accurate and up-to-date. Therefore, the author and the publisher accept no responsibility for any inaccuracies or omissions and specifically disclaim any liability, loss, or risk, personal or otherwise, that is incurred as a consequence, directly or indirectly, of the use and/or application of any of the contents of this book. While inspired by actual events, all case studies, events, locations, organizations, persons, and characters contained in this material are completely fictional. Any resemblance to any events, locations, organizations, persons, or characters, real or fictional, living or deceased, is entirely coincidental and unintentional. There is no guarantee that websites mentioned herein will remain active.

If you do not agree with, and do not wish to be bound by the above terms, do not read this book. Immediately return it to your place of purchase, or send it to the publisher, with a copy of your receipt, for a refund.

About the Author

Jeff Hajek, MBA, is a continuous improvement expert and an authority on managing change at the front line. For more than fifteen years, Jeff has played a critical role in guiding teams through major transformations in the workplace.

He has extensive leadership experience, a robust business background, and a deep understanding of the needs of the teams in the trenches. His efforts have spurred Lean success at a variety of companies—from small businesses to *Fortune*® 500s, and from the front office to the shop floor. This rare blend of knowledge and practical know-how uniquely qualifies him to help companies enhance their bottom line—by developing the skill set of their front line.

Jeff is a successful author, speaker, and entrepreneur. He is a graduate of the elite United States Military Academy at West Point, and is the founder of Velaction Continuous Improvement™, LLC, a company dedicated to maximizing Lean success by creating win-win solutions for the front line, their managers, and their companies.

For more information, please visit: *www.Velaction.com*.

Acknowledgments

First and foremost, I want to thank my wife and children for the opportunity to write this book and to own a business. They are an inspiration to me and without their love and support, this book would not have been possible. They are the reason I kept working when my eyes started to glaze over from the countless hours at my computer.

I'd also like to thank my family and friends for helping build a foundation that led me to this point in my life. My sister-in-law, Lisa, deserves an individual note of appreciation for her endless supply of support and encouragement to our family during this process.

A few other people deserve special mention. I am very grateful to Kathleen Bernard, a manager and Lean enthusiast at Starbucks®, for her optimism and valuable commentary, and to John Byrd, CEO of Productivity Plus, for his wisdom and friendship.

I also want to express my appreciation to the teams I have worked with throughout my career. I learned so much from you.

Thank you as well to the team behind the scenes: Michele DeFilippo, Stephen Evans, Susan Kendrick, and Charles Tichenor.

Foreword

THIS BOOK ISN'T JUST ABOUT LEAN. It's really about all forms of continuous improvement; Lean is just the most widely used method. Other approaches include the Toyota® Production System (TPS), Just-in-Time (JIT) manufacturing, agile manufacturing, Six Sigma®, Theory of Constraints (TOC), flow production, and countless other internally developed systems.

These methods have some significant differences, but they still share many common traits, tools, and techniques. Each is used for solving problems, and each causes substantial changes in the lives of employees and their managers. The nuts and bolts of the systems—things like brainstorming, flowcharts, data collection, and many other tools—show up in several of the improvement philosophies.

This book is intended for individuals who are going through any stage of a continuous improvement transition. While some sections specifically address Lean, you can apply the majority of the content to all of these philosophies. This book can help you, no matter what improvement methodology is changing your life.

Introduction

YOUR FUTURE IS BRIGHT. You may find that hard to believe right now, especially if you are in the middle of a major change. Transitions can be hard and can dampen your spirit. However, you will soon see a light at the end of the tunnel.

Unfortunately for many frontline workers, that light looks like it is shining only for your employer. As your boss has undoubtedly told you, Lean works for companies. You have probably heard stories about amazing gains that other businesses have made—companies that have come back from the brink of bankruptcy, or that have used Lean to become the dominant player in their markets.

The part of the story that is often left out, though, is how Lean makes you feel. The fact is, at times, Lean can be unsettling, difficult, and overwhelming. While this is most common during their initial exposure to Lean, people anywhere on their continuous improvement journey can experience these challenges.

This gap in information creates a major problem. You hear how great Lean will be, and then experience something completely different. It is a recipe for a job satisfaction disaster. This book tackles that problem and gives you insight into what you might go through during the hard parts of the transition. More importantly, it shows you the brass ring—what Lean can do for you personally, and how you can share in the benefits that Lean offers your company.

Those gains might currently seem out of reach for you. You might think that you are stuck, like you do not have any options. But when you finish reading this book, you will see that you *do* have choices—lots of them! You will learn how to make changes in how you approach your job—changes that will make things better for you. You will also discover practical, easy to implement strategies that will help you clear the hurdles that you will encounter in a Lean company.

You will face one decision, however, that is far more important than any other. When you finish reading this book, you will have to decide if you want to continue feeling the way that you do right now about your job. If you are like many people, you want more. More satisfaction at work. More recognition for the value you bring to your company. More days when you wake up excited about your job instead of dreading it. More occasions when you look up at the clock and are surprised that it is already quitting time. More instances when you have energy left over for your life outside of work.

It is probably hard to envision that these things are within your reach, especially if you are currently going through a rough patch. Keep this in mind, though. You have an amazing potential to change your life for the better in a Lean world.

How do I know this? Because in my career, I have had the good fortune to encounter a wide range of people and organizations. I have worked closely with frontline employees and with executives, in industries as diverse as electronics, the military, and heavy manufacturing. My path has crossed many functions—service, administration, and fabrication, as well as injection molding, painting, assembling, marketing, engineering, accounting, and more. Despite all the differences in industries, job descriptions, and personality types, some common themes emerged.

The first is that Lean can make people feel isolated. Whether someone is a manager of a human resources department or a welder on the shop floor, he can often feel very alone in dealing with the substantial and often unwelcome changes that have landed squarely on his doorstep.

The second theme is that employees probably didn't have much say in the decision to start their Lean journey. And it is a journey. People embarking down the Lean path are like the early pioneers loading up the wagon trains and heading toward the great unknown—all in the hope of creating a better life. The difference, though, is that the settlers *chose* to go on their epic adventure. The frontline workers starting Lean, in all likelihood, did not. And yet, there they are, going down a path that they probably would rather not be taking.

The final and most important theme is that attitude is everything during a transition. People who are upbeat and accepting of changes tend to do well in a Lean environment. People who are successful at continuous improvement also tend to view their jobs more positively. So, which is the chicken, and which is the egg? Do people who thrive in a Lean company feel more cheerful as a result, or do optimistic people just do better with Lean?

It doesn't really matter which happens first—the two go together. The more optimistic and proactive an individual is about change, the more likely she is to be successful overall; as she achieves Lean success, she becomes more accepting of change and gets more satisfaction at work as a result. This doesn't mean that every person with a positive attitude will do better than every person with a negative one. It just means that an optimistic view about a change takes an individual further than she would otherwise go.

A story that highlights these themes has stuck with me throughout the years. I facilitated a *kaizen* event (a weeklong improvement project) at a factory early on in its Lean voyage. The team was pretty typical—some people jumped right on board with Lean; others positioned themselves as opponents. Most just hung out in the middle, nervously waiting to see what was going to happen next. One person in that group was a clear skeptic, but had not yet decided to fight Lean. He spent a lot of time in the back of the room with his arms crossed across his chest. He did what he was asked to do by the team members, but he didn't take it upon himself to do anything extra; and he clearly lacked the enthusiasm of the Lean supporters. We finished the week with some solid gains in the manufacturing area, and then went back to our busy jobs.

Some months later, when I was walking across the shop floor I saw him again. As I passed by his station, he proudly held up a strange-looking tool he had created with his manufacturing engineer—two wrenches welded together into a new device.[1]

Was the new tool a huge deal? Probably not. It likely saved only a few minutes each day and prevented some occasional scraped knuckles. Was what the tool *represented* important? Absolutely. In that moment, he wholly embodied the spirit of continuous improvement by putting the principles of Lean into action. He had created his own solution. He made his job better. He improved his satisfaction.

As we were chatting, I saw a pronounced difference in him from when we had worked together during the *kaizen,* but the transformation obviously didn't happen overnight. It probably began when standardization made his job better. He might have started to like having structure to his workday. Perhaps he began to see how *andon* (warning) lights brought him the help he needed when there were production problems. At some point, he likely started looking forward to switching to new stations so he could have some variety in his job. Only after he had some experience, did he take on the challenge of solving a problem completely on his own. He took the initiative to get rid of a thorn in his side—one that he probably would not have even noticed several months earlier.

His life got better when he chose to help himself. He could have just plodded along in a situation that he didn't like, but he chose not to. He acted in a way that improved his circumstances. Chances are, the good feelings that he created for himself carried over to personal relationships and other aspects of his life outside work.

What does that story mean to you? Well, the initial question to be answered is who "you" are. This book is, first and foremost, for frontline employees and junior leaders who are the heart and soul of any company. You are the unsung heroes of the business world.

---

[1] Always keep safety in mind! Qualified personnel should approve any custom tools.

You do the real work that provides the value that customers want and, more importantly, pay for. You are also the ones who pay the biggest price for Lean, and at the same time have the least say in the changes that are happening around you.

In fact, there is a good chance that you don't even have a choice about reading this book. Your boss might have handed it to you as a homework assignment. Why would she do that? Because the goal of this book is to help you find win-win solutions for both you *and* your company. The strategies discussed later in this book work for one main reason: they serve not only your interests, but they meet your manager's needs as well. *Whaddaya Mean I Gotta Be Lean?* helps you improve your satisfaction, and your boss gets a more effective employee in the process. *Both* parties get what they want.

With that in mind, the secondary audience for this book is the leadership in your company—to give them a better understanding of how you think, what you need in your job to be successful, and how Lean impacts you in a different way than it does them. It also reinforces the message that your satisfaction supports corporate goals such as improved profit or better customer service—things that are critical for a business's survival.

This book also supports your leaders. When you become more engaged, more satisfied, and better at problem solving, you free up your manager's time—something all bosses need more of! This allows him to work on the parts of his job that he wants to do, like implementing strategy, rather than the things he has to do, like resolving employee complaints.

Bottom line: when you take charge of your satisfaction, you, your manager, and your company all come out ahead.

As you read this, know that your managers and executives are learning along the way, just like you are. They will have to choose whether they see Lean as a tool to get better performance out of their workers, or whether they view it as a partnership with their teams. If they choose the former, they will still be able to show progress on measures related to quality, delivery, and cost (QDC).

If, however, they choose the latter, they can have a satisfied, productive, engaged workforce—and achieve *world-class* gains in the process.

So, let's go back to what that story about the new tool means to you. The purpose of that anecdote is to make you aware that you can do things to make your Lean experience better. Your company and your leaders play a big role in how Lean affects you, but they do not play the only role. You actually have a great deal of control. It doesn't matter whether you are a Lean novice or an expert, or whether you are an advocate or completely opposed to it. Unless you are one hundred percent satisfied, you can improve your situation. Choose not to settle for things as they are now. Continuous improvement applies not only to your company, but to your life as well. Tomorrow will be no better than today unless you do something about it.

That's why I created this book. I wanted to help people discover their ability to improve their situation. It is disheartening to see frontline employees suffer needlessly at work—especially when there are solutions that can make things easier. I want the experience that I have gathered over the years to help more people bridge the gap from "what is" to "what can be." I want them to achieve fulfillment in a Lean environment.

Think of your Lean experience as a journey. Each day is different, filled with new challenges and ever-greater opportunities. As you progress down the continuous improvement path, you can do it the hard way and go it alone. Or you can benefit from the experience of those who have gone before you. So, grab your walking stick, lace up your boots, go to the next page, and start your Lean adventure with a travel guide in hand.

CHAPTER 1

What's in it for you?

IMAGINE THAT YOU LIVED SEVERAL DECADES AGO. You wake up one brisk morning to a brightly shining sun, throw on a jacket to beat back the morning chill, and head out to run a few errands. You can see your breath in the air as you walk down the street and set your sights on one of the few shops that is open at this early hour—the neighborhood bakery. As soon as you step through the door, smells immediately warm you from the inside . . . hot cinnamon rolls, a variety of sweet pastries, and the comforting aroma of freshly baked bread.

You walk up to the counter and ask Stan, your neighborhood baker, for a loaf of the usual—his mouthwatering homemade white bread, steaming hot and fresh from the oven. After the usual chitchat, he turns to retrieve a loaf, but then suddenly does something unexpected. He asks you if you want it sliced.

You are stunned. He has never asked you that before, but you immediately grasp the magnitude of this wonderful new option. You won't have to clean up the crumbs that fall all over your kitchen counter. You won't have to wash a knife. You'll have perfectly even slices, and sandwiches will take a fraction of the time. Oh, and your morning toast will be ready in an instant. Sliced bread, whenever you want it. Then, you start to worry that there must be a catch. It's *got* to cost extra. But, no—Stan tells you his competition down the street has been slicing their customers' bread for a while. Now his shop has to do it to keep from losing business.

So, you say, sure, you'd love to have it sliced, and you hear a long suffering sigh from behind the counter. Lou, Stan's right-hand man, is not all that pleased about your decision—he is the one who has to do the slicing. Lou still has all his other, regular work to do and now has this new task on top of everything else. You see him throw a quick, angry glare at Stan's back when he thinks no one is looking and you hear him grumbling to himself as you pay for your purchase.

Sliced bread wasn't going to go away, no matter how much Lou wished it would. The change that Stan forced upon his assistant spawned one of the most well known expressions of all time: "Why, that's the greatest thing since sliced bread!" Bakery patrons everywhere welcomed the change with open arms. Slicing spread like wildfire to shops everywhere. Its popularity guaranteed extra work. Even if Lou had tried to resist the change, he would never have had a chance.

If Lean is changing your life in the same way that sliced bread altered Lou's, you are walking in his shoes. And, like sliced bread, Lean is here to stay. It is not going anywhere, and for precisely the reason that sliced bread stuck around—both are good for the customer. Unfortunately, you are experiencing just what Lou had to go through. Your boss is telling you to do something that you probably don't want to do, and it is reducing your satisfaction.

Anyone who has ever gone through a big transition can relate to what you are going through right now with Lean. The pattern repeats itself all the time. A change comes along. It could stem from a new invention or perhaps customers who want different services. Maybe increased competition is spurring your company to look for more efficient ways to deliver products and services. Whatever the trigger, companies react by shifting the way they do business. Employees might become dissatisfied during the transition. Then they adjust—or at least most of them do—and eventually, "the new way" simply becomes "the way." Then another change happens. And then another. And another. The cycle continues.

Lean is just one of many changes that have affected people in the workplace. But, in fifty years, "Lean manufacturing" will be a term for the history books—not because the concept will fade away. Just the opposite. Consider the example of "interchangeable parts manufacturing." Nobody uses that term nowadays. Why not? Because interchangeable parts are used everywhere. Customers expect that the parts they buy will fit together. That concept is no longer a novel idea. Lean will be like that, too. The "Lean" in "Lean manufacturing" will fade away as Lean principles become even more widespread. Eventually, people will just assume that manufacturers are Lean.

Until then, though, you are in Lou's position: you work in a business where your boss is asking you to do extra tasks for a customer. Your world is now different, but not by your choosing. In the midst of change you now have to figure out how to find satisfaction.

Why is being satisfied at work so important?

Let's take a step back and consider why being satisfied with your job is so important. Take a look at the following pie chart. A week contains 168 hours. Where do they all go? About a third of those hours are spent sleeping. About half of the remaining time is spent at work, getting ready for work, or going to and from work. That leaves you only about half of your waking hours for yourself. Slice off a large chunk of that time for television, and even fewer hours remain.[2]

Wait a minute, though. That does not mean the leftover hours are all for fun and games—you still have to complete your chores, sort through mail, run errands, prepare and eat meals, and do the tidal wave of other things that make up your daily schedule. You

---

[2] (Yang, 2004). *UC Berkeley News* reported that the average American watches 170 minutes of TV per day.

might also have ongoing commitments to friends and family that take up some of your free time, as well.

The end result? The amount of time that is *really* yours pales in comparison to the amount of time you spend working. Your personal situation may not be exactly the same as the one in the example, but you get the idea—you do not have a lot of time to yourself outside of work. So, logic dictates that the place where you can make the biggest impact on your overall quality of life is to figure out how to be more satisfied at work.

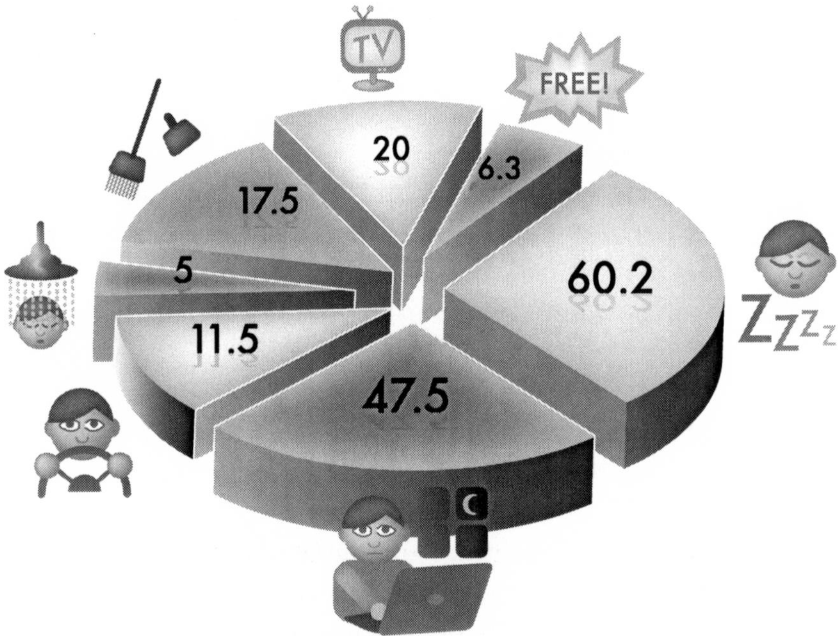

You spend over half of your waking hours at work. Shouldn't you be satisfied with your job?

So, what is job satisfaction?

So, what does job satisfaction really mean, anyway? For the purpose of this book, job satisfaction results from having the reality of your employment match the expectations that you have about your job. To complicate matters, job satisfaction fluctuates. Since working conditions are rarely static, your contentment rises and falls as things around you change (and Lean certainly changes things).

Imagine if you could measure satisfaction with an instrument like a speedometer. At the far left of the gauge, you would find someone who hates his job and can't stand going to work every morning. On the opposite end, someone else would have to be dragged away from her desk at the end of the day. Where are you on that scale? Unless you are one of the lucky few in the "very satisfied" range, there is room for improvement in how you feel about work.

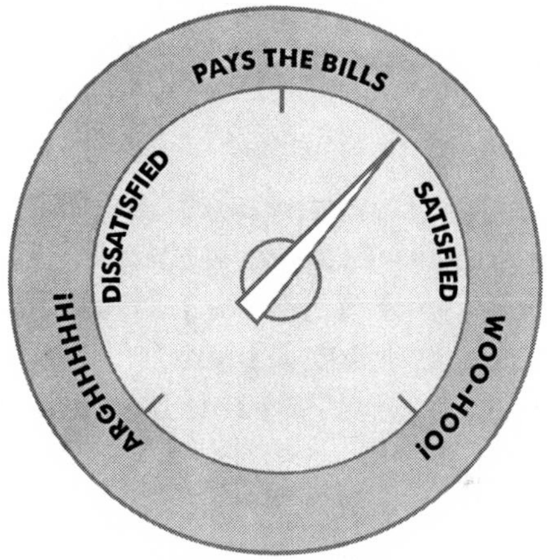

Where does *your* job satisfaction level fall?

When it comes right down to it, job satisfaction is a relatively simple concept. There is a bunch of stuff you expect, and then there is what you actually get. The closer those two things are to each other, the more satisfied you are.

Now, not all aspects of your job affect your satisfaction in the same way. In the 1950s, a psychologist named Frederick Herzberg presented the idea that the issues that affect job satisfaction fall into two main categories.

The first, he called "hygiene issues." These are the "must haves"; these factors make you less satisfied if they are missing, but don't add much to your satisfaction when they are present. An example of a hygiene issue is being safe from injury on the job. Your job satisfaction doesn't increase each time you leave work with all your limbs intact. However, if you think those limbs are at risk, your job satisfaction takes a big hit.

The other category contains factors called "motivators." In this group, more is better. If autonomy is important to you, more freedom to do things your own way makes you more satisfied in your job.[3] If you figure out how to increase your motivators, both in number and strength, you will see improvement in how you feel at work.

The list of factors that affect job satisfaction is practically endless. Some of the most common are listed here:

- ***Pay and Benefits.***
  - *Salary.* Does your company offer competitive wages or overtime opportunities if you want them?
  - *Benefits.* Does your employer provide health insurance, dental insurance, or 401(k) plans?
  - *Perks.* Are there "extras" like free meals or on-site day care?

- ***Relationships.***
  - *Relationship with bosses.* Is your boss competent? Do you like her leadership style? Do you trust her? Trust can be an important factor. One group of economists actually tried to figure out exactly how much it matters. They found that a moderate improvement in trust can provide a boost to job satisfaction equal to a thirty-six percent pay raise.[4]
  - *Relationships with peers.* Do you enjoy the people you work with? Employees consistently rank this as one of the most important factors for satisfaction.

---

3 (Syptak, Marsland and Ulmer, 1999)

4 (Sahadi, 2006)

- ***Job Factors.***
  - *Enjoyment.* How well do you like what you do?
  - *Importance.* Do you think your job matters?
  - *Autonomy.* Consider how much control and influence you have in your day-to-day role. Can you change things in your job?
  - *Variety.* Do you get bored doing the same thing day after day?
  - *Seniority.* Does your time on the job affect promotions, job security, and how benefits are administered?
  - *Being appropriately placed.* Are you in the right job that plays to your strengths?
  - *Skill set.* Do you have the expertise to do your work?
  - *Flexibility.* Does your company provide flexible schedules?

- ***The Company.***
  - *Reputation.* How is your company viewed?
  - *Job security.* Do you believe your company is stable? Are you worried about layoffs?
  - *Prestige.* Do you help provide a popular product or service?
  - *Company policies.* Are policies fair?

- ***Working Environment.***
  - *Safety concerns.* Do people get injured on the job?
  - *Physical factors.* Are dirt, heat, and lighting conditions problematic?
  - *Tools and equipment.* Do people have high quality tools that make their jobs easier?
  - *Length of commute.* Do you have a long commute that reduces your free time and raises your stress?
  - *Control.* Do you have choices about personal space, overtime, and time to socialize with coworkers?

As you read this list, some items undoubtedly struck more of a chord for you than others did. Every person has his own way of ranking these factors.

Job satisfaction is in the eye of the beholder.

Suppose, for instance, you and a coworker both have to work a lot of overtime. You might love the extra money, since you have two kids in college or a big mortgage or a vacation you want to take. On the other hand, your coworker might be a star softball player who hates missing his games.

Job satisfaction is defined by the individual.

As you see, one size does *not* fit all when it comes to job satisfaction. It would be a big mistake to approach any discussion on the subject without understanding that only one person can define it—you.

How does being satisfied help you?

Job satisfaction has a long list of benefits for employees.

Employee Benefits of Job Satisfaction:

- ***Life satisfaction.*** How satisfied you are on the job affects how content you are in general.[5] Tough times at work can strain personal relationships. Have you ever had a bad day on the job and found yourself snapping at someone at home because of it? Nearly half (forty-two percent) of workers report that work pressures affect their personal relationships.[6] The more fulfilled you are at work, the more content you can be at home and in your life in general.
- ***More energy.*** You might have noticed the difference between "good tired" and "bad tired." Good tired is the feeling of being pleasantly worn out after playing eighteen holes of golf on a sunny afternoon. Bad tired comes from your job draining your batteries so you have less energy to face the pile of work on your desk, and less drive to sign up for that evening class you always wanted to take. Job satisfaction helps keep those batteries charged and make things easier all around.
- ***Workplace rewards.*** Satisfaction makes people more engaged in their jobs. This can lead to better performance along with other benefits—bigger pay bumps, better assignments, and faster promotions.
- ***More stability.*** If you like your job, you are less likely to want to leave. Staying with your current employer helps you avoid the hassles of a job search, the possible loss of benefits, and the challenge of being a new employee on the bottom of the totem pole.

---

5 (Centre for European Labour Market Research, 2006)

6 (The Marlin Company, 2001)

- ***Lower stress.*** Some stress is okay. It helps you perform better in certain situations, like sports or when trying to get that last-minute shipment out the door. However, feeling chronically stressed is a problem. This is the feeling that many people get when they no longer like their jobs. Never-ending pressure accumulates over time and often ends up at home with you at the end of the day. As a result, stress and job *dissatisfaction* go hand-in-hand. Reducing your stress can help you avoid many problems.
  - High stress causes weight gain for several reasons:
    - Stress-related food cravings tend to be for unhealthy foods.
    - Stress increases cortisol (a stress hormone), which can slow metabolism.
    - High stress levels can increase abdominal fat storage, leading to greater health risks.
    - Weight gain tends to reduce self-esteem and makes people less energetic.
    - Long hours (a cause of stress) and reduced energy (a result of low job satisfaction) make weight control difficult. When time is tight, people tend to exercise less.[7] Plus, stress from working long hours can mean more trips to fast food restaurants.
  - Stress can cause several health problems:
    - Elevated blood pressure.
    - Back and neck pain.
    - Dizzy spells.
    - Anxiety and tension.
    - Sleeplessness.
    - High cholesterol.
    - Ulcers.
    - Increased cardiac risk.

---

7 (Scott, 2007)

  - Migraine headaches.
  - Diabetes and asthma (both worsened by stress).
- Stress lowers the body's immunity and increases the risk of infection.
- Stress-related illness can cost you a lot of money to treat.
- High stress can cause you to use up your personal days.
- Chronic stress raises the likelihood of smoking, alcohol abuse, and drug addiction.[8]

Most employees are not satisfied

Ask yourself if your job is as rewarding as you want it to be. If you are like most people, the answer to that question is, "No!" In one survey, less than fifty percent of the American workforce said they were satisfied with their jobs. This is down from around sixty percent two decades earlier.[9] At least part of the reason for this increase in dissatisfaction is because people also think that their work is getting harder. In fact, sixty-two percent of employees reported that their workload had increased over the previous six months.[10]

What influences job satisfaction?

So, you now know how job satisfaction can be beneficial to your life, but you may still have questions about what contributes to job satisfaction. Employees commonly believe that much of it originates from corporate policy.

But take a step back and contemplate where *your* satisfaction comes from on a day-to-day basis. Regardless of the work you do, several factors influence job satisfaction. Relationships with your coworkers, trust in your manager, personal space, and advancement opportunities all tend to affect your level of fulfillment.

What do these examples have in common? They are all local rather than corporate-level, factors. Company policies certainly

---

[8] (National Institute on Drug Abuse, 2005)

[9] (Amble, 2007)

[10] (Schwartz, 2004)

play a role, but they don't dictate how well you like the person who works next to you; they don't make your manager trustworthy; they don't appreciate your hard work or recommend you for a promotion.

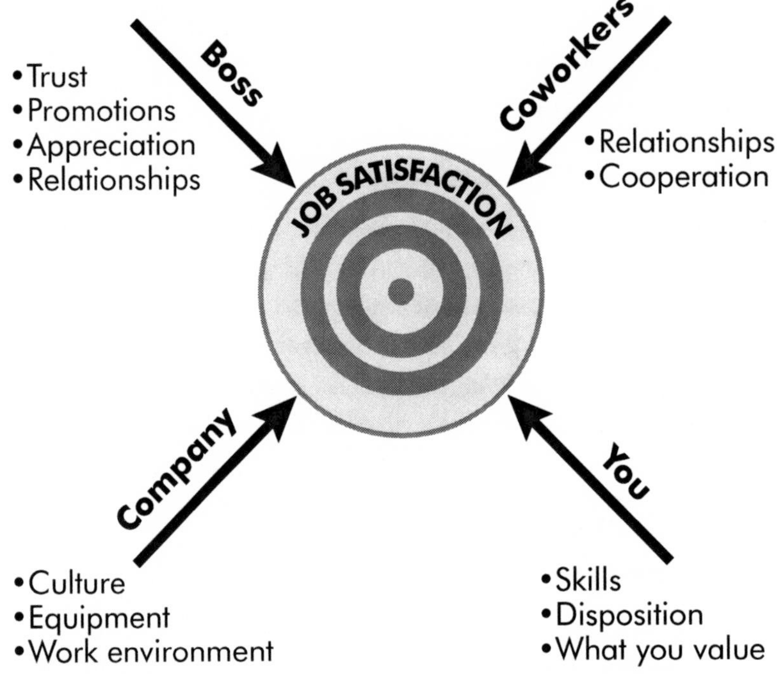

Many local factors play a role in determining your job satisfaction.

On the surface, it might seem to be a problem that so many local factors can affect your satisfaction. The reality is that having a lot of local influencers is actually good for you. Some companies treat their policies as if they were written in stone. If you had to change those corporate policies in order to improve your satisfaction, you'd be facing an uphill battle. However, having so many local factors gives you many options to increase your contentment on the job. Chances are, you have a lot more input at the local level (i.e. with your manager or coworkers) than at the corporate level (i.e. with your CEO). And that leads to one of the most important questions you can ask about your satisfaction . . .

Who's responsible for making you satisfied?

Many factors and many people play a role in your satisfaction. Shareholders, executives, managers, consultants, coworkers, customers, vendors, and even your own family and friends—they all have a hand in determining how you feel about your job. As you might guess, not everyone on this list has your personal fulfillment as his or her number one priority. Each person has his own needs and agendas that compete with yours. If your coworker gets what he needs for his own satisfaction and he can help you out at the same time, he is on your side. If your needs are in opposition to his, who do you think he will try to satisfy first?

There is one person, though, that you can count on to have your best interest at heart. The most important person that influences your satisfaction is the person you see in the mirror every morning.

You are not only the one with the most vested in improving your satisfaction; you are the one with the most control over it.

That's right. *You* can do more for your own satisfaction than any other person or group can, both at work and at home. With a little creativity, you can learn to do countless things to improve your situation; this book will teach you how.

Understanding that you have the power to change your satisfaction level is important, *but* it is only one piece of the story. The other piece is harder to hear. It is about responsibility.

Basically, two types of people will read this book. The first looks outward for fulfillment. He believes that *the people who surround him* should take responsibility for improving *his* satisfaction. He thinks that life would be perfect if his manager would just give him a raise or if a certain coworker would just be a little less short-tempered.

Sometimes, the "outward looker" gets lucky. Maybe his boss is facing high turnover. She might boost salaries to keep employees from leaving her department. Perhaps the irritable coworker gets busy on a project and is out of the office for a while. In both cases, the gains are *side effects* of the boss and the coworker each doing what *she* needed to do to meet *her* needs. Once their needs change (and needs always change) the satisfaction for the "outward looker" goes away.

Rarely will anyone at work make a change *only* because they want to satisfy you. People will try to meet your needs—as long as it meets *their* needs as well. If you rely on other people to improve your satisfaction, you are in for a roller coaster ride.

The second type of person is the "inward looker." She understands that *she* is the one who is ultimately responsible for her own satisfaction. She knows that other people can influence her circumstances and that she will always face obstacles to being satisfied. But she also knows that it is *her* job to react to those barriers and to overcome them. She realizes that she always has choices. This type of person generally responds well to adverse conditions. She chooses not to be a passive bystander, but prefers to take action to make her situation better.

What is the best way to take charge and improve your satisfaction? Pick actions that make your situation better, but that benefit other people at the same time. Think about it. If something that helps you hinders your coworker, you'll have to work twice as hard to make it happen. She will protect her own satisfaction and try to block you. If, however, that coworker sees that there is something in it for her as well, she will not only let you do it, but she might even help you get what you want.

Let's say you decide that you want to personalize your shared cubicle. You might tack up posters of a musical group that you like. Unfortunately, your coworker does not like that band and resists your efforts, making things difficult for you. Instead of posters, then, you might choose to bring in some plants, which you know your coworker is okay with. Working on your green thumb wasn't your first choice for making your cubicle homier, but you still like having the plants at your desk. The added benefit? Your coworker might add to the indoor garden or help take care of it. While you would have preferred the reminder of that memorable concert instead of the plants, creating an adversarial condition and damaging a relationship is too high of a cost—especially when a small change could benefit both of you.

When you create win-win situations, you encounter much less resistance and get more of what you need.

In the next chapter, we will explore the corporation's role in your satisfaction. For now, though, just assume that you are on your own at the local level. This doesn't mean your company won't do anything to help you; it just means you'll need to use a little finesse when you make changes so that your employer realizes it is getting something from you as well. If you understand how your company thinks, you will have a better shot at getting what you want.

Your company must believe it is getting something in return for spending money to improve your job satisfaction.

For instance, you might argue that the company doesn't pay well enough, and you might claim that big raises will help improve retention. However, if nobody has been quitting over pay issues, the company may not believe that higher salaries will do anything to keep employees from leaving. If they don't think they will get something in return—better retention, in this case—for the raises, guess what? Your paycheck isn't going to budge. On the other hand, if the company really does have a high turnover rate and it really does pay below average, your argument holds water and you may see a change.

Everyone is different

As you move forward in this book and start to take steps to improve your job satisfaction, consider this: not every person runs at the same speed or lifts the same weight. Just as physical characteristics determine certain abilities, your basic personality influences your level of job satisfaction. Some studies even suggest that a genetic predisposition increases the likelihood you will feel a particular way about your job.[11]

If you have always been the half empty type, you might be surprised, and even a little disheartened, to learn that your DNA affects your job satisfaction. You might think that it means your satisfaction is predetermined. It certainly is a challenge to fight your genes, but your genetic makeup doesn't guarantee you will have low job satisfaction. It just influences it. You can do things to compensate for the way you are wired.

Let's look at a more obvious example of how people overcome their genes to get what they want. Pretend, for a moment, that you have fair skin. Since you know you are prone to burning if you stay outside longer than fifteen minutes, you understand that you need to take some action to protect yourself if you want to spend a day at the beach. You will have to put forth some extra effort to avoid the pain of a bad burn.

You could slather on sunscreen, sit under an umbrella, put on a long-sleeved shirt, or wear a hat with a big brim on it. You have to decide if enjoying a day of sun and surf with your friends is worth the time and energy of the prevention.

Similarly, you will have to ask yourself the same question about work. You must decide if the advantages of being satisfied with your job are worth some extra effort on your part.

How can job satisfaction change?

You now know *what* contributes to it, *who* contributes to it, and most importantly, whose job it is to manage it—yours! If you want to actually improve it, though, you have to also understand the specifics of *how* satisfaction changes.

---

[11] (Segala, 1999)

Overall, managing job satisfaction comes from understanding what matters to you and simply making sure that there are more good things than bad things at work. Since satisfaction is unique to each person, not surprisingly, the issues that are important to you may not matter as much to your coworker.

Take a look at the **Satisfaction Contraption** in the illustration. In essence, it is a scale. On one side of the beam is the Good Stuff bucket; on the other side is the Bad Stuff bucket. At the base are the "Must Haves." When the Good Stuff bucket is heavier than the Bad Stuff bucket, satisfaction outweighs dissatisfaction. Obviously, the reverse is true as well.

When your Good Stuff outweighs your Bad Stuff you are satisfied.

Does your company provide a great health plan? Drop that "block" into the Good Stuff bucket. Does your boss let you have a flexible schedule that allows you to spend more time with your kids? Another "block" goes in. The more important something is to you, the bigger the "block".

But wait—not everything at work is rosy, is it? Your neighbor on the assembly line is difficult to work with. Drop that "block" into the Bad Stuff bucket. Has an angry customer ruined your day? The negative side starts to get heavier.

Now, remember when we talked about "Must Have" conditions (hygiene issues), like safety? If you are concerned that you are in harm's way, you would drop a safety "block" into the Bad Stuff bucket. If, on the other hand, you don't worry about getting hurt at work, you would place the "block" on the base, labeled "Must Haves." Why not put it into the Good Stuff bucket? As you recall, your satisfaction level doesn't increase when a "Must Have" requirement is met.

So, the Satisfaction Contraption is pretty simple, right? More good things than bad things mean more job satisfaction. More bad than good, and maybe you should be dusting off the old résumé.

Of course, like most things, the Satisfaction Contraption is not quite as simple as it first seems. Why not? Because situations and people change constantly.

After you become a parent, being away from home on all those work-related trips you previously enjoyed may not be so desirable. You pull the travel "block" from the Good Stuff side and drop it right into the Bad Stuff bucket.

In essence, the "blocks" change when you do. Sometimes, though, the impact of an event on your satisfaction is temporary—the effect, positive or negative, fades over time. If you look closely at the Satisfaction Contraption again, you will notice that the buckets have holes at the bottom. Why? Well, because the short-lived "blocks" act like ice. As they melt and drain out, the weight of the bucket decreases, changing the balance on the scale.

Say your boss takes you out to lunch—a perk "block" gets put into the Good Stuff bucket because you value the sense of appreciation you get from the experience (and because you like having saved a few bucks on a nice meal). The impact of that lunch is probably fairly limited, though. You might not even remember it a month down the road. The positive effect of that "block" soon melts and drains away. The impact of a negative event, like an argument with a coworker, can also drain away over time as well.

That's not to say that these short-lived "blocks" can't accumulate and have a lasting effect. When temporary events pile up faster than they melt, the scale can move a lot in either direction. If you quarrel with a coworker every day, you just keep piling those "blocks" in the Bad Stuff bucket. The "blocks" are added faster than they can melt away. Does your boss give you constant encouragement? If so, he is always refilling your Good Stuff bucket with manager support "blocks" that keep your satisfaction level high.

One final thought about the Satisfaction Contraption. Everyone's is unique. The "blocks" have to matter to you to make your satisfaction level change. You may work next to a coworker who loves chatting throughout the day. The coworker adds a "block" on the good side because the conversation is rewarding to him. You, on the other hand find it distracting. It becomes a Bad Stuff "block" for you.

The same holds true for your company. The benefits and working conditions that your employer provides only add to your satisfaction if you value them. This situation obviously creates a risk of confusion—your boss might offer you a plum assignment, but not realize that it conflicts with your child's performance as a star in the school play. He thinks he added to your satisfaction, but he inadvertently dropped a "block" into your Bad Stuff bucket.

Items received from a boss matter only if the employee values them.

Remember, just like value is always determined by the customer, job satisfaction is always determined by you. The best way that you can tip the balance of that scale in your favor is to help educate your boss. Teach her what is important to you so that she has a fair chance of helping you get it.

Managing your Satisfaction Contraption

Many factors contribute to your job satisfaction; the bigger question is, what exactly can you do to tip the scale in your favor? Despite how it may feel sometimes, you are not helpless in your search for fulfillment at work. In truth, you have quite a bit of control. The leap you need to make, though, is to switch from the belief that you are carried by the currents to the philosophy that you are able to chart your own course. Later in the book, you will learn a lot of practical strategies that you can use to get to your final destination: being more satisfied at work. First, though, here are a few general principles to remember:

- ***Add to your Good Stuff bucket.*** Once you figure out what factors are important to you, actively seek those things out. Don't just focus on big ticket items like getting a promotion. Look at the small, easy-to-do items, too, like taking walks during lunch.
- ***Remove items from your Bad Stuff bucket.*** If you can eliminate problems on your own, do it! Keep your workspace neat to avoid unpleasant conversations with your boss. Make an effort to resolve that nagging problem with your coworker.
- ***Change your perspective.*** Most adults are pretty set in their ways, but seeing situations from a different perspective can spur change. Imagine you've always hated your company's tardiness policy. But, now, let's say you've got a new supervisor who doesn't really enforce it. Before long, a few of your coworkers start abusing his leniency, and you have to do extra work when they are running late. These new circumstances might lead you to change your mind about the policy that you had been dead set against.
- ***Life changes.*** Think beyond the current moment. Are there any life-changing events you anticipate in your future? If you know you are getting close to starting a family, you may decide a promotion is the route to your dream house in the suburbs.

Advancement often requires degrees, which you can't earn overnight. Managing your satisfaction gets easier when you plan ahead.

- ***Periodic cycles.*** Satisfaction can have a natural ebb and flow to it. You might like working overtime when the weather is bad, but you can't stand being inside when the sun starts to shine. Your work cycles might also change—perhaps you work retail and like it most of the year but hate the holiday rush. Your Bad Stuff bucket gets a chunk of coal thrown in every winter during the busy season. Plan for the variations.
- ***Lifestyle changes.*** On occasion, people make a conscious decision to change what is important to them. Before you began to diet, you loved the mouthwatering taste of chocolate cake. But as you started to create a healthier lifestyle and you watched the numbers on the scale steadily drop, that dessert started to hold less and less influence over you. The same thing happens at work. Early in your career, your biggest priority might be getting out on time so you get to a pick-up game of basketball at the gym. Maybe at some point, though, you head up a special project team and discover you have natural leadership talent. You might change your priorities, and start working toward a promotion.
- ***Education.*** Here's an interesting statistic. In a Salary.com study, fifty percent of people felt they were not paid fairly. When job description and qualifications were taken into account though, only twenty-two percent were actually underpaid.[12] This fact illustrates, again, it is the gap between expectations and reality that causes loss of satisfaction—the pay is not the problem, but rather it is the *belief* about being underpaid that creates the bad feelings. Learning more about a situation and setting realistic expectations goes a long way toward balancing the Satisfaction Contraption.

---

[12] (Salary.com, 2007)

CHAPTER 2

What's in it for your company?

CLEARLY, YOU HAVE THE BIGGEST STAKE IN YOUR JOB SATISFACTION. But what about your company's stake? Where do your leaders stand on the subject? Does your job satisfaction even matter to them? To understand the answer, you first have to understand one simple rule of business:

No profit = No company

The key point for you, is that no company = no job! When it gets right down to it, the bottom line *is* the bottom line. So, the question becomes, does it profit your company to help you become more satisfied with your job?

The answer is that a business has to weigh the benefit they get from having a satisfied workforce against the cost of making that workforce more content. Believe it or not, your company already spends a lot of money trying to improve your satisfaction. They pay your salary and probably pay for vacation time, insurance coverage, a retirement plan, training, and other benefits. Is that cash well spent? Are the benefits to the company greater than the costs?

Overwhelming evidence says, yes, it *is* in the best interests of a company to keep its workers satisfied.

As a rule, businesses that focus on job satisfaction are more profitable than those that don't.

How much more profitable? *Much* more. Companies with satisfied employees routinely have better profit margins than those who don't.

Let's take a look at *Fortune*® magazine's "100 Best Companies to Work for" list. The "Best" companies (during an eight-year study) had an average annual return on investments of fourteen percent. Compare this number to the average annual return for the whole stock market over the same period: six percent.[13]

The rankings on the "100 Best" list are determined, in large part, by employee surveys—surveys that include questions about job satisfaction. It would be difficult for a company with dissatisfied employees to make it onto the list. This strongly supports the premise that companies with an emphasis on employee satisfaction not only beat the market, but give it a sound thumping! The "Best" companies, over a fairly long period, more than doubled the performance of the average companies that make up the stock market. This evidence seems to indicate that spending money on employee satisfaction provides a strong return on investment.

If you think eight percent isn't a huge margin of victory, look at the numbers over time. Let's say the average "Best" company and the average non-"Best" company both had a share price of ten bucks at the beginning of 1998. At the beginning of 2006 (assuming a constant return of 6.1% per year), the average company's price would be up to $16.06. And, what would those extra percentage points mean to the average "Best" company? About $12.00 more per share!

---

[13] (Edmans, 2008). The actual annualized returns are 13.9% and 6.1% from the beginning of 1998 to the beginning of 2006.

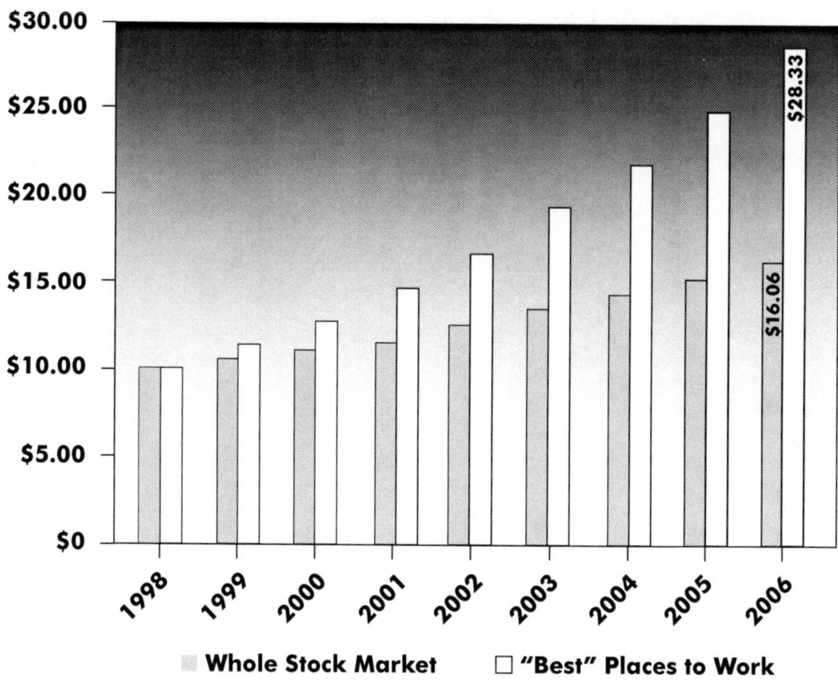

How do the "Best" companies compare to the whole stock market?

Do you see why your job satisfaction should matter to your leaders? Is there any question which group of stocks would provide a larger profit for the company, or yield bigger bonuses for the executives?

Now, you may not worry too much about your boss's income, but here's something that might hit closer to home—besides your satisfaction, that is. Let's say that your Great Aunt Thelma, rest her soul, passes away on your thirtieth birthday. You were always her favorite, so she leaves you ten grand to invest for your retirement. You get to wondering, what's the difference between an average company (at 6.1%) and a "Best" company (at 13.9%) over the thirty-five years until you retire? Invested at an average company, and left alone, the ten grand would turn into a hair under $80,000. If, however, you invested in a "Best" company, you would nearly be a millionaire!

$10K Invested for Thirty-Five Years

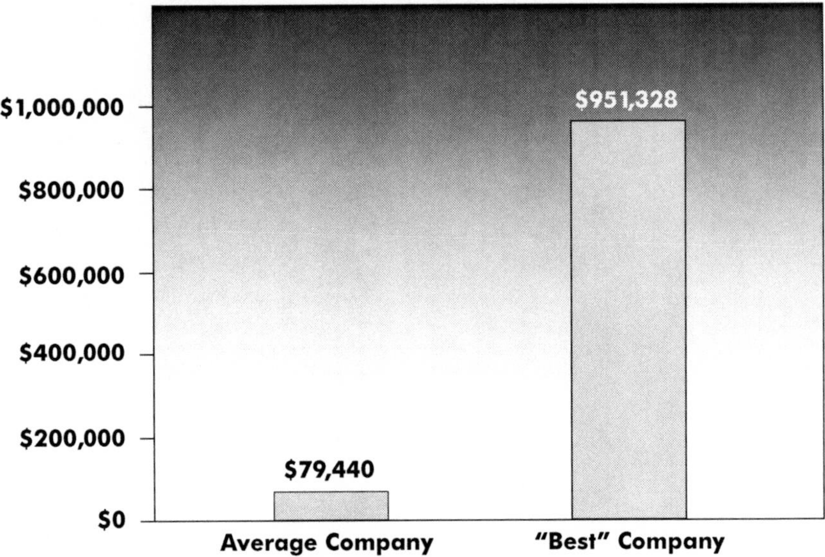

Which stock would you rather have in your 401(k)?

Companies on the "Best" companies list share another significant benefit:

The employers on Fortune's "100 Best Companies to Work for" list usually stay in business for a very long time.

The average age of the companies on this "Best" list was eighty-five years! The average company in America lasts only twenty years—the owners of the companies that don't last either sell the company or shut it down.[14] To you, an employee, longevity means job security, and consequently, increased job satisfaction.

[14] (Colvin, 2006)

Strong company performance means more resources for employees to do their jobs right, which continues the cycle of success.

These thriving, long-lived companies tend to increase their advantage over struggling ones. The businesses that have been around a long time have the resources to do things right. They can invest in timely and appropriate maintenance, computer upgrades, quality equipment, and proper personnel levels. They can also spend money on team building and training. These actions serve to increase corporate performance, which fuels even greater job satisfaction. Success breeds more success.

How does job satisfaction increase profit?

High employee satisfaction translates to profit. A content, engaged workforce translates into *real* dollars to a company. While this section is primarily a summary of employer benefits, don't skip it. As you start taking steps toward making your job better, it pays to know what the company will get out of it. Remember, you'll be more likely to get the things you ask for if both you and your company win.

Employer Benefits of Having Satisfied Employees:

- ***Better Customer Service.*** Content employees make customers happy. Happy customers mean more profit. Some time ago, Sears® completed a study that showed a five percent improvement in employee satisfaction adds 1.3% to customer satisfaction. How does that affect sales? A 0.5% increase in revenue![15] Half a percent might not sound like much, but for Sears (now combined with K-Mart®), it adds up to about a quarter *billion* dollars. The opposite is also true. Dissatisfied employees are

[15] (Corporate Leadership Council, 2003)

more likely than satisfied employees to upset customers. And customers are nearly four times more likely to complain about bad service than they are to compliment good service.[16] So, if employees do not treat customers well, word gets around.

- ***Decreased health care costs.*** Increased employee satisfaction equals less stress, which equals lower health-related expenses. Health care costs can be significant, especially if a company is self-insured. Stressed employees can cost business an average of $600 more per year in health care costs than other employees.[17]

- ***Fewer sick days.*** Just as lower stress leads to better physical health and a reduction in the number of sick days used; higher satisfaction reduces the number of "I just can't take it anymore" mental health days. When busy and overwhelmed coworkers have to fill in for absent employees, quality and productivity suffer, and morale drops. More than a *million* workers are absent every day because of stress-related reasons![18]

- ***Lower turnover.*** Satisfied workers are less likely than dissatisfied ones to look elsewhere for work. In fact, forty percent of turnover is related to job stress (closely linked to job dissatisfaction).[19] The impact of having people jump ship is substantial. Replacing an employee costs between $3,000 and $13,000[20] and eats up time that could be better spent on other company initiatives.

- ***Easier recruiting.*** Having a reputation for being a great place to work attracts stronger candidates.

- ***Less time spent on human resources issues.*** Satisfied workers have fewer complaints in general, so supervisors and managers

---

16 (Kotler, 2000)
17 (Schwartz, 2004)
18 (The American Institute of Stress)
19 ibid
20 ibid

can focus on hitting their targets rather than smoothing over problems.

- ***More motivation and engagement.*** Satisfied workers are more likely to do the extras that make a company great. This includes showing initiative, offering suggestions, and volunteering for project teams.
- ***Satisfaction is contagious.*** Employees key off each other, so having energized, and satisfied people on work teams increases the well-being of those around them.
- ***Satisfaction makes changes easier.*** People contest changes less when they are more satisfied overall. Angry people are more resistant to change.

The bottom line is that higher job satisfaction in employees will improve a company's quality, delivery, and cost. When employees are dissatisfied, the business pays a high price.

How does job satisfaction help managers?

As you read earlier, a big portion of your job satisfaction comes from the people you interact with on a daily basis. One of the most influential of those individuals is your boss.

To be really effective in finding job satisfaction, it is critical that you understand how your boss benefits from your contentment.

Managers commonly face the challenge of spending a significant portion of their day on personnel issues. As a result, they can't spend as much time as they want on "big picture" projects or improvement efforts.

Dealing with dissatisfied team members can quickly consume a manager's time. An employee with issues and concerns might end up addressing them with his boss for an hour a month. If that manager has forty employees, she could spend as much as a week each month trying to resolve these issues. There is not a manager in existence that wouldn't like to take some problems off her plate and free up five or ten hours a month to work on strategy or other pressing projects.

Just like you, your manager wants to do well in her job. When her teams are more satisfied, she is more satisfied because she spends less of her time smoothing out problems and more time hitting her targets. Remember: a satisfied manager usually means more satisfied employees.

Does job satisfaction increase individual productivity?

Your satisfaction leads to clear benefits for the company and your manager—this is relatively undisputed. There is one question, though, that remains only partially answered. Does job satisfaction increase individual productivity? This is, literally, the million-dollar question. A great deal of money rides on getting a definitive answer. As it stands, despite the number of claims that there is a strong link between individual productivity and satisfaction, there is enough dissenting evidence to raise some questions about the strength of the relationship.[21] How strong this link is remains to be seen.

Regardless of how future research turns out, the question being asked—if satisfaction affects individual performance—only addresses part of the issue. Many studies have looked only at whether a satisfied employee can get more work done in a day than a dissatisfied one. What about the extra labor that *dissatisfied* employees cause, though?

Look at the big picture. Some correlations to job satisfaction are well established. Job satisfaction, job stress, and absences, are clearly linked, for example. Low job satisfaction and the resulting absences indirectly reduce productivity. The stand-in worker is

[21] (Corporate Leadership Council, 2003)

unlikely to perform as well as the absent one—effectively lowering productivity because of poor job satisfaction. It is also important to consider the impact of dissatisfied employees on sales. What happens when a dissatisfied employee upsets a customer? Someone else has to spend time smoothing things over. Or, what about the time spent training a new worker, hired to replace a dissatisfied employee who quit? In each of these cases, a dissatisfied employee caused an increased workload and lower overall productivity, even if his pace wasn't actually slower.

There is, however, one important piece of data that specifically affects Lean companies. Evidence indicates that as work complexity rises, the link between job satisfaction and productivity strengthens.[22] In other words, the more complex a job, the more employee satisfaction will play a role in how productive a worker is. Why not in uncomplicated jobs? One possibility is that employees in simpler jobs are more closely supervised than those in complex ones. Dissatisfied people perform similarly to satisfied people, not because they want to or show initiative, but rather because the boss is right there telling them what to do. In complex jobs, people tend to operate more independently, so initiative and motivation—both byproducts of satisfaction—increase productivity.

In a Lean company, this difference becomes very important. After all, Lean increases the complexity of *all* jobs. Lean bosses expect employees to participate in identifying problems and in making efforts to fix them. Lean workers must understand how to develop processes, not just how to follow them. They must learn measurement systems. They have to join continuous improvement projects. In a Lean company, no job is an uncomplicated job.

As an example, let's take a look at the working world of ditch diggers. Other than a strong back and a willingness to do hard work, this position does not have many requirements.

When a company becomes Lean, however, a constant drive starts for the worker to be able to do more. Say, for instance, the

[22] (Job Satisfaction)

current ditch-digging speed is fifty yards of ditch per day; then, under Lean, next year's goal might be fifty-five. In order to do that, all the ditch diggers will be required to come up with ideas on how to dig more efficiently. Maybe one solution will involve new tool designs.[23] Perhaps better ditch locations will avoid hard dirt and rocks. The ditch diggers will likely have to join project teams to keep improving productivity.

So, yes, once they become Lean ditch diggers, their jobs become more complex. And as companies raise the complexity of their employees' work, job satisfaction becomes more important to productivity.

What about team productivity?

Most discussions about productivity and job satisfaction focus on the individual level, although an even more essential issue to examine is the impact on team performance. One study found statistical confirmation that teams with high job satisfaction perform at higher levels than those with low satisfaction.[24]

Why? Satisfied people are better corporate citizens. They help each other more. They are more willing to spend time training each other. They share process information. They communicate better. They don't waste as much time on office politics. The end result is a team that works well together.

For an example of how this works, look to your favorite professional sport. Every league has a team that achieves more than what its fans expected it to accomplish. Some sports analysts would say the team has "chemistry." Others might attribute the team's success to strong coaching. In most cases, though, if you look closely, you will see a team full of players who are satisfied with their jobs. You will also see a noticeable lack of disgruntled, outspoken players that disrupt the team. Instead, each team member plays to his

---

[23] Let's clarify the term "**tool**." It can mean a physical tool, like a wrench or hammer, or a Lean tool, like 5S or *kanban*.

[24] (Goenner, 2008)

strengths, and helps those around him perform better. Those kinds of teammates are fun, and satisfying to be around.

And, speaking of keeping teams satisfied . . .

Why doesn't your company focus more on job satisfaction?

As much as employees would like job satisfaction to be important to their companies, the truth is, in most cases, it is not the number one priority. Sure, some companies—as seen on the "100 Best Companies to Work for" list—show by their actions that worker satisfaction is important to them. Other companies *say* that satisfaction is important, but their choices are not consistent in supporting that message. And still other companies don't invest much in their people at all—they view them as expendable and treat them like they would any other resource. Most businesses fall somewhere in the middle of these extremes.

This raises an interesting question: if the link between job satisfaction and profit is so clear, why is it that more companies do not make satisfaction a priority? Several reasons explain—or justify—why companies are not taking action to improve satisfaction, or why they are not benefiting from their efforts:

- ***They don't understand the connection between satisfaction and profit.*** Most company initiatives start with a financial analysis. Unfortunately, it is difficult to precisely measure how satisfaction will pay off or when. Many of the benefits are intangibles that slowly and indirectly filter through to the bottom line. For instance, if a boss learns that he scored low on "fairness" in a satisfaction survey, he might consider making some changes. He might have a tough time, though, figuring out how to prove that assigning work more evenly will *really* drive a 2.1% increase in productivity during the next quarter. No, managers usually want immediate improvement and exact data to support their decisions and actions. If they can't figure out how to measure the results of their efforts, they may not be willing to take the risk.

- ***They don't believe a connection exists.*** A company's focus on job satisfaction will mirror how it values employees. In the not so distant past, labor was viewed as an expense, a cost to be minimized. Spending money on satisfaction directly opposed the goal of reducing labor expenses. The more modern, and alternative, way of thinking about the workforce is to treat them as an asset. If a company invests in its employees' job satisfaction, the returns can be substantial.

- ***They are focusing on other initiatives.*** In this world of limited resources, companies have to pick and choose where they are going to place their efforts. A company may *want* to improve its culture but may instead have to struggle with a major competitor or face a crisis that is taking up its time and money. In either case, management moves satisfaction to the back burner.

- ***They don't know how to make employees satisfied.*** A company may believe satisfaction is important but not have any understanding about how to provide it. It is easy to get bogged down by the sheer quantity of information available on how to set up satisfaction programs. The company leaders may pick an ineffective strategy and falter in spite of their good intentions.

- ***They know what to do, but are not effective.*** Knowing *what* to do and knowing *how* to actually do it are two entirely different things. Once a company figures out how to satisfy its employees, it still has to determine a process and implement the changes. Some companies go awry with well-intentioned, but poorly executed, programs.

- ***They think their employees are already satisfied.*** This line of thinking usually involves three potential issues. The first is that companies routinely underestimate how important satisfaction is to their employees. The second is that they don't truly know *what* their employees want. The third is that companies innocently mistake how well they are doing on meeting the needs of employees.

- ***They focus on the average, instead of the individual.*** Some companies have a one-size-fits-all approach to job satisfaction, which leads to corporate policies that don't adjust well to individual needs. This approach tends to end up as a one-size-fits-*none* result. In those cases, despite the company's investment in employee benefits programs and its efforts to improve job satisfaction, workers still end up being dissatisfied.
- ***They use only corporate policies and ignore local factors.*** Individual managers play a huge role in how satisfied their employees are. Remember, factors like poor communication and not trusting bosses are often cited as reasons for low satisfaction. A corporate policy to "communicate better" will probably not make a manufacturing manager on the shop floor more effective at keeping his team informed. Instead, a cultural shift and local training would be necessary to bring about this change. Unfortunately, not many companies evaluate how their managers are contributing to their employees' well-being.

Basically, then, the reasons a company does not improve job satisfaction fall into one of three main categories (1) the company doesn't know how, (2) the company's efforts are just not effective, or (3) the company doesn't care. The last one is the most difficult situation to be in because it means you are on your own in improving your satisfaction. Fortunately, that is not an impossible task, but it certainly will take a fair amount of work to overcome. The first two, however, hold promise. Companies in those categories already *want* to increase their employees' satisfaction—all they need to do is figure out how—with a little help from you along the way.

A word of caution, though, when figuring out where your company stands. Don't confuse a company's lack of focus on *your* satisfaction with the belief that employee satisfaction in general is not important. If your needs are unique, the cost may be too high for the company. They will probably do the things that benefit the greatest number of employees first. Remember, your company must perceive that its efforts to build satisfaction will pay off.

Is your job satisfied with you?

This is a tough question and one that not many employees even think to ask. But it is fairly safe to say that not everyone is good at their job. In fact, about half of the people in the world are below average in their performance! (Guess what? While that sounds harsh, if you think about it, isn't that what "average" means?)[25] So, how does this apply to you at work? It means that some of your coworkers—not *you,* of course—probably do not perform as well as they think they do.

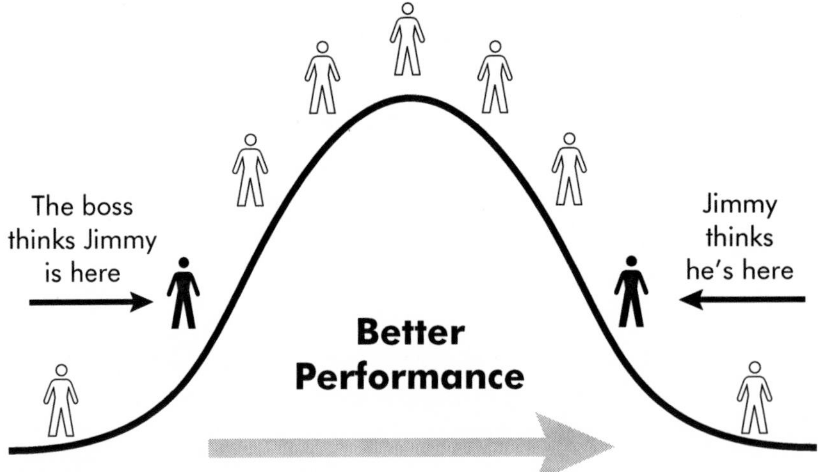

How does your boss view you?

Try to imagine the following situation at your next company meeting. What would happen if the CEO asked all the above-average employees to sit on the right side of the room, and the below average

[25] For you mathematicians, the correct term is really 'median', but 'average' is in more common, though incorrect, use.

ones to sit on the left side? Assuming that everyone would sit where they believed they belonged (and not sit on the above average side to avoid embarrassment), is the split likely to be even? Not a chance. The right side would be standing room only, while tumbleweeds would roll through the barren space on the left.

Why might a "left-sider" think he belonged on the right?

First off, remember that job satisfaction is measured in the eyes of the beholder—which is you. Job *performance* is measured in the eyes of your boss and the company you work for. Most people tend to evaluate themselves using their own criteria instead of their boss's. That being the case, you won't effectively measure your job performance. Why not? Because, what you believe is important might not even matter to your boss. In addition, the things that you think are trivial might actually be a big deal to your manager and the company.

Second, many people have difficulty with honest, objective self-evaluation. They blame their poor performance on external conditions. Think about children playing little league. A common excuse for the missed pop fly is, "The sun got in my eyes!" It is easier for kids and adults to explain away poor performance rather than to face up to it and change it.

Since you can't judge yourself impartially, you might have trouble knowing if your job is satisfied with you. What happens when you think you're doing a great job but your boss doesn't? Easy answer: right or wrong, the boss's opinion is the one that matters.

Don't give up, though. Here are a few ways you can change your boss's thoughts about your performance:

- ***Take action.*** Change your behavior to match what she wants.
- ***Change her perspective.*** Make sure she knows about the things you are doing that match what she wants. She might know about your wrong behaviors, but be unaware of all the good work you do.

- ***Educate her on your processes.*** Help her realize the importance of the things you're doing. Bosses don't always know what *really* happens down in the trenches. Teach her.
- ***Communicate better.*** Ask her for input. If you aren't sure what she really wants, ask; don't just assume that you know.

To make performance even more difficult to evaluate, when a big transition like Lean comes around, all the rules change. Your boss will judge your performance in a new way. Lean not only changes your job, it changes how you are evaluated as well. Make sure you know the new rules, or you will be starting behind the eight ball.

You are all in it together

Finding satisfaction is, first and foremost, *your* responsibility. But your company also has a lot to gain from your fulfillment and can be a powerful ally in this endeavor.

If your leaders have chosen continuous improvement as a way of life for the business, they are open to change and they are trying to make the company perform better. Your satisfaction can contribute to their goals, especially if you can demonstrate that your needs are aligned with the company's objectives. Do that, and you are likely to get more of what you want at work.

CHAPTER 3

Why do you have to be Lean?

What's happening in the world?

THE WORLD IS IN FLUX, AND IS AFFECTING YOU in ways that are changing your life. For the most part, the changes have been good for you—as a consumer. You have more choices than ever before and better service. Dollar for dollar, manufactured products are more affordable, more feature-rich, and more reliable than ever. For you, as an employee, however, the changes may have dramatically altered your workday. Consider this story . . .

Your son, Jimmy, and the neighbor's boy, Bobby, both open lemonade stands right next to each other. They start out charging fifty cents a glass, and both make a decent profit. Unfortunately, the world begins to change.

Lemonade continues to sell well in your neighborhood, but has also become a hot product in the Far East. Global demand has gone up, but there are still only a handful of places in the world that can grow lemons. As a result, lemon producers are having a hard time keeping up with orders. Then a frost hits Florida, and growers announce a citrus shortage. The kids' raw material costs rise.

Increasing population, higher energy prices, and fewer raw materials drive up costs. Increasing costs shrink profit.

The boys try to raise their prices to keep making money. They start charging sixty cents, but that price is just too high. Another kid sees an opportunity and starts selling soda down the street for fifty cents. She starts raking in the dough. Lemonade sales drop so the boys have to roll back their price to fifty cents. Only now, though, they make less profit than before because the material costs remain high.

If a business raises the price of a product too high, it won't sell. Customers will buy a substitute item instead.

One day, you see the neighbor boy, Bobby, reeling out an extension cord across his lawn. He sets up an automatic juicer, so he can be more productive and won't have to add his sister to the payroll. Bobby understands that the machine can squeeze more juice from the lemons than he can by hand. He decides to pass some of his savings along to his customers and charges a nickel less. Suddenly, your Jimmy is behind the times.

Your company's costs have to be as low as, or lower than, the competition.

Your son is not to be outdone and the next day, Jimmy has a juicer set up as well. In addition, he has found a company on the Internet where he can buy the cups for less than he had been paying at the local store. A few days later, a delivery truck rolls up, and Jimmy receives the package of custom-printed cups.

Better transportation and communication makes the world smaller. Businesses in London, England, now compete with businesses in London, Kentucky for the same customers.

As the summer progresses, business starts to get slower for the boys. People pass by just as frequently, but they don't seem to be spending as much. Most just walk right past the lemonade stands. The boys shave a nickel off the price of the lemonade, and business starts to pick up again.

When times are tight, customers are more selective about where they spend their money. They look harder for a good deal. They pay for the things that they "must have" first, like groceries, gas, mortgages, and maybe even cell phones. People might not have much money left over for "nice to haves" like dining out.

One day, you hear a little girl shriek out front. Apparently, she found a bug in the lemonade she bought from Bobby. His sales plummet when she posts a video of the bug on the Internet.

People talk. They will tell each other about a company's products and services. This is especially true when they are unhappy about something.

One night, you look over Jimmy's shoulder, thinking he is doing homework on the computer. He is actually looking at the website of a ginseng vendor in Thailand. His customers started asking for it a while ago, and now he sees them walking by with bottled ginseng lemonade bought from a kid in Arizona.

Customers constantly change their preferences. If your company doesn't give them what they want, the competition will.

As the summer winds down, Jimmy and Bobby have the luxury to sit back and wonder what the next year will bring. They know that their customers will still demand high quality lemonade, but next year, buyers might want it even fresher. Instead of having it poured from a pitcher, customers might want it squeezed right into their cups. They won't want to wait longer for it, though. In fact, they might even prefer a drive-through to speed things along. Some might request a snack to go with their drink. The point is that the boys have two options. They can sit back and conduct business as usual, or they can make the changes that they need to in order to stay competitive year after year. One thing is clear in their business and likely for your company as well:

Customer expectations are always rising.

What was good enough yesterday is nowhere near good enough today. Consumers have grown accustomed to having new and improved features in every product launch, *without* a new and improved (higher) price. They want products cheaper. They want them more reliable. And they want them right now. When a company fails to fulfill those requirements, buyers will find a new place to go. Your company will very quickly go out of business if it doesn't meet its customers' needs. If your company goes out of business, what will happen to your job?

How can a company respond?

So where does this story about a couple of kids fit into your life? The pressures they were facing are the same ones that confront your employer. If your company wants to continue to do business, it has to be profitable. That gets harder and harder to do as the world evolves. Your company will have to try something new to keep making money. That "something new" is likely to have a significant impact on what you think about your job and how you feel about coming to work every day.

A company can react to increasing pressure in many ways. Some responses are short-term belt-tightening methods: reducing benefits, or hiring and pay freezes, for example. While these methods may provide immediate relief, they do so with a high long-term cost. If employees feel wronged or customers lose trust in the company, they will jump ship for the first alternative that comes their way.

Some options are longer-term fixes: exploring mergers and acquisitions, expanding research and design, or purchasing new technology. The company might even try to grow the business. These are risky moves, since they all take a lot of money and may or may not pay off.

Businesses have one more option: Lean. Over the years, Lean initiatives have proven to be an effective way to combat the pressures currently facing companies. Lean, when done well, makes substantial gains in quality, delivery, and cost. Because it has proven so effective, nearly seventy percent of America's manufacturing companies are using some form of Lean.[26] More than half of those use it as their primary means of continuous improvement.[27]

Executives are always looking for proven strategies, and Lean fits the bill. If Lean techniques didn't work, Lean would not have the appeal it does, nor would it have the staying power that it has shown. Executives quickly discard ineffective methods.

The decision to be Lean

At some point, your company's leaders decided that Lean was a good idea for your organization. To understand who those

[26] (Blanchard, Census of U. S. Manufacturers—Lean Green and Low Cost, 2007)
[27] (Blanchard, Census of Manufacturers—What's Working for U. S. Manufacturers., 2006)

leaders are, let's take a look at how decisions are made and how companies operate.

Many Lean efforts start out in response to the demands of shareholders. Think of these investors as the owners of an old steam locomotive—the *Shareholder Express*.

The *Shareholder Express*

The owners of the train provide the fuel—coal—for the firebox, which heats the boiler that powers the locomotive. In the case of a business, the fuel is not coal—it is the money that the shareholders invest. Without coal, the train stands still; a business would do the same without money. But, stoke the firebox of a locomotive with coal, and the train gets going; stoke a business with money, and that business will gain forward momentum, too.

Once a train gets going, it needs someone to guide it to its destination. That "someone" oversees the train as a whole and keeps every aspect of it running smoothly. On the train, that person is the conductor. In a business, there might be an entire group in place to perform that task—the executive team. Its members would set the course and direction of the business, but they would not handle everyday operations.

Someone has to take care of those details, though. So, just as the engineer has to monitor dials and pull levers and flip switches to keep the wheels of the train turning, a team of managers must handle the technical, day-to-day operations of a company.

On the *Shareholder Express,* when the engineer decides to adjust the temperature on the boiler, he sets a team into motion. The team members fill hoppers, adjust water flow, close pressure valves, and decide how much coal to shovel into the firebox. In business, supervisors and other frontline leaders direct you, the frontline employees, to carry out the instructions of the managers. The frontline workers are the ones powering the company—answering phones, making widgets, and doing all the day-to-day work that keeps the company on track.

Without its fuel and crew, a steam locomotive sits still. Without shareholders, executives, managers, supervisors, and you, a business could not function, either. In both cases, it is in everyone's best interests to make sure that the train and the business keep moving along. If anyone stops, everyone loses.

Now, let's look at the main decision makers in more detail. **Shareholders,** and their voracious appetite for high returns and rapid growth, drive Lean decisions. Some of their income comes from taking a part of the company's earnings as dividends, but the lion's share will normally come from the value of the company itself. That's why shareholders are so interested in growth.

Without boring you with the details, here's a simplified look at how the stock market works. Investors calculate a company's stock price by adding all the stuff it owns (its assets), subtracting its debt, and adding an estimate of what it can earn down the road (potential profits or future earnings). If stock buyers expect that a company's future profits will be higher than current profits, like when Lean cuts costs, the stock price will rise.

The Stock Price Equation

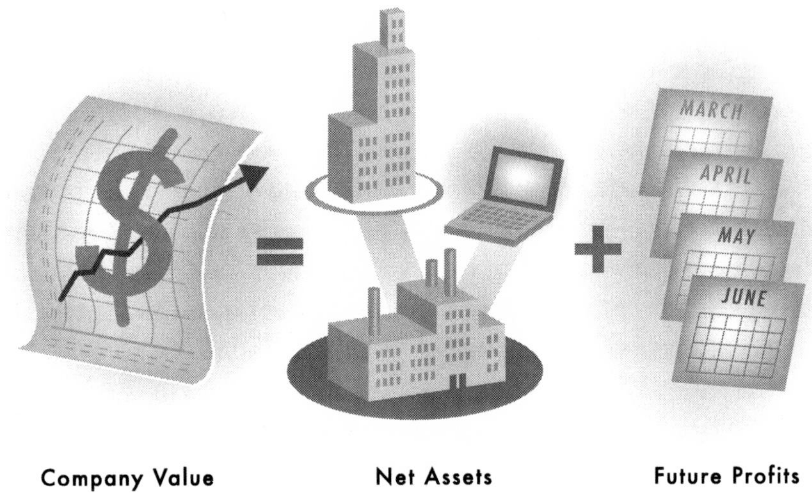

How share value is determined.

Executives, at the urging of shareholders, try to keep the stock price going up. Frontline employees often assume that a high share price somehow changes the pressure that shareholders exert on the corporate leaders. Here's a secret, though . . .

Share price doesn't really matter to shareholders.

It sounds crazy to say that, but think about it for a moment. If the stock's price is low, shareholders want more; if it's high, they want more. And they always want to see the stock grow at an increasing pace. In addition, no matter how high the price gets or how fast its value grows, they will not tell a company to back off and take it easy. Do you think they call up in October and say, "You've already hit your annual sales goals—why don't you shut down for the rest of the year?" Obviously not.

So, how much profit is enough? That's a tough question, but there are two things to consider in search of an answer. The first is opportunity. If the shareholders *think* that the company should be making more, they will want more.

The second is return. Companies have to deliver higher returns than safer investments, like government bonds, in order to attract new investors. Generally, the rate of return (the amount "returned" from an investment) must be high enough to convince investors to part with their money. That rate depends on the amount of risk involved in the investment. Bigger risks require bigger potential rewards. Savings bonds are pretty safe, so investors only expect a low rate of return. Because companies can fail, they have to have a higher rate of return to convince investors to hand over their cash.

Because of their demand for profit, shareholders tend to get painted in a bad light by employees. Very few frontline workers think it is *their* responsibility to make money for the shareholders; most just view it as a by-product of doing their jobs. In other words, most frontline employees try to reduce costs not because it will boost the company's stock price but because their boss says it is part of their job and they want to do well at work.

The relationship between shareholders and employees is built on shaky ground in the first place. Stockholders commonly believe that if employees get paid higher wages, enjoy better benefits, and have easier workloads, then they, the shareholders, will lose profit. Employees, on the other hand, do not want to accept lower pay, fewer benefits, and greater workloads to increase profits for the benefit of stockholders.

What complicates the relationship even further is that most employees don't consider the risks that shareholders face. Investors take a chance on their initial investment, but also live with the everyday possibility that the stock price could tank, costing them a large part of their savings.

What makes matters worse is that these two groups have little or no interaction. Each sees the other as a nameless, faceless entity whose purpose is to try to take something from them! This absence of contact helps feed the image, on the part of employees, that investors are wealthy people who live in mansions and have lots of big, expensive toys. In reality, shareholders fall into three basic categories:

- ***The "Big Investor."*** The most common vision of a shareholder is the "big investor." She is an individual who tends to own enough shares to have a voice in the company.
- ***The "Institutional Investor."*** "Institutional investors" are groups that hold people's money and invest it as a block. These "institutions" might be insurance companies, mutual funds, or retirement programs. Most people who invest in companies do so through an institutional investor.
- ***The "Little Guy."*** The "little guy" is the small investor who manages his own portfolio. He may even invest directly in the company he works for. There are a lot of "little guys", but individually, they don't have a lot of clout.

Since many employees invest in their own company through a stock purchase or a 401(k), *you* or someone you work with could, in fact, be a "little guy" shareholder. In that case, in all likelihood, you are quite happy when your share price goes up—just like the other investors.

Regardless of how you feel about shareholders (or owners of private companies, for that matter), remember this: without their initial investment, your company would not exist. With no company, you would have no job. Don't forget: a rising tide lifts all boats. If the company is doing well, the shareholders get the lion's share of the financial benefit, but employees receive their own sets of rewards: a less stressful working environment, fewer supply and equipment cutbacks, and more opportunities.

The shareholder's role in Lean decisions is simple. They push for more. If a little bit of Lean adds a little profit, it follows that more Lean will add more profit. Since shareholders love profit, they will naturally put pressure on the company's leadership—specifically, executives and managers—to deliver it.

Executives have a tougher job than shareholders. Shareholders have to figure out where to invest their money. Executives have to come up with an evolving plan that will make the company increasingly profitable. They must react to new technologies that threaten to make current products obsolete. They have to stave off competitors who are trying to steal customers. And that battle for market share is not only local. International companies constantly enter the mix as borders become more open and a larger number of countries industrialize.

Executives probably look confident, but in reality, they hold onto their jobs only as long as they are performing well. Do you want to know the really tough part for executives? Their failures are very public. When companies fire them, there is often a press release, literally announcing it to the world. Imagine your family and friends reading in the evening paper that you lost your job because of poor performance.

As a result of these pressures, executives are constantly looking for ways to deliver more profit to their shareholders. Lean always seems to eventually pop up on their radar. When it does, they rely heavily on their managers to implement it.

Managers generally are not involved in the decision to try Lean. Rather, they are the ones figuring out the nuts and bolts of how to make it work. They go through training, hire people to run *kaizens*, and decide where to try Lean first. They establish the processes that support continuous improvement. Once executives set managers in motion, these mid-level leaders are the ones who decide the "how" of implementing Lean.

How does the Lean ball get rolling?

So, now you know who is making the decision about continuous improvement, and where the push for more profit comes from. But what makes these leaders direct the company down the Lean path?

Much of the reason lies in the fact that the business world is relentless and merciless. Companies that don't thrive and grow get swallowed up or tossed aside. Another reason is the same old argument many of you used with your parents: "Everybody else is doing it!" The difference in this case, is that the people who are doing it are making it work with impressive results. A little research will yield many, many case studies that describe the gains made by Lean. A third reason for directing companies down the Lean path revolves around managers who talk to colleagues and hear about the enviable results other companies have achieved with Lean.

So, the need to survive, to thrive, and to grow drives most Lean conversions. To illustrate this let's look at a common manufactured good, like a pair of scissors. When many different companies make the same product, controlling costs in every aspect of its production is critical. If one competitor is able to significantly reduce the cost of its products, it spells serious trouble for the rest of the scissor manufacturers out there.

Lean might be the only option that will allow your company to stay in business. Perhaps your company is facing intense cost pressure from suppliers of raw materials, which drives the price of the final product higher. Maybe consumers are insisting upon faster delivery or retailers are wanting smaller shipments. Maybe customers are demanding better service. Lean might be the only answer for troubled companies. Fortunately, nothing motivates people to change as well as a crisis.

Lean, however, should not be limited to use only in bad economic times. It also can help strong companies leap to the next level. In these cases, the business may be doing well, but it sees an opportunity to use Lean to leapfrog up the market-share ladder. Often this can be the best occasion to start Lean. When times are good, a company has more flexibility and more resources to devote to improvements. Unfortunately, it is much harder to rally employees behind a Lean conversion during a period of comfort and record profits.

So, what's Lean supposed to do?

In short, Lean does more with less. It eliminates waste so employees can focus more on productive work. As a result, companies get more done with the same number of people. In addition, Lean companies generally have quicker delivery times and higher quality levels than their non-Lean competitors. Lean also has a nice side effect. When it reduces inventory, it frees up funds, or **working capital**—money that can go back into the corporate coffers and be available for other purposes, like financing growth.

Growth is one of the two basic ways a company can increase profit. The other is to cut costs. Each way has its own benefits and drawbacks.

When money is saved it drops straight through to the bottom line. In other words, each dime the company can shave off expenses goes right into profit. The primary drawback is that the amount of money saved is limited by how much money the company takes in. A company can never save more than it gets paid, so reducing costs alone is not a viable long-term option for growth and increasing profit.

Increasing sales, the other method of increasing profit, does not have the same limitation as cutting costs. As long as someone comes up with a constant supply of new ideas for selling more products and services, the company's profits can keep rising. As expected, increasing sales does have a downside: beating out the competition takes effort, and it is often expensive.

Managers, fortunately, don't have to choose one strategy over the other to be Lean.

Though most people view Lean primarily as a cost-cutting measure, it also makes products easier to sell by shortening delivery time and improving quality. Reducing costs and increasing sales both raise profit.

Let's revisit Jimmy's lemonade stand to see how Lean helps a company grow and increase profit. On top of producing some of the world's best lemonade, Jimmy is also a dedicated ballplayer. He currently has his eyes set on a new first baseman's glove, which he wants to get for next year's baseball season.

Since this is an additional expense, Jimmy will need to earn an *extra* $50 to buy that mitt. His business is doing pretty well—he expects to sell about 5,000 cups this year. He's got quite the operation!

Right now, it costs him about $0.45 to make each cup that he sells for $0.50. To make that extra $50, he has two choices. His first choice is to cut his costs. How much would he have to save per cup to scrape together an extra $50? He would have to shave $0.01 from each sale, a mere 2.2% change. His other choice is to sell an extra *thousand* cups—a twenty percent increase in sales that would be challenging in any industry much less in the neighborhood lemonade business.

Now, which route do you think Jimmy will choose? He's a smart kid who is good at math and wants to play a better ballgame next year. Will he try to sell a thousand more cups of lemonade, or will he work at squeezing that penny out of the cost for each cup?

Jimmy's Options

Which is easier—saving a penny per cup, or selling a thousand more drinks?

In this case, it makes sense for Jimmy to spend his energy using Lean to reduce his costs. But what about when he turns sixteen and wants to buy a car? College is also looming on the horizon. Cost cutting will only take him so far. At some point he will need to grow his business and increase his profit to reach his goals. Fortunately for him, Lean will help him do both. It will assist him with his cost-cutting efforts this year and will lay the foundation for expansion in the future.

The actions he takes to squeeze out that penny will also let him make lemonade faster, and with higher quality. Those factors will make it easier for him to sell his drinks.

Besides, now that he is going to be Lean, Jimmy won't have to tie as much of his cash up in ingredient inventory. Therefore, he will have money available to construct new stands and to place advertisements in the local paper. Jimmy is well on his way to being behind the wheel of a used car.

While the story about Jimmy is make-believe, the results real companies get using Lean methods are not. It is common for Lean to help companies produce twice as much and still be able to meet customer demand in a fraction of the time.

However, gains are not limited to the shop floor. In administrative areas, Lean is making significant inroads—with great results that are only going to get better. Relatively speaking, Lean in the office is in its infancy compared to Lean on the shop floor. As the collective knowledge about Lean in the office grows, progress is going to accelerate. It's a good thing, too—more than sixty percent of the costs of doing business come from administrative and other non-production areas.[28]

Retail can also benefit from Lean. Well-managed stores can supply what customers want, when they want it, and *still* stock as much as a third less inventory. They can even typically show productivity gains up to twenty percent in the process.[29]

---

[28] (Tapping and Dunn, 2006)
[29] (McKinsey & Company)

Executives salivate about such results. Senior leaders, though, seldom act without some degree of certainty that they will succeed. So, in looking at all the improvement methods out there, what makes corporate leaders believe Lean is the best choice to make their profit bigger?

Where's the proof?

First of all, proof lies in the tremendous amount of information available about Lean. Vast resources abound on the subject—books, training, case studies, and even websites chock full of Lean wisdom. If Lean did not work, such information would have no readers.

Further evidence can be found by looking at how many people are available to help implement Lean. Take a few minutes on the Internet and search "Lean consultant." There is a long, long list of firms, both commercial and non-profit, who want to help your company do more with less. If Lean did not work, there would be few businesses paying for Lean services, and hence, few Lean consultants.

Sometimes, though, the biggest proof of something comes not from what is available but from what isn't. So, what don't you find? Specialists who claim to "un-Lean" a company; consultants who teach batch manufacturing (the opposite of Lean); information on cleaning up a Lean disaster. There is simply *not* a market for these things. Once a company goes Lean, it stays Lean.

Think about what that means to you.

It means that you will not be getting away from Lean anytime soon. So if you are hoping that Lean is a fad you will be holding your breath for a long, long time! Lean has staying power and it is not going away. With that in mind, rather than fight reality, why not accept that your company will be Lean and will not be going back. Then you can direct your energy into what really matters to you: increasing your job satisfaction.

To figure out how to do that, you'll need to understand more about Lean itself.

CHAPTER 4

What is Lean?

Who should read this chapter?

THIS CHAPTER IS AN OVERVIEW OF LEAN TERMINOLOGY. It packs a lot of information into a very small space. If you are a beginner at Lean, don't let yourself get overloaded when you look at it the first time. Start out with a quick read, with the goal of just getting yourself oriented to the language and terminology of Lean. As you start doing projects or hearing people talking about Lean, come back and re-read specific sections in more detail to gain a better understanding of the concepts of Lean. For example, if your boss is talking about getting rid of inventory, come back, jump over to that section, and see if you can figure out just why she is trying to do that. This type of technical material is much easier to understand when you read it with a real-world use in mind.

If you already happen to be well-versed in Lean, at least take a few minutes to skim over this chapter. At a minimum, it will be a good refresher. At best, you'll gain some more knowledge and new perspectives on how Lean works.

A brief history

The origin of Lean depends on how broadly you interpret the term. In narrow definitions, Lean focuses on reducing inventory and improving operations.

The broad definition of Lean is that it is a philosophy of relentless waste reduction. It involves any effort to do more with less.

With that in mind, here are some examples of Lean concepts that can trace their roots way back in time:

- ***Separating people from machines.*** Windmills have been making people's lives easier for hundreds of years. They allowed workers to labor less with their muscles and think more with their heads. This separation enabled people to accomplish more in the same amount of time.
- ***Standard Work.*** Frederick Winslow Taylor published *Principles of Scientific Management* in 1911. His writings laid the foundation for Standard Work.
- ***Assembly line production.*** Despite the popular belief that Henry Ford invented the assembly line, examples of the concept are known from as far back as the early 1800s. Henry Ford, more accurately, was the one who made the assembly line popular.
- ***Focusing on quality.*** Quality has always been important to manufacturing. The introduction of interchangeable parts in order to speed up production drove an even greater need for consistency. The parts had to fit together properly. And contrary to the belief that Eli Whitney invented interchangeable parts, the concept was actually already in use in the late 1700s.[30]
- ***Process improvement.*** Someone had a sore back from hauling veggies to market, so he slapped a few wheels on a box and the

[30] (The Eli Whitney Museum & Workshop)

cart was born. If you look even farther back, cavemen were chipping stones into scrapers. As basic as these ideas seem now, they are classic examples of process improvement.

Despite these earlier examples, most people trace the roots of the modern version of Lean to the **Toyota Production System (TPS)**. In post-World War II Japan, the market was fragmented and resources were limited. The typical methods of production used throughout the world were not suited to the Japanese situation. In response, Taiichi Ohno, widely considered to be the father of TPS, created a strategy to lower costs and improve quality. Through his efforts, TPS was born.

Over the years, countless companies and organizations have modified TPS and integrated it into their culture. These offshoots were designed to match each company's unique situation. Because of this, Lean exists with as much variation as general concepts like management or human resources. Most continuous improvement efforts, though, will have the same point of focus: the customer.

In addition to the many "flavors" of Lean, its concepts overlap many other programs, methods, and philosophies. You may have heard of Six Sigma, the Theory of Constraints (TOC), Just-in-Time (JIT) manufacturing, agile manufacturing, flow production, and, of course, TPS. In practice, many of the basic ideas are shared, borrowed, tweaked, and blended into a business system that meets a company's specific needs.

With that in mind, be flexible in applying the concepts in your company. Learn the specific ways that your current organization does things.

The big picture

One of the most important cornerstones of Lean is its focus on the customer.

Every step in the process of getting your product or service out the door should add some kind of benefit to the customer. You will frequently hear the term **value stream** to describe this concept. Leaders commonly show this flow visually on a **value stream map (VSM)** and use this tool to highlight areas of waste. More importantly, they use it to plan a path to improvement.

Some Lean leaders accept only pencil and paper VSMs. The premise is that VSMs should not be drawn in an office; they should be completed while the employee is watching the process he is documenting. The downside? VSMs can take longer to change and are harder to send to people. A good compromise is to always draw it at the process location, then transfer it to computer if there is a good reason to do so.

Take a look at this value stream map for Jimmy's lemonade stand. Don't get caught up in trying to understand every little detail; just get an overall feel for it so you can picture what a value stream map looks like when you hear it mentioned.

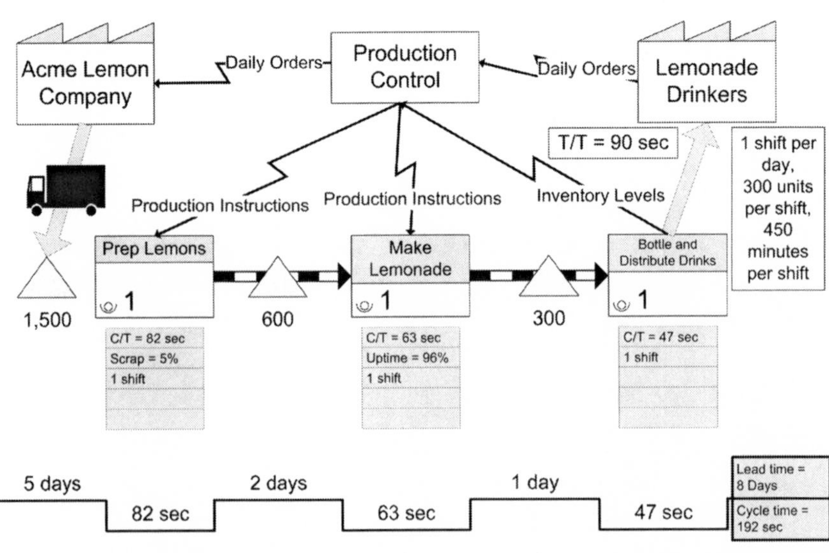

Sample of a Current State Value Stream Map

Value can only be defined by the customer. It comes from what the customer wants,* not *what the company thinks the customer should have.

Customers want solutions to problems, not specific products. For example, no customer came out and said, "I want an MP3 player." What they said was, "My CD player is too bulky," or, "My CD player skips," or perhaps, "I want to carry more songs around with me." The MP3 player solved those problems.

By keeping the customer front and center, Lean helps companies focus on the things that add value. To do this, everyone has to understand and speak the same language.

Say what?

Once you start down a Lean path, much of the terminology can sound a bit foreign. Technical words can be unfamiliar in any new field, but in the case of Lean, you'll find a heavy Japanese influence. This comes from the fact that TPS, which originated in Japan, is the most commonly copied Lean system in the world. But even the English entries (such as "value stream") can sound like a different language. This chapter focuses on the most common Lean terms that you will encounter. It is certainly not exhaustive, but it is enough to give you a strong start.

New languages go hand in hand with new cultures—in this case, the **continuous improvement culture**.

A continuous improvement culture is a setting in which everyone in a company not only sees the need for improvement, but actually contributes to the effort of fixing problems and making processes better.

The more people that contribute ideas, the greater the improvement and the faster the pace. Employee involvement is only one piece of the puzzle, though. Several principles fit together to create a strong culture. Many Lean systems use a picture of a house to show how these all interact. The steps name the fundamentals that build a solid foundation for a continuous improvement culture. The pillars are typically Just-in-Time and *jidoka* (both will be described in more detail later). The middle of the house shows the core of the company—people, methods, materials, and machines. Finally, the roof generally shows the benefits of the culture.

The Lean House

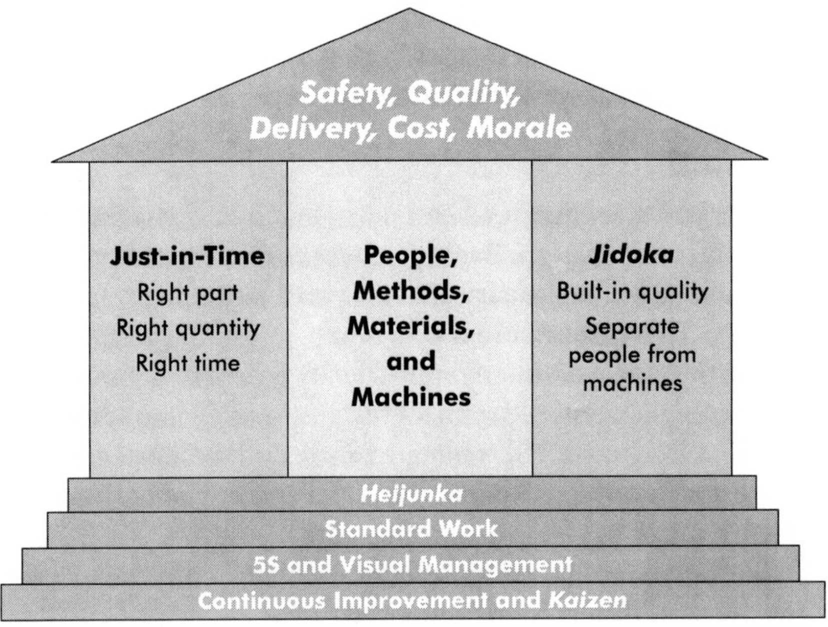

Companies often use a diagram similar to this one to summarize their Lean programs.

Learning Lean

There is a lot to learn about Lean. Employees typically receive Lean training in one of four ways:

- ***An orientation or training event for a large audience.*** This is a good way for a company to build exposure to Lean and to quickly let workers know what is going on around them. Knowledge lessens the fear of the unknown. But, usually, Lean sticks with people best when they are able to immediately put its concepts into practice, and big events simply don't provide that opportunity. Trainers also have a difficult time making sure that students fully understand the concepts.

- ***One-on-one or small group mentoring sessions.*** Imagine you have an assignment to organize a copier area. You might turn to your mentor, whether your boss or a coworker, for a quick lesson. He might even give you some advice on how to get started and where to find the supplies for the job. These sessions vary widely in effectiveness because they depend not only on the mentor's knowledge of Lean, but also on his skill as a teacher. On the plus side, one-on-one training is generally very timely—you put the lesson to use right away. You also have the opportunity for immediate feedback. Your mentor can easily tell if you really understand the information, and adjust accordingly. After all, the mentor is focused on you, and often observes as you try out your new skill.
- ***Formal training.*** Formal training in Lean exists in many formats. Contracted instructors can come to your company. You can attend seminars. Some companies have permanent Lean classrooms for their own employees. You can go to training centers that are in the business of providing Lean education. Some universities even have a variety of Lean courses available. Formal classes can cover pretty much any level of Lean topic you can imagine. The down side of formal training is the cost, in both money and time away from work. Plus, it isn't tailored to the student, and its lessons are seldom put into immediate use. These limitations can reduce how much knowledge people actually absorb and retain.
- ***Just-in-Time training.*** Just-in-Time training comes right before a *kaizen*—a short project, usually a week long, that makes

sweeping changes to improve a process. Most *kaizen* events start with a module of training that is needed for the current part of a project. In other words, students use the information from a Monday morning training module on a Monday afternoon. This JIT type of instruction tends to be effective for one specific reason: trainees use the lesson right away. Many *kaizen* trainers, or facilitators, will continue teaching classes throughout the project to help teams reach their goals. Trainers can come from inside the company or they can be hired consultants.

Waste not, want not

One of the most important Lean concepts is ***muda***—wasteful activity. Taiichi Ohno, identified the following **Seven Wastes.**[31] Try not to get too wrapped up on deciding which form of waste something is. It doesn't really matter which category you assign it to. If something is *muda,* eliminate as much of it as possible.

What You Already Know

Your time and money are valuable. You don't like waiting for appointments, sitting in traffic, or having to throw out food that was left over after a meal.

1. ***Defects.*** Defects in products—when items don't work properly—are clearly a waste. But defects can also happen in processes, such as building the wrong model or delivering a part to the wrong location. Defects obviously require work to correct. Worse, if they make their way downstream to a customer, the poor quality can reduce profit in the form of lost sales. Defects give otherwise loyal customers a reason to look elsewhere for a more reliable product. Where can defects be traced back to?

Every defect is caused by an error in a process.

[31] (Ohno, 1988)

The obvious solution then is to find where the errors occur and fix the process. Defects for Jimmy and Bobby include the obvious—spoiled lemons or bugs in the lemonade, but spilled drinks, sticky cups, or incorrect change are all types of defects as well.

2. ***Overprocessing***. This is generally viewed as anything in excess—any unnecessary steps or processes that do not add value to the end product or service. Jimmy would be overprocessing if he shook up his lemonade in a sealed container and then stirred it as well.

3. ***Transportation.*** Moving material from one place to another wastes time and energy and includes a risk of loss or damage. At first glance, transportation may seem necessary; but, it is normally the result of a non-Lean layout. Sometimes, this type of waste is so bad that when a particular route is traced on top of a factory map, it looks like a bowl of tangled spaghetti! This type of waste can be present in an office as well— if you have to carry a file down a hall to a fax machine and then walk it back to a file storage room. Jimmy might have had this form of waste if he frequently carried lemons, water, or cups back and forth between the house and the stand.

4. ***Motion***. While moving material or products from one location to another is transportation waste, the unnecessary movements of workers or tools is a waste of motion. Wasted motion takes time and uses up energy, especially if the tool or equipment is heavy. Other examples include the following:

    - Re-orienting parts to get them into a new position.
    - Walking between work stations to get tools.
    - Shuffling files to get to the right one.
    - Flipping a tool around in your hand to get it ready to use.

If Jimmy took phone orders, and had to walk into the house each time the phone rang, that would be an example of wasted motion.

5. ***Time.*** Waiting for parts, letting glue set, watching a machine work, staring at the hourglass on a computer screen—all this is waste. Jimmy would be wasting time if he stood by watching his juicer squeeze lemons.

6. ***Inventory.*** An excess of inventory ties up money that could be used for other things. It also slows down the speed of production, which matters most when custom products or perishables are involved. It is important to remember that inventory includes not only supplies of raw materials but also finished products awaiting sale. Jimmy has inventory waste when his stockpile of lemons and sugar exceeds his immediate needs.

7. ***Overproduction.*** Overproduction occurs any time an upstream process produces more than a downstream process can use right away. The result is always the same. Inventory piles up along the value stream. Overproducers generally have a reason for making more than needed. Workstations might be far apart, and big batches reduce travel time. Maybe the overproduction is a hedge against maintenance problems. Perhaps machines take a long time to switch between parts, so the operators run large lots. Regardless of the reasons (most of which are avoidable), overproduction is wasteful. Slicing lemons faster than they can be juiced is an example of overproduction in Jimmy's roadside operation.

   Many people have the misconception that overproduction does not exist outside of the manufacturing sector. It certainly looks different in office or service environments than it does in manufacturing, but it is present. It is primarily apparent when work is pushed onto the next step and hits a **bottleneck** (an obstacle that slows down progress), where it will sit for a long period before being touched again.

When work gets passed on without any regard for how backed up the next worker is, the system soon gets swamped and bogs down. For example, an overworked engineer may routinely have design change requests piled into a stuffed inbox. What's the result? Being backed up adds work—prospecting to find the right document, trying to prioritize, and answering the inevitable calls of, "Where's my stuff?" Notice that these things are actually other forms of waste. That is because:

Overproduction creates or hides all the other six types of waste. For that reason, it is widely considered to be the worst of the Seven Wastes.

You can also think of excess capacity as overproduction in service environments. For instance, when a plane takes off, the airline is paying to move all the seats, whether they are empty or full.

Excess capacity in the office (and in service) is overproduction and costs money.

How does less mean more?

One of the central themes of Lean is inventory control. Obviously, you've got to have enough material available to meet the pace of your production targets. More than what you need *right now,* though, and the waste of too much inventory starts to add up. The alternative to piles of inventory is to utilize a **Just-in-Time** strategy to make sure that the right materials are in the right place in the right quantities, shortly before they are needed.

> ***What You Already Know***
>
> *You know not to buy a five-pound box of strawberries if you live alone and only need a handful to make your milkshake. The lower bulk price may seem like a good deal, but it's not if the berries get moldy and end up in the trash before you can eat them.*

This includes finished goods, raw materials, and components, as well as partially finished products, which are sometimes called **work-in-process (WIP)**, or **work-in-progress.**

Unfortunately, relying on excess inventory is like an addiction to painkillers. It trades a whole range of long-term, big problems for some relief right now. It enables a company to hide such problems as poor suppliers, low quality, long distances, and large setup times. Inventory doesn't solve the problems—it just masks them.

Once a company starts using inventory to compensate for poor processes, problems become hard to find and even harder to get rid of. In the end, the waste of excessive inventory becomes evident in the following ways:

- ***Inventory costs money.*** Inventory ties up cash that could be used for other needs. If your company has a million dollars in inventory, it can't spend that money on buying new computers or setting up a new production line. Buying small quantities gives a company some financial flexibility, since it spreads expenses out over time. That way, the company doesn't have to come up with a big chunk of cash all at once. If Jimmy spent too much money on lemons, he might run out of cash to pay for sugar or make change for customers.

- ***Money loses value over time.*** Like cash that is tucked in a mattress or buried in the yard, money that is tied up in inventory loses buying power every day. If it doesn't earn interest, it loses ground to inflation.

- ***Inventory goes bad.*** Buying perishable resources in bulk doesn't make sense, even if it *is* packaged into a "great deal." It needs to be used or sold before it goes bad. Lettuce spoils, so grocery stores only buy what they can sell quickly. Jimmy obviously can't buy lemons too far in advance for the same reason. To a lesser degree, even things like computer hard drives "spoil" because bigger, better, faster ones come along to make the old ones obsolete. The real kicker: your company might even have to pay for the costs of disposal, especially if the inventory contains hazardous materials!

- ***Inventory takes space.*** More inventory takes up more space. More space costs more money. So . . . less inventory can save your company money because less space is needed for storage.
- ***Theft and other losses.*** A sprinkler head breaks and the warehouse gets doused with water . . . An unethical visitor develops sticky fingers . . . Rodents find a home in some storage boxes. Sometimes items just get misplaced. In any case, if you can't find something when you need it, the company has to spend money to buy replacements. Even if your company pays for insurance to offset losses, more inventory means higher premiums.
- ***Inventory has to be managed.*** Inventory is constantly being shuffled, consolidated, counted, logged, and cleaned. The company might even have so much on hand that it needs to buy a forklift, which means a driver, insurance, and fuel, plus bigger aisles.

Get organized

5S is an organizational philosophy that results in a safer, cleaner, more efficient workspace. The term 5S comes from a series of Japanese words, all starting with the letter *S*. The English versions, coincidentally, contains 5 "S" terms as well. Granted, some of the Japanese words can be translated into more than one English equivalent, so you might see other terms used in different sources. For the scope of this book, however, let's use the following terms for 5S:

> **What You Already Know**
>
> *Finding a fork takes longer if you have to look through a disorganized pile of flatware thrown into a drawer than if you look in a neatly sorted divider. If the divider has shapes that outline the spaces for specific utensils, you can tell right away that you don't have any clean spoons.*

1. ***Sort.*** Get rid of any unnecessary items that clutter the work area, and continue to do it on a regular basis. This is equally true whether on a shop floor or in a cubicle.

2. ***Simplify.*** Organize all work areas and arrange resources so they are easy to find and get to. This includes providing safe and ready access to such items as tools, supplies, and computer files. Keep the items that are used most frequently closest to where they are needed. An example: keep a stapler in a designated spot next to the copier, rather than storing it in a cabinet.

3. ***Straighten.*** Tidy up work areas and make them easy to keep clean by designing ways to prevent dirt from accumulating in the first place. Get rid of unneeded flat surfaces that collect dust and clutter. Then set up systems that prevent it from reappearing. If you can't eliminate a messy job, use 5S to make the grime gather where it can be easily cleaned—use chutes, grates, small fans, vacuums, etc. Prime areas to target include desks, shelving units, areas where cutting or grinding is done, and the space around copiers and printers.

4. ***Standardize.*** Make things visual and obvious by labeling or marking locations of resources. That way, you'll be able to easily tell when something is low in stock, out of place, or missing.

5. ***Sustain.*** Make a habit of practicing good 5S techniques—your boss should designate a portion of every day to maintaining your work area. Why daily? For some reason, clutter attracts more clutter. Staying on top of your 5S keeps messes from getting a foothold.

5S is best summarized as "A place for everything and everything in its place."

Jimmy has to keep his customers happy. Having established places for his materials and resources—his ingredients, spoons, pitchers, and glasses—enables him to serve his customers quickly. Plus, a stand that is clean and organized makes a good impression.

What you see is what you get

Visual management builds on 5S. It uses organization and standardization to make abnormal conditions stand out. When these problems are so obvious that they jump out at you, they are easier and faster to solve. Two specific types of **visual controls** are *andon* lights and *kanbans* (both will be explained shortly).

> ***What You Already Know***
> *You know that a red traffic light means to stop, and a green light means to go.*

The ultimate goal of visual management is for anyone with a basic understanding of the process in question to be able to recognize that an area has a problem *and* know what to do about it. In fact, there are basically only two rules for establishing a successful visual management program:

- ***Make abnormal conditions easy to spot.*** Use the "ten-foot rule"—make sure an abnormal condition can be *easily* identified from at least ten feet away. A red *andon* light is a perfect example because it is so easy to recognize from a distance.
- ***Know what to do.*** Have a plan for reacting when something is wrong. Knowing an issue exists is only the first step. Visual management includes having an established reaction plan that spells out what to do about the problem.

The more obvious visual management is, the more effective it will be. As your company becomes more and more Lean, visual controls and reaction plans will sprout up everywhere. On the surface, all these signals can seem a little over the top and somewhat restrictive. People typically balk, at least initially, at having their workday dictated by flashing lights. The truth, though, is that they increase your freedom because you don't have to spend your time watching a mechanized process or checking things over and over. Visual controls free you up to do more important things.

Visual management is used to turbocharge Lean efforts.

As mentioned, an ***andon***—the Japanese word for paper lantern—is one type of visual control. In Lean it acts as a signal to identify a problem. The light that flashes on a phone when someone is on hold is an example of an *andon*. The most common *andon* lights you will see in manufacturing are those used to signal that help is needed on an assembly line or to announce that a machine is having problems.

Outside of work, you use *andons* as well. Consider the dashboard of your car. Warning lights come on to indicate abnormal conditions. The "door ajar" and "seat belt" lights both tell you that a problem exists. You also know what to do about it. You don't need to do a "pre-flight" inspection of the car to make sure everything is in working order—your car's visual controls save you that time and get you on the road faster for a worry-free drive.

Jimmy could also benefit from visual controls. He might use a marking on the pavement to indicate that the line of customers is too long and that he needs to call his sister for help. The visual control tells him something is out of the ordinary and that he needs to take action to fix the problem.

What You Already Know

Your newspaper ends up on your porch every day, even if you are out of town. Mail order rental DVDs are the opposite—you don't get a new DVD until you turn in the one that you just watched. Returning a DVD is a signal to the movie distributor that you are ready for the next one on your list.

No pushing!

Pull is a core principle of Lean that helps control inventory and production. The premise of pull (vs. push) is that workers do not start production until someone downstream (nearer the customer) needs or asks for a product. Demand drives production.

Pull is controlled by many methods: *kanban* cards, signal lights, empty spaces on the floor, or even colored ping-pong balls in a chute. In the following diagram, a downstream worker takes a product from a rack. The empty space signals the upstream supplier that it is time to restock, and even indicates which item to produce. This illustration depicts a version of pull known as a **supermarket**. If the supermarket is full, there is no demand and production waits. That prevents inventory of that item from piling up.

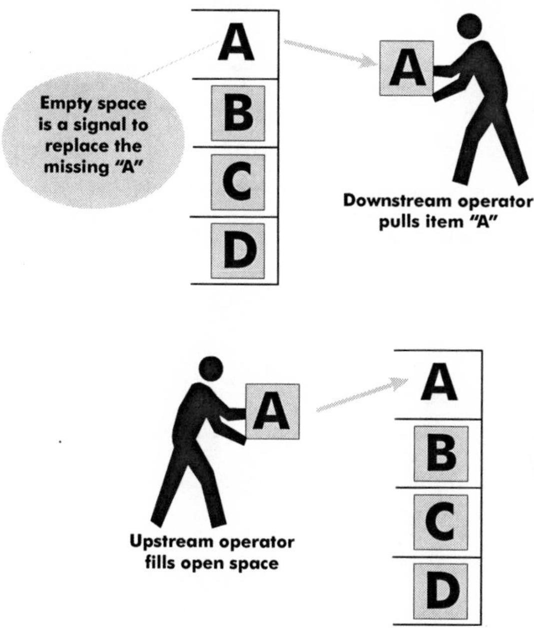

Pulling from a supermarket.

The biggest advantage pull has over **push** is that pull prevents overproduction. In push systems, people build to a pre-determined schedule that may or may not agree with the actual demand at that moment. The upstream process churns out parts from a list without really knowing what the downstream process needs. In a pull system, each step of the supply chain is tightly linked; in push, the upstream and downstream supply chains are disconnected. The effect? Pull systems respond well to changes in demand, or to operational difficulties; push systems do not.

Can I take your order?

A ***kanban*** system is a low tech, yet very visible way, of managing inventory levels. The cornerstone of the system is the ***kanban* card,** which contains all the information you need to transport, produce, or order the proper amount of material.

> ***What You Already Know***
>
> *You know that when you get toward the bottom of a box of checks, you will see a re-order form. You send the order to be filled and use the last couple of checks as you wait for your new ones to arrive.*

<table>
<tr><th colspan="4">Part Description</th><th colspan="2">Part Number</th></tr>
<tr><td colspan="4">Smoke-shifter, left handed.</td><td colspan="2">14613</td></tr>
<tr><td>Qty</td><td>20</td><td>Lead Time</td><td>1 week</td><td>Order Date</td><td>9/3</td></tr>
<tr><td>Supplier</td><td colspan="3">Acme Smoke-Shifter, LLC</td><td>Due Date</td><td>9/10</td></tr>
<tr><td rowspan="2">Planner</td><td rowspan="2" colspan="2">John R.</td><td colspan="3">Card 1 of 2</td></tr>
<tr><td>Location</td><td colspan="2">Rack 1B3</td></tr>
</table>

Sample *kanban* card

The most common *kanban* system uses two bins. As soon as one bin is empty, the worker drops a *kanban* card in a collection point, and starts using parts from the second, full bin.

In the meantime, whoever received the dropped card starts the next part of the replenishment process. Purchasers place orders, material handlers move parts, and upstream operators start production.

So, two things are happening at the same time. An operator is pulling from his second bin, slowly reducing the number of parts. Meanwhile, the order is making its way to the supplier, where it is filled and shipped to your company. (The handwritten dates on the laminated *kanban* card indicate when the order was placed and when it should arrive.) The quantities in the bins are predetermined. If all goes smoothly, the parts arrive to fill the empty bin just before the other bin runs out.

A *kanban* system works because the cards trigger very specific actions. Everyone in the organization recognizes the cards, and knows exactly what to do with them. *Kanbans* may seem out of place in the age of computers, but work extremely well because they are so visible.

While the typical *kanban* is a laminated card, sometimes an empty container itself is the signal. When the container, bin, or rack arrives at an upstream process or supplier, the recipient knows to fill it up.

Kanbans are far more common on shop floors than they are in offices. The most likely place to see a *kanban* in an administrative environment is in the supply cabinet. For example, in a full stack of fifty forms you might see a laminated red sheet of paper with replenishment instructions inserted ten sheets from the bottom. This sheet acts as a *kanban* to trigger restocking as the supply gets low.

Kanban systems don't, by themselves, reduce inventory. They just maintain it at whatever level the company sets. Reducing inventory levels comes from process improvement like shortening **lead times** (the time from order to receipt of goods) or reducing batch sizes.

What You Already Know

The recipe for your Uncle David's famous enchiladas isn't very tasty if you don't follow the directions exactly. You know that the dish is easily ruined if you: add ingredients at the wrong time, if you and your spouse duplicate a spice, if the stove isn't at the correct temperature, or if you forget to take it out after the proper amount of time. You intuitively know that a consistent output (or, in this case, an edible result) requires consistent input.

Having high standards

Lean calls for uniformity. This means that a person provides the same service or makes a product the same way every single time. It also means that Joe and Sue come up with the same results, even if they work different shifts. **Standard Work** is the "recipe" that brings consistency to the table. It has several requirements:

- ***Standard Work defines the sequence of operations.*** It should not only include *what* to do and *how* to do it, but also *when* to perform a task. The order matters.
- ***Standard Work assigns work to a single position.*** If the job requires two or more operators, each should have his or her own Standard Work that says who does what tasks. If duties are not specifically assigned, processes will be inconsistent. Operators can easily forget steps if each one thinks the other did it. Or, if the work is not coordinated properly, workers end up standing around waiting for each other.
- ***Standard Work designates Work-in-Process (WIP).*** A worker should only be working on one item (or set) at a time. If the Standard Work says to assemble only one wiring harness, you—as the worker—would do that, and only that. If the Standard Work says to prep a set of four items at once (like a set of tires), you do that. A good workstation will make it difficult to do more than is outlined in the Standard Work, since the area will be set up to support only the specified WIP.
- ***Standard Work should be balanced to a product's takt time.*** ***Takt* time** defines how frequently a company must be able to produce a product in order to meet its customers' needs. It is the pace of demand. If your shift is eight full hours and your customers (on average) order twenty-four widgets a day, you know you have to produce three per hour. So, every twenty minutes you need to churn one out. Your *takt* time is twenty minutes. The length of time it *actually* takes to complete Standard Work is called **cycle time.** If the cycle time is longer than the *takt* time, say, twenty-three minutes for the example,

the process can't meet customer demand. If the cycle time is shorter than *takt* time, workers will be standing around, waiting—and wasting time.

Standard Work offers the following benefits to Lean businesses:

- ***It improves quality.*** Consistent, repetitive inputs lead to predictable, high-quality outputs.
- ***It provides a basis for planning.*** Companies can plan production more quickly and more accurately when they know how long a process takes (cycle time) and what resources it needs to complete it.
- ***It lays a foundation for improvement.*** It is difficult to improve a process that changes every time someone does it. Stabilizing the process provides a starting point for improvement. It also ensures that any improvements are shared with the whole team, instead of just a few workers who know the best practice.

Standard Work, in its pure form, is most applicable on the shop floor. In the office, its use is a little murkier. Consider a customer service representative answering phone calls. The inherent variation in what the customer wants makes Standard Work the wrong tool to document how to answer a phone call. Other tools, like process flowcharts are much better suited. Still, in other office jobs, Standard Work fits like a glove to provide results that are consistent and work that is well-defined. Repeatable, low-variation processes like receiving checks from customers or placing purchase orders are good examples. Standard Work is normally documented on three forms:

- ***Standard Work Sheet.*** This form visually shows the flow of work. It follows the operator's route as well as where WIP is needed to make the process flow.

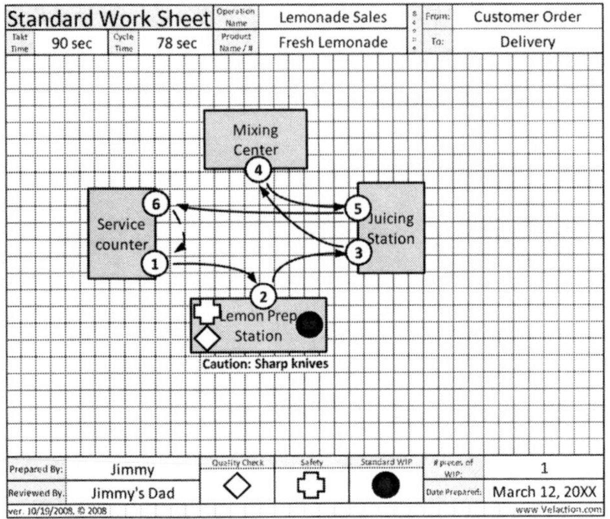

Sample Standard Work Sheet

- ***Standard Work Combination Sheet.*** This form shows how operators and machines interact, as well as how much time the operator spends walking from task to task.

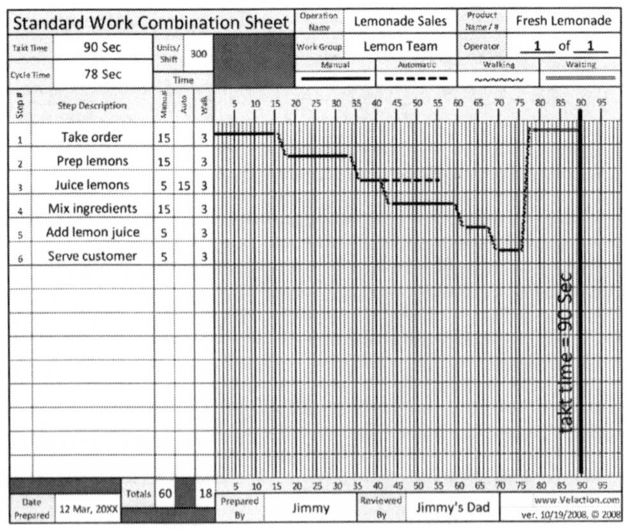

Step #	Step Description	Manual	Auto	Walk
1	Take order	15		3
2	Prep lemons	15		3
3	Juice lemons	5	15	3
4	Mix ingredients	15		3
5	Add lemon juice	5		3
6	Serve customer	5		3
	Totals	60		18

Sample Standard Work Combination Sheet

- ***Work Instructions.*** These come in a variety of formats but all provide the specific details needed to do the steps described in Standard Work. Continuing the analogy from earlier, if Standard Work is a recipe, then work instructions would be specific directions on how to do the steps. For instance, a recipe might instruct the chef to "brown the ground beef." Work instructions would explain, in detail, how to do that. In the manufacturing of go-carts, for example, Standard Work would say, "install tires." Work instructions would specify the part numbers needed, the tools required, the torque to apply, and other specific details.

How do you measure up?

Lean operates on the philosophy that you have to understand what is going on with a process in order to be able to improve it. Measuring the details of an operation provides that understanding. As a result, Lean companies tend to set up extensive **measurement systems.** Unfortunately, this doesn't always sit well with employees.

Most people hate being measured.

Notice the mismatch in employee preferences and company needs. For many people, when they leave school, the daily appraisals stop. No more pop quizzes to find out whether they did their reading assignment. No more handing in homework to get graded. Sure, you probably still get an annual performance review at work, but many employees think of those more as a boss's personal opinion than as facts about the quality and consistency of their work.

What You Already Know

Many people have their cholesterol level and blood pressure checked periodically. To make an evaluation of your condition, the doctor would compare your current numbers to your previous ones and then to society-wide averages. If your measurements are higher than they should be, some sort of action might be required—prescription medicine, for example, or cutting down on the double cheeseburgers and fries.

In a Lean company, though, ongoing assessments are a way of keeping the organization on track. Production is measured; quality is tracked. Graphs, charts, and stopwatches are everywhere.

In well-run operations, measuring processes gives an immediate indication of problems that the company must correct.

Metrics, also referred to as **measures,** are the specific items that are evaluated. For instance, "productivity" is a metric that monitors output over a set unit of input (parts per hour, for example). Workers generally correct obvious problems as soon as they see them. Subtle issues might go unnoticed, but they won't slip by the metrics. When one of these measures shows a change, the people responsible for the process can immediately launch an investigation to find the cause.

These changes can be trends—such as a downward move that could mean a machine is wearing out, a computer is getting bogged down with spyware or a virus, or a saw blade is losing its edge. Wild variations might point to a step in the process that can't deliver consistent results. Such changes are general indications that something is going on in the process. And once that something is identified, it has a better chance of being fixed.

On the sample run chart, there are two noticeable changes. First, the dip on March 18 indicates a one-time problem that caused a single day of lower productivity. Perhaps a machine broke down. Second, on March 25, productivity jumped up and stayed there. A *kaizen* team likely implemented a process improvement on that date.

Identifying a problem using a metric is only the first step. Metrics *must* be acted upon, or the effort to collect the information is wasted. In other words, knowing about problems is useless unless something is done to find a solution. Most good Lean systems will also monitor **countermeasures**—the actions that teams use

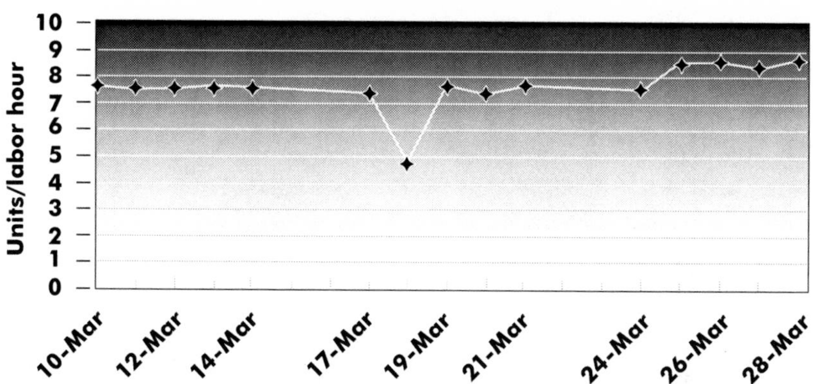

Run charts make changes in metrics easy to notice.

to get a process back on track. This follow-up plan, which involves employees at all levels, is another reason that Lean works so well.

Managing the metrics

The use of metrics to highlight problems and track solutions enables **daily management,** which promotes keeping teams on track through regular, frequent leadership involvement. The most noticeable component of daily management is the team meeting at the start of a shift, sometimes referred to as a "**stand-up.**" In these gatherings, leaders and employees review that day's numbers and come up with specific actions that will keep teams and processes on track. While daily targets are the primary focus, these sessions also review progress on long-term goals. Since measuring processes can be so valuable to the team, why do people dislike being measured?

Most people just want to be appreciated and recognized for their hard work, not scrutinized.

They fear getting in trouble for not being as effective at their jobs as the star performers. Unfortunately, some managers will use measurement systems to weed out the lowest performing employees. This makes metrics a sensitive topic between managers and employees. Fortunately, most leaders will use information to help the team and the process—and you.

The fact is, managers know when a person is not performing well. Guess what? Measures seldom enlighten leaders about who the highest performers are or who is just trying to get by with the least effort. Bosses usually already know. And so do you. And so do your coworkers. Ask yourself this: who are the best performers on your team? Who would you want to take with you if you left to start your own company? You know the answers to those questions without having to look over a chart or graph.

For the moment, let's stress the positives about measurement systems. On a large scale, measurements can be used to recognize teams for outstanding performance and to drive process improvement. Metrics also help establish reasonable improvement goals so teams don't feel overly pressured.

Additionally, metrics are great for building consensus. They provide real information, which is far more reliable and valuable to employees than a boss's opinion. Managers who understand the value of measures tend not to make important decisions off the cuff, or with their "gut feelings." Employees are more likely to support a decision when they can see the data that drove it. After all, good decisions make employees' lives easier.

On a smaller scale, measures can assist you directly. In fact, knowing where you stand lets you take action, even if your boss does not address the issue with you. A measurement system gives you an unbiased view of how you are stacking up against your peers. Some workers don't care how well they are doing, as long as they don't get fired. The great majority of employees, however, want to do well at their jobs.

While managers can use measures to provide information about individual workers, the real purpose of metrics is to point out variation. They highlight unusual situations and provide specific details that leaders and teams can act upon. Performance and satisfaction are both raised when specific problems get solved.

When measures don't match expectations, or when they change dramatically, it's time to investigate. So, what things can a measurement system help identify?

- ***How processes stack up.*** If a team's performance is all over the map, the process itself is probably a problem. If only a few people are off the average, it probably means those individuals are not following the process.
- ***Best practices.*** If someone is doing markedly better than others, two reasons exist. The first is that he really is faster. The second possibility is that he has figured out a better process—one that others could, and should, duplicate.
- ***Additional tasks.*** Some metrics suffer because the worker is doing unmeasured tasks in addition to measured ones. Someone has to take out the trash, right? The task makes productivity look worse than it really is, since it takes people away from the measured work.
- ***Working with others.*** Some employees become the unofficial "go-to" person. They are typically highly experienced or are star performers. Their productivity numbers fall, though, when coworkers frequently come to them with problems. This highlights a need for more effective training.
- ***Special situations.*** Sometimes, high performers end up getting the toughest assignments—the hardest station on an assembly line, or the most demanding customer in the office. Their numbers then look worse because they have the biggest challenges.
- ***Poor training.*** When a person does poorly on his metrics, a good manager will start out by watching him. This can immediately identify if the issue is related to poor training.

Obviously, productivity and quality are dependent upon doing a job the right way.

- ***The employee is in the wrong job.*** Hiring methods are not always perfect and occasionally a person does end up in a job they can't do. Other times, a person could perform well, if she wanted, but just doesn't like the job. Both of these issues affect performance. Metrics help in these situations by providing objective evidence of the person's results. When an employee is in the wrong job, the only solution is often moving the worker to a more appropriate position.

In each of these situations, good leaders will take corrective actions. Even better leaders will have their teams trained to be able to act on the measurements themselves.

What You Already Know

Gardening in your back yard is probably best done with a shovel. You wouldn't rent a backhoe to plant a bush.

Bigger is not better

Many people believe that big complicated machines are more efficient than smaller, less powerful options. They can be, of course, but in many cases, big is not the right size for the job. For example, think about how a large, centrally located printer is used.

Sure, the cost per page is lower for the big printer and the unit probably prints faster than a smaller model. To retrieve documents, though, people have to get up from their desks and venture out to track down their print jobs. The trip adds cost because of the inefficiency of the *whole* print process.

One solution is for employees to batch their print jobs so they only have to walk over to the print center once a day, instead of each time they print out a document. Sounds like a good solution on the surface, but it adds other problems. Downstream coworkers end up waiting longer for the document, since the batching disrupts flow.

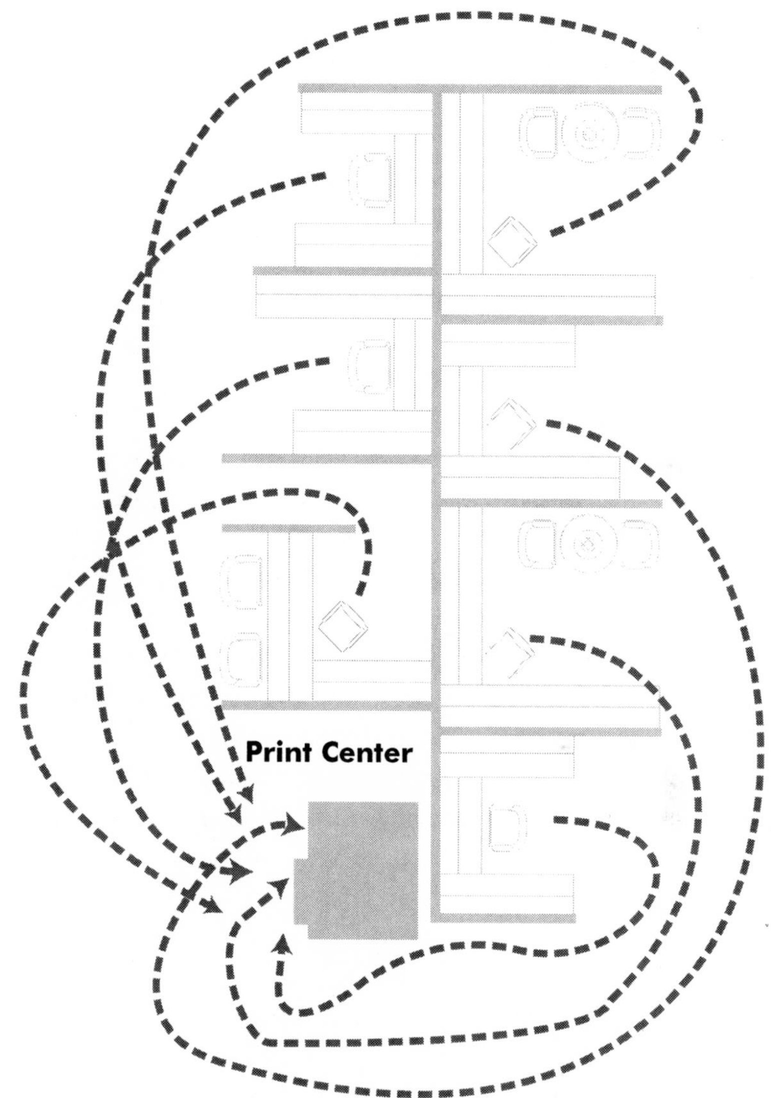

Large machines can create waste.

When people go to get their documents (waste of transportation), the trip away from their workstation is a big interruption. Since all the employees are probably batching their print jobs, the piles can be large. Workers have to sift through reams of paper (waste of motion). Sometimes, they will not be able to find their document, or they will grab someone else's by mistake (defect waste).

They might not detect printer problems—jams, being out of paper, or some other service issue—because they are not close enough to see the warnings. The entire stack of printouts might even be ruined if the printer left streaks down each page (*more* defect waste). Finally, their print job might be at the end of the print queue and they have to stand around watching as everyone else's papers pile up (waste of time).

The *muda* that is added in dealing with these issues could easily eat up any per-page savings advantage the big printer has. Smaller, more centrally located printers can often save money in the long run.

In manufacturing, the same problems are even more apparent. Big machines that produce large lots (batches) are expensive, so they have to support several product lines to make them cost-effective. This means they are not positioned to make products flow well. Rather, big machines tend to be organized by function—folding is done in one location, cutting is done together, and drilling is in another location. Instead of walking those long distances between machines for only one part, workers often save up for a more worthwhile trip.

Batch machines also take a long time to switch over from one product to another (see changeover in the next section), adding pressure to build more units before switching to the next product.

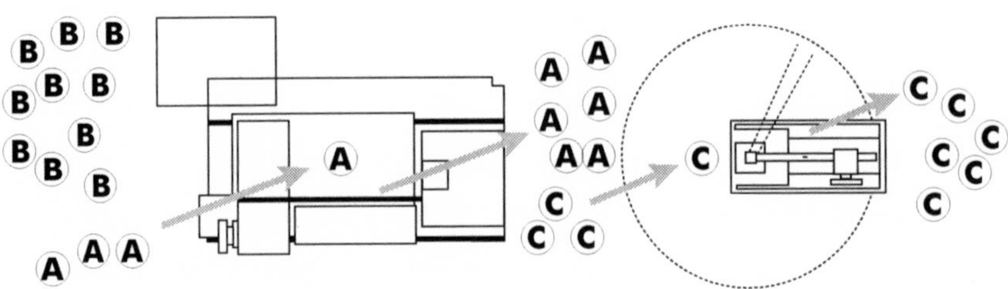

Big machines cause large lot sizes.

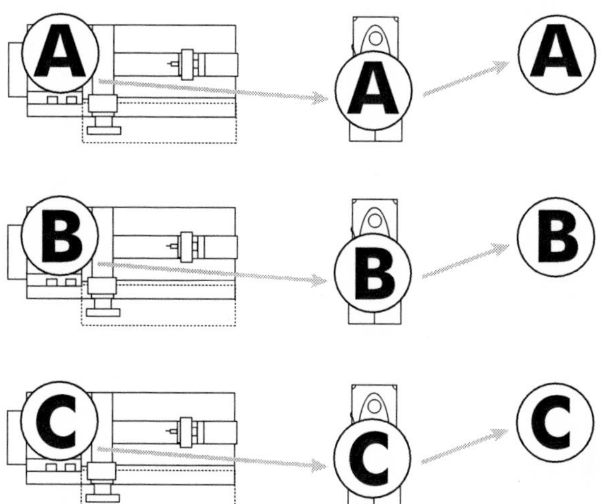

Having the right-sized machine for a job helps products flow better.

When the speed of a large machine is the only thing that is considered, the "cost per part" might appear cheap. When all the extra work and inventory caused by overproduction are added to the equation, the parts aren't so inexpensive after all.

In many cases, several small machines are a better option than a single big machine. That is where the term **right-sized machines** comes from. It means matching the size and capacity of a machine to the specific task it will be performing. Having smaller machines dedicated to specific processes also means no sharing and, therefore, no waiting to use the machine. Another benefit: right-sized machines can be located near their upstream and downstream processes, making parts flow better.

Changeover

When a machine is shared by different product lines, operators have to switch between parts. This process is called **changeover,** or **setup.**[32] During the transition time from one product type to

[32] Lean experts can't seem to agree on whether setup and changeover are the same thing or have subtle differences. Don't worry about this, though. Just use the terms however your company does.

another, the machine is not producing. Because of this sometimes lengthy downtime, once the machine is up and running, it has to produce large batches to make up for lost time. These long production runs drive up inventory costs and tie up cash that could be used elsewhere. **Setup reduction**[33] is, therefore, among the most critical tools in Lean. Reducing setup time is what lets a batch manufacturer turn the corner to becoming a Lean enterprise.

> **What You Already Know**
>
> *Years ago, people watched home movies on film. They didn't do it all that often, though, because it took forever to pull out the screen, find the box of reels, set up the projector, feed the film by hand, start the projector, and focus it. Just getting everything ready could take a long time, so families seldom watched just one—instead they made a night of it.*
>
> *Once people started getting the family recordings on videocassette, though, the process got easier. It didn't take nearly as long to set up. They just popped in the tape and fast-forwarded to the right spot.*
>
> *Now, many people have their videos on DVD. They just insert the disk in the player and press a menu button to get to exactly the scene they want to see.*

Compare batch manufacturing to grocery shopping. The farther you live from a store, the more you tend to buy when you get there. For example, if you lived way up in the mountains, you would buy lots of food, maybe once a month. If you lived across the street from a store, you might pop in for small purchases every day or two.

The more often you shop, the less you buy. That means you have more flexibility in budgeting and planning for your meals, right? The mountain man can't easily change to a different meal if he gets a craving for something not on the menu plan, or if he suddenly has dinner guests. The city dweller can react with hardly any notice. Old friend stopping by? No problem!

Big purchases also raise your risk of big inventory damage. If you only have a small pantry of food and get an ant infestation, your losses are limited. If you just stocked up your mountain cabin,

---

[33] Despite the sometimes interchangeable use of "changeover" and "setup," you will rarely, if ever, hear the term "changeover reduction."

you might lose weeks of food. Small stockpiles are also less likely to spoil. What is the difference in the two situations? The setup time it takes to drive to and from the store.

The takeaway is that short setups are like living close to the store. As setups get shorter, batch sizes can get smaller. And as batch sizes get smaller, production can get closer and closer to **single-piece flow**—the holy grail of Lean manufacturing. That's when an item starts moving through production and never waits in a pile of inventory anywhere in the process.

While setup reduction is most commonly used in reference to machines on a production floor, the concept can also apply to the time it takes to shift between tasks in an office. A materials team may have to review supplier performance, estimate upcoming demand, and place orders. Each task takes a little setup, or preparation time, such as pulling up the right spreadsheet. Some estimates peg this psychological changeover at up to forty-five minutes for complex tasks. Administrative personnel can spend as much as twenty-eight percent of their day switching from task to task.[34] As a result, the team likely tries to do a large batch of each job before moving on to the next type of work. As on the shop floor, if the changeover time was smaller, the office staff could do more changes and stay on top of things better.

Even Steven

Most companies are not blessed with even demand from their customers. They may get orders for eighty units today and a hundred tomorrow, but none the next day. One approach used to deal with this phenomenon is to try smoothing out demand. Airlines frequently

> ***What You Already Know***
>
> *You try to add some balance to the chores that you do. You don't cook on Monday, clean on Tuesday, launder on Wednesday, and wash dishes on Thursday. You tend to allocate your time and do a little bit each day to keep on top of everything.*

[34] (Ferriss, 2007)

offer last minute reductions on fares to avoid letting the plane fly with empty seats.

But even if companies succeed in shifting some demand, they may still experience peaks and valleys. Restaurants use happy hours to lure some of the dinner crowd in at an earlier time. Despite their best efforts, though, they will still have a much greater demand around 6:00 p.m. than they do at 3:30 in the afternoon. In the case of a restaurant or similar business, not having the capacity to meet demand can cause it to lose customers, money, and reputation.

Here, physical products have a big advantage over services. This is where ***heijunka,*** or **level loading,** comes in. An electronics store probably doesn't have a steady, evenly spaced line of customers coming in to buy computer keyboards. The demand varies. Add this up for all the retailers selling that keyboard, and the electronics manufacturer would be in quite a bind trying to meet that exact demand. So, the manufacturer levels its production to meet the average demand, and puts some stability into its processes.

Once the workload is stabilized through *heijunka*, process improvement really takes off. You no longer have to battle demand variation on a daily basis—whether total numbers or the quantity of each product type (the **model mix**). Lead times drop rapidly as you pull waste out. You can reduce inventory at a faster rate. After all, with a more even mix of production, you need fewer parts on hand at any given time—you don't have to store as many parts to cover possible daily spikes for each model.

Heijunka does require some close attention. Product planners still have to keep on top of what customers are ordering and determine if fluctuations are short-term variations, or if they are part of a larger trend. If the latter is the case, the company will have to adjust its production levels.

Don't touch that

Jidoka all started many years ago at a textile plant. Because the threads on looms would frequently break, an operator had to monitor each machine so he could shut it off if a problem came up. Eventually, an engineer devised a method to combat this problem—when a string broke, the loom stopped automatically and signaled a worker to fix the problem. This system came to be called *jidoka,* or **autonomation**—automation with a human touch.

> ***What You Already Know***
> *You know that you don't have to hang around the laundry room, waiting to shut off the dryer—the machine will do it automatically. And, you know that if the load in the washing machine gets out of balance, the machine will automatically shut itself off before it shakes apart. These are examples of jidoka.*

Using *jidoka,* a machine can identify an abnormal condition. It can then react, usually by shutting down to prevent damage to itself and the part. Finally, the machine will signal a human operator, typically with an *andon* light and possibly an audible warning. Instead of pairing one operator with one machine, a single operator can monitor multiple machines at once. When a problem signals the operator, he locates the condition, fixes it, and re-starts the process.

Jidoka is an integral part of the continuous improvement culture. The *jidoka* process has four steps:

1. ***Identify the problem or abnormality.***
2. ***Stop production and signal the operator.***
3. ***Correct the abnormal condition and, if needed, come up with a short-term fix or "workaround."***
4. ***Develop and implement a permanent solution.***

As mentioned already, *jidoka* prevents damage to malfunctioning machines and improves quality by stopping production on machines that are making bad parts. It increases productivity by reducing waste. And another big benefit is frequently overlooked:

Jidoka respects people's intelligence.

Employees should not be asked to stand around doing a basic task that requires little skill when their talents could better be used elsewhere.

Go with the flow

What You Already Know

Traffic on some roads—ones with wide straight stretches and limited access—flows smoothly. Other roads—the ones with many side streets and stoplights—are often more reminiscent of parking lots than of major thoroughfares. Yet other roads normally move well, but can get log jammed with an influx of cars—near a stadium, a mall, or a major employer, for instance.

Flow is the smooth, continuous way that a product or service moves effortlessly down the value stream toward a customer. In Lean teachings, production is frequently compared to a meandering river, full of pools and backwaters. But as companies lower the water level—in other words, as they reduce inventory—the pools start to drain and the water stops flowing into those backwaters. The lower water level also uncovers all the rocks (waste) that impede flow. As Lean efforts continue, the meandering river starts running faster and faster, eventually turning into a smoother, straighter channel.

If you dropped a stick into the meandering river, it would take forever to make its way downstream, and might get caught up in whirlpools or flushed into those little backwaters. You couldn't guess when it would reach its destination. Once the river was streamlined, though, the stick would zip along the current at a steady pace.

Lean reduces lead times and improves predictability—and makes customers happy as a result.

Flow is not a means of becoming Lean but rather a result of your company's Lean efforts. A business has to use many Lean tools to reach this end state.

The opposite of Lean

The opposite of flow is **batch and queue.** This is the default manufacturing method, in which products and services are produced and transported in large lots and then sit while waiting for the next step. These stacks of partly assembled materials disrupt flow and create huge amounts of waste.

One common example of batching and queuing in the office environment is a database that only updates once a day. An example of this is when your bank does not post transactions to your account in real time. Instead, your transactions are queued and batch processed overnight. In those cases, your deposits and purchases from one day are not reflected on your account until the next day.

What You Already Know

You know how disheartening it can be to see huge piles of laundry waiting to be washed, or piles of dishes stacked in the sink. You know how easy it is to miss paying a bill on time when a huge stack of mail is waiting for your attention. Doing a little bit at a time always seems easier than digging out from under big piles.

Lean manufacturers tend to call non-Lean companies "batch manufacturers." (Not surprisingly, those companies don't tend to call themselves that. They refer to themselves simply as manufacturers.)

Lean manufacturers are not the only ones trying to improve processes. Batch manufacturers, in fact, make use of many tools that are thought of as Lean hallmarks. As examples, 5S and visual controls are frequently used. Batch manufacturers run *kaizen* style events, and track their performance as well. Some may even have a continuous improvement culture.

A batch manufacturer tries to figure out how to efficiently produce large quantities of parts at the same time. A Lean manufacturer works on improving the flow of parts (preferably one at a time) through the production process.

It is true that batching can create local efficiencies. The SuperBatch 3000 machining center might, in fact, kick out widgets thirty percent faster than a right-sized Lean machine. But, batching systems cannot avoid inefficiencies in other areas:

- ***More space is used for storing inventory.***
- ***More quality problems occur when long runs of defective parts are produced.***
- ***More time is spent coordinating large production runs.***
- ***More people are involved in expediting.***

Lean looks at whole value streams, not just one process.

Putting it into practice

Whether Lean or not, a company that wants to get better can't just settle for knowing the various improvement tools. They actually have to put them to use.

There is one area where an important difference between non-Lean and Lean companies starts to emerge. Lean businesses place the authority and some *responsibility* to help make changes on the front line. Employees are expected not only to help with the improvement process, but also to own a little slice of it. Sometimes this is in the form of participation on a *kaizen* event and sometimes by simply implementing an idea on the spot.

Some Lean organizations are good, or even great, at engaging their frontline teams. What keeps the other companies from having more effective involvement by employees? Managers might have trouble letting go of authority to make changes, or they may not think that their employees have the right abilities. Many managers underestimate how smart their teams are, so leaders don't provide enough training to build skills. Managers are not the only ones selling employees short, though.

You, the frontline employee, probably underestimate yourself more than your boss might. You are smarter and more capable than you think you are. Lack of confidence and anxiety about failing can make you nervous about attempting changes on your own. If you practice Lean correctly, you *will* make mistakes—in fact, you will make a lot of them. But you will also make some great things happen. Ponder this quote from Ingvar Kamprad, the founder of the furniture giant, Ikea®.

Only those who are asleep make no mistakes.[35]

Mistakes come in two basic forms. The first is a mistake of inaction. It happens when a need for improvement exists, but nothing is done about it. The second is a mistake of action. It happens when someone tries to fix something and fails. Inaction in the face of a need is always a mistake—there is no chance of improvement. Trying to make an improvement, even if the attempt failed, at least had the potential to make things better.

What is the chance that a dissatisfied employee will take risks if he is already feeling bad about his job? What is his chance of becoming an engaged employee? Why would he make changes for the sake of the company, if he feels let down by his employer?

Job satisfaction is the secret recipe for an engaged employee. An engaged employee is the secret weapon for Lean success.

So, what's next? Let's dive into the world in which Lean operates. It is important to examine some things that you don't want to hear about, but that are critical for you to know: the Hard Truths about Lean.

[35] (Ferriss, 2007)

CHAPTER 5

The Hard Truths about Lean

RARELY IS LIFE SIMPLE ENOUGH THAT SOMETHING is all good or all bad. For example, taking a vacation is fun and relaxing; but you also have to part with your hard-earned cash, wait in long lines at the airport, and battle your way through the deep pile in your inbox when you return.

Lean is no exception. Some of its challenges are directly related to the changes Lean brings. Others just come from the way things are in the world today. Regardless, these difficulties rarely get addressed head on. Why not? Because they are hard to talk about and often result in strong emotional responses.

Most of what managers tell you about Lean relates to why Lean is fabulous for a company, terrific for consumers, and good for you. For all the benefits that Lean offers though, some Hard Truths need to be discussed—truths that will impact you and your manager in some way or another.

These realities are not easy to deal with, and no one on any level wants to hear them, much less talk about them. So, why do we bring them up? Because knowledge is power. Understanding these truths will not only help you get more of what you want, they will assist you in deciding where you can spend your energy most effectively. There is little point in wasting your time beating your head against a solid brick wall. The wall won't budge and you end up frustrated, with a massive headache, and are no further along than when you started. The trick to being successful lies in knowing which walls to avoid and which obstacles can be overcome.

Let's consider an example. If you live in Montana, one Hard Truth is that it gets extremely cold during the winter months. You have two basic choices to make in regard to that cold truth. You can fight the reality, denying that it is cold. But that won't raise the temperature. You can talk to the governor about making it warmer. But what are the chances of that making any difference?

Fighting reality doesn't change the situation; it just makes you miserable.

No, you are far more likely to find contentment in the Big Sky state if you accept the truth that the temperature is going to be frigid. This lets you make some alternative choices: taking up snowshoeing, buying warm clothes, enjoying the wilderness. If you ignore reality, and choose not to stock up on firewood, you *will* end up with frostbite.

Now, this analogy isn't meant to suggest you give up on trying to change the Hard Truths. Instead, it should encourage you to invest your energy and emotion wisely when working in a Lean environment.

You can choose how you react to a situation.

Sure, you can still choose to protest and spend a lifetime fighting the existing reality—you may even find some success. You also might get lucky. Some of these truths will change over time as the world continues to transform, without any effort at all from you. The point, though, is that the truths associated with Lean are well established. They probably won't change overnight. And when they do change, it is generally the result of a monumental effort from a lot of people.

Fighting reality takes your energy away from what you *should* be trying to accomplish—accepting Lean and working around its limitations. Effectively managing your energy will go a long way toward achieving your goal of finding satisfaction at work.

Focus your effort in areas where you can make a difference in your job satisfaction. Don't squander your precious energy by repeatedly banging your head against a solid wall.

After you read this chapter, take a few minutes to reflect on the aspects of Lean you are struggling with. Be honest with yourself and decide whether any of the things that are causing you grief are Hard Truths that you won't be able to change. Now, let's take a look at some of these Hard Truths.

You, the consumer, caused Lean

Every time you tap your foot, waiting impatiently for service; every time you buy the less expensive of two products; every time you complain about poor quality—in all of these circumstances, you are telling a business that you—the consumer—want more from the company. Through your purchasing decisions, you let them know that if they don't deliver what you want, you will go somewhere else to find it. Companies have to look for a way to meet customer needs while remaining profitable. To do so, many of them eventually find their way to Lean. This is one of the many Hard Truths about Lean: it exists because consumers—you—want it to exist.

Lean is good for you

Lean has already been really good to you—maybe not as an employee, but as a consumer. In fact, Lean is a big reason why many prices have come down. You wonder, "Lower prices?" Okay, so not all prices have come down over time. Healthcare and education costs have been skyrocketing.

But, look at some other products. Gasoline prices jump dramatically from time to time; however, would you believe that the cheapest-ever *real* (inflation-adjusted) cost of gasoline in the twentieth century came around 1999?[36] Many people find it hard to believe that the trend in gasoline prices has ever been anything but upward. They also don't think of the oil industry as a shining example of Lean.

You may never have realized that oil production uses a lot of equipment to get that black gold from underground to your gas tank. The companies that make steel for refining equipment, the industries that build heavy machinery for drilling, and the businesses that provide vehicles for transporting oil products are almost certainly using Lean somewhere in their value streams. Think of how much higher gas prices could be if Lean efforts hadn't been reducing the oil companies' costs.

Manufacturing is an area in which Lean really shines. Sure, you can buy some really expensive, top-of-the-line items, but for many mainstream products, prices *are* coming down. Electronics are a good example of this. Pick any technical device in your home—computer, audio equipment, cell phone—and think back a few years. How much more do you get for your money right now? Sure, you might pay for new features that didn't exist in the past, but if you are really comparing similar items, you could probably find a lower price. Television, bike, and toy manufacturers, and even fast food chains all provide more for less. Why are these prices dropping? Because Lean has driven out waste all along the value stream. Components are cheaper. Assembly is faster. Engineers design products with Lean in mind.

In addition to driving down prices, Lean shortens product cycles. That means new generations of manufactured goods can

---

[36] (Moore and Kerpen, 2003)

roll out more quickly, making eager consumers happy. Happy customers mean more Lean.

Resistance is futile

When products and systems work well, customers are loyal and stick with them. Customers normally need a reason to move on to something else.

Companies are the same. When a business discovers how well continuous improvement works, it gets addicted to the results that Lean delivers. So, the company becomes more enthusiastic about Lean and devotes more resources to it. Toyota has been using its version of Lean since shortly after World War II and the program still continues to grow.

Once your company starts going down the Lean path, it is unlikely to ever leave it.

This news is probably hard to hear if you are hoping that Lean will be a passing fad.

Accepting that the change to Lean is permanent enables you to move on and start applying your energy toward finding satisfaction in a Lean environment.

Lean can create internal conflict

Think about how people feel about sport utility vehicles (SUVs). Drivers love the size, safety, and versatility; at the same time they frequently dislike how fuel inefficient and environmentally unsound the vehicles are.

Some internal conflicts are more deep-seated. A father might struggle with the conflicting demands of being a good parent. On one hand, he wants to be a good provider, which probably means working long hours. On the other hand, he wants to be available to his children and spend more time with them.

On the job, you probably believe you are a good employee, but you may also resist the changes that your company wants to put in place. This type of situation can create a lot of stress. The truth is that most people struggle, to some degree or another, with the changes that Lean presents.

To illustrate this point, imagine a team with a strong work ethic. They view themselves as hardworking employees and want to put in an "honest day's work." But then Lean comes along and eliminates most of the waste in a process—like watching a machine run or walking to a department in another building to get a signature. Those easy, mindless chores gave them a breather during the busy day and let them stretch their legs, chat with a few friends, and take a break from the monotony of their work. As Lean streamlines these tasks and replaces them with more productive, active work, employees resist the change.

Teams can want to be productive workers, but still expect some downtime throughout the day. But think about this situation from the other side. If you are the one paying a plumber a huge hourly rate, do you want him standing around watching water go down a drain or walking back and forth to his truck twenty times while he is on *your* clock? Probably not.

The challenge you will face in the Lean workplace is finding a way to balance the opposing thoughts you are sure to have.

The good old days weren't that good

People tend to remember more of the positive aspects about the past than the negative. In general, people look back fondly at the good old days. While some things "way back when" were easier, lots of things were not.

Take cell phones. Some people complain about them; but, if they are so bad, why are they so popular? Sure, they can be like an electronic leash, but they also make life easier. You can call home to let your family know that you are caught in a traffic jam and are running late. You can even call for help in an emergency—before cell phones, you might have had to walk several miles for assistance if your car ran out of gas.

In addition, countless industrial and technological advances continue to benefit humanity. Crop yields are way up. Infant mortality is down. Vaccines cure many diseases. Advances in science have improved the quality of life for many.

People, though, have a tendency to remember the good stuff from long ago and the bad stuff from recent times. That pits the worst of Lean against the best of the good old days—an uphill battle because those good old days are a tough act to follow.

Here's an example. A family-owned company had been around for many years. But time passed and competition got tougher, forcing the family to sell to a holding company (a company that owns other companies) that specialized in Lean. Years after the sale, long-time employees still looked back with fondness to the times of plenty that they remembered before the sale. They never recalled the circumstances that led to the company being sold off. No amount of evidence could make them believe that times were better *now,* despite record profits, skyrocketing margins, growing market share, and higher product quality.

The comparisons they made were not reasonable since they were not evaluating the state the old company would have been in today. Had it continued on its earlier, non-Lean path, the company would likely have failed at some point. A truer comparison would have been between the current job with the Lean company, and what their old job would have been like if the prior owners had not sold—non-existent.

This demonstrates the very real and ongoing problem with Lean transformation—that emotions dominate logical reactions and color employees' perceptions about Lean.

Without Lean, something else would take its place

If Lean had never been invented, do you really think your life would be any different? Would your leaders have just stopped trying to make the company more productive and more efficient?

No. If your company was not using Lean, it would be using some other improvement method. Lean found a home in your company, not because your CEO wanted to be Lean, but because she wanted to increase the bottom line (profit) in order to stay in business. That need would have still existed, regardless of whether or not Mr. Ohno ever got the Lean ball rolling.

Not everything is Lean's fault

The old saying "stuff happens" is true in any environment. Lean, though, becomes the scapegoat for this "stuff," even though similar problems occurred long before Lean showed up. Run out of parts? It's Lean's fault. Missing deadlines? Guess where fingers start to point.

Sherlock Holmes was famous for gathering *all* the evidence in a case before making conclusions about a crime. Frequently though, employees gather selective facts; the ones that support *their* cause. Some people expect Lean to be bad, so they find confirmation of their theory everywhere they look. Good results are disregarded, and anything bad is attributed to Lean.

The fact of the matter is that Lean is not perfect, especially when it is first introduced. But remember, many problems were present before Lean came riding into town. You probably ran out of parts before *kanbans* were in place. Deliveries were late long before your company swapped production systems.

When Lean is implemented, it becomes easy to find problems. This is because Lean slowly removes inventory—effectively taking away a safety net and exposing processes to their underlying problems. When those issues get uncovered, they must be fixed. The difficulties were there *before* Lean; they were just not as apparent. Uncovering problems is a far cry from causing problems; Lean is not always to blame.

Lean takes time and effort

If Lean was easy, everyone would be doing it well. All companies would be getting astronomical gains, and profits would be going through the roof. Is this what is happening? No. Why not? Because changing a culture is not a quick fix; nor is it an easy one. Lean takes effort, not only in the transition period but also in staying on the Lean path for the long haul. Lean requires real commitment, especially during the rough spots when things don't go according to plan.

While Lean must start at the top, there has to be buy in at *all* levels of an organization. This is worth emphasizing. For Lean to reach its full potential, *all* employees (especially the front line) must be willing to put effort into change.

Not only is it difficult to get everyone to participate in continuous improvement, it also is a challenge to build up the internal talent that is needed to do Lean well. Becoming really good at Lean usually takes many *years.*

Lean success just increases competition

Despite all the effort you put into making your company Lean, it will never be enough.

Why? Because Lean raises the bar for all businesses. Let's say that your company makes some amazing gains, and profit goes up this year. Do you think the competition is going to stand by and let you steal all of their customers? Some competitors won't be able to keep up and will eventually go out of business. Others will try to figure out what you are doing. And they will copy it. If your company stands still, the competition will eventually catch up and even pass you by. To prevent that, your business has to keep moving forward faster than the competition.

Look at the world of professional sports. Over time, the quality of play has continually improved. Despite all predictions that world records cannot be broken, new ones are constantly being set. This happens in the business world as well.

You work on a barter system

Most people believe that they get paid money for their work. But that is only part of the deal. The whole truth is that employment is not a simple transaction. Granted, you give your time and the company gives you a salary, but much more than that check changes hands—on both sides of the table.

What do you offer? Time, experience, creativity, loyalty, motivation, and productivity, just to name a few. What does the company bring? Opportunity, job security, insurance, retirement plans, education, and training, plus much more.

When you experience a transition in Lean, the negative aspects—the costs you must pay—overshadow what you get in return. You might even compare how hard things are for you with how easy people at other companies have it.

Perhaps you hear about free dinners or massages at other companies. What are the employees "charged" for those benefits? The price may be pulling all-nighters at their desk in order to meet deadlines. The Hard Truth is that the grass is not always greener on the other side and you probably benefit more than you think you do.

You sell to the company

In virtually any transaction, the customer and supplier relationship is defined by the flow of money: customers pay suppliers. Good suppliers believe that "the customer is always right." Companies must pay attention to the needs of their clients or risk losing business.

So, who is receiving the money in your relationship with your boss? Since your paycheck comes from her, doesn't that make her your customer? Now, what was that expression about customers? Probably not exactly what you want to hear, but you can bet that your manager sure thinks about it that way.

Many employees have a double standard. When you, as a customer, are shelling out money at a restaurant (a supplier), you have certain expectations. You anticipate that you get the product you want, when you want it, how you want it, and you demand to get your money's worth. If you ordered a thick, juicy, medium rare prime rib and ended up with a dry, old piece of meat that was so tough you could give it to your dog as a chew toy, you probably would not be very pleased. You might even choose to avoid that establishment in the future. You would probably vote with your feet, and your wallet, and let that steak house know that they didn't provide you with the value you expected.

But when the role is reversed at work, and you are the "supplier," the rules change. You might label bosses with high expectations as unreasonable. You might get angry with a manager who fires a marginally performing friend in the cubicle next to you, even though you "fired" the steak house for the same reason.

What would you do differently at work if you had to pass a performance evaluation at the end of each day in order to be invited back to do your job the next morning?

Now, an employee-employer relationship is more complicated than simply ordering a meal, but it does offer something to contemplate. Every time you go out to dinner, you evaluate the restaurant. How many times do you keep going back to a restaurant that doesn't meet your expectations? The Hard Truth is that your company gets to do the ordering and they pay you to deliver.

Everyone wants more

Most employees think that the people above them on the business ladder are overpaid. Skilled workers hear that a CEO made millions in stock options, and are stunned, envious, and angry that anyone would get paid that much. This feeling is so common that "corporate greed" has become a buzzword in the media.

Guess what? Some people resent you in the same way. An inexperienced or unskilled worker might look at a machinist and think they get paid an insane amount for "just cutting up some metal." A minimum-wage earner may think assembly line workers get paid more than they should.

Most people think they are underpaid and believe anyone making more than them is overpaid. Unless you are on the bottom of the totem pole, someone is probably looking at you and thinking you are overpaid for what *you* do.

Why does this matter? Because Lean will likely increase the bonuses of your managers and executives; and give the shareholders bigger returns. That has the potential to reduce your job satisfaction if it exaggerates your belief that your boss is overpaid.

New hires don't see things the same way you do

When current employees are asked to be Lean in their jobs, they may be very vocal about how bad the new ways are. Put a person off the street in the same role, and they may not complain at all. In fact, a new employee may even comment about how smoothly the process flows. This shows that the process itself is not the problem. Rather, the struggle comes from the fact that established employees feel forced to change and that lack of say in the matter breeds hard feelings.

Employees and managers shoot at different targets

Let's say your supervisor just ran his December numbers and found that your team had improved productivity by seven percent from the previous year. When he told you and your coworkers, you were pleased and very proud of your accomplishment. When he told his manager, she asked what had kept him from hitting the eleven percent improvement rate that your team had gotten the prior year.

Pay close attention to the point of this story. Managers tend to set much higher targets than you do. You can end up with bad feelings when you and your leaders interpret the same results in different ways.

Lean, like life, is not always fair

A source of frustration for many employees is that continuous improvement efforts are applied where they are needed most. That means that resources may not be evenly distributed throughout the company. In other words, some workers will bear a large Lean burden because their area has to go through more changes than other departments. Other areas may not get the Lean resources they want, because another group has a greater need. Lean will not and *should not* be applied evenly, but it still can create some ill will.

The pie won't get split up evenly

This concept was touched on earlier, but it is worth looking at again in more detail. How do employees, managers, executives, and shareholders go about splitting up the company's earnings?

On the surface, it appears that the shareholders get the first slice, since theirs is often the biggest. It doesn't really work that way, though. In reality, things start at the front line. The workers get paid first, but their reward is the lowest. You get paid whether the company does well or not. For instance, if the company misses its earnings marks, paychecks do not get any smaller. Managers, the next rung up the ladder, often get a good chunk of their pay in bonuses. They get more than frontline workers, but their pay fluctuates, depending on how the company has performed over the short term and how well they have met department goals. Executives get paid even more, but much of it is often in stock options, which depends on how the company performs over the long term. Finally, the shareholders get their piece of the pie, but only when the company does well. They are also the only group that can actually lose money when the company isn't profitable and the stock falls.

So, as you can see, there is unevenness in the size of the slices of the profit pie each group gets. This disparity is based, at least in part, on the risk each group has. The front line bears relatively little risk in how well a company does from day to day. As the risk level increases from management to executive to shareholder, the pieces of the pie become larger.

Your pay is based on scarcity, not value

Many people like to think that the amount of training, the importance of the job, or the abilities of the employee have something to do with how salaries are determined. Not true. It is, rather, the scarcity of a person's skills that drives the pay level.

Higher-level skills indirectly increase pay, but only when few people have those abilities. Why do great ballplayers in the pros get paid so much more than average ones? Because not many players can bat over .300.[37] Teams are willing to pay for that very rare skill.

Arguably, teachers, police officers, and trash collectors all have a much higher value to our everyday lives than ballplayers, but get paid much less. Why? Because more people are available with the skills to do those jobs. For the same reason, manufacturing and office jobs tend to be easy to fill. Many people are available who are both willing and competent to step in.

This scarcity of skills creates a conflict for you with your coworkers. You are competing with each other. Those of you with the best skills—whether you are top machinists, or naturals at Lean production—are hard to find. Your pay will likely be higher than your coworkers with more easily replaceable talent.

Managers are people, too

The thing that many employees forget about their manager is that he has his own boss just up the ladder. Believe it or not, managers are just like you. They feel overworked and underappreciated. They get overwhelmed and stressed out by deadlines. Managers try to perform well in their jobs. But chances are, when they are having trouble, you tend to have a hard time, too.

---

[37] For you non-baseball fans, hitting a fastball is considered by many to be the hardest thing to do in sports. Hitting it so that nobody can catch it three out of ten times is even harder, and more uncommon.

Remember, a manager might have to pick up the kids from daycare, pay the bills, and fix that leaky faucet, just like you do. They worry about many of the same things such as their health and retirement.

It's easy to lose sight of this when your manager has to make a decision that you don't like. You might immediately jump to the conclusion that the manager has no compassion. Perhaps your boss's manager has given your boss a directive, and she has no choice. Perhaps what you want is simply not possible. Maybe your manager doesn't know how to do something, doesn't have the budget, or can't come up with the other necessary resources. It might even be that, since most decisions don't make everyone happy, you just drew the short straw this time.

True, some managers really don't care about their staff. But they are rare exceptions. Generally, any hardship that a manager causes you is a result of the pressure she is under. Lean adds to her challenges, especially during the early period of a transition. So, do yourself a favor and give your manager a break, or at least take a minute to consider why she is doing something. Not only will you make her life easier, but you will likely reap the benefits of having an appreciative boss as well.

Perceptions matter more than reality

Imagine that you are preparing breakfast for your kids, Tommy and Sally. They are thirsty, but there is only one bottle of juice left. You decide to split it equally between the two of them. You didn't get to the dishes last night and only have two mismatched glasses in the cupboard. One cup is tall and narrow, and the other is short and wide. You distribute the juice and immediately an argument erupts about who got more.

Sally got the short, wide glass and is not pleased that her younger brother got "more than his fair share." You try to tell her that it was evenly doled out (you poured half of the bottle in each glass), but her mind is made up and you are unable to change it in the face of her conviction. She stomps off with a scowl on her face muttering under her breath that she doesn't want the juice anyway and that you always liked Tommy better. Your morning quickly heads downhill and you end up frustrated and irritable that she won't listen to reason.

So, what does this have to do with Lean? Perception is everything and no one likes to be around someone who complains all the time—your boss certainly doesn't. Your manager will be tolerant of some moaning and groaning about the unfairness of Lean and will listen to your concerns (if you express them appropriately), but at some point employees have to get on board with Lean or get left behind. Your manager doesn't have a choice about being Lean, and if you want to remain in this company, neither do you.

Not to say that you can't have misgivings, but you have to be able to demonstrate that you are at least willing to try. If your boss believes you are attempting to adapt he will give you a break. When it comes time for assignments, raises, and promotions, who do you think he is going to favor? Those team members that make an effort to support the company's initiatives or those who resist, throw up roadblocks, and generally make his life more difficult?

Sure, you might be able to fake your Lean support for a short time. It is very hard to appear engaged for the long haul, though. You will eventually be found out and you will be labeled a Lean opponent—a title that is very difficult to get rid of and one that will make life difficult for you in the future.

Do you know how your manager would label you right now? Your boss has probably formed his opinion of you based on a series of snapshots in time. Sometimes, it is not your lucky day and your boss walks up behind you, and he overhears you criticizing the most recent change in your department—your reputation gets tarnished. If this was a single incident, you probably have nothing to worry about. But if your manager hears nothing but fault finding from you, rest assured, you will soon have a problem on your hands.

What if you are really willing to give Lean the good old college try, but you suspect that your boss views you in an inaccurate way? Ask him the next time you have a one-on-one meeting. Find out what you would have to do to change his opinion, if it happens to be different than how you view yourself. But what if you are really anti-Lean? Then you have some soul searching to do. The important thing to remember is that managers act on their perceptions. It is critical that you understand what your reputation is in a Lean environment.

Moving forward

Talking about these Hard Truths is an important step toward improving your job satisfaction. If you ignore these realities, you can do very little to make your job better. Time and time again, fighting reality just makes people bitter, angry, and worn out, and it doesn't change a thing—except maybe move you closer to getting a pink slip. Instead, let go of some of that struggle, and choose to put your efforts where you have a better likelihood of improving your well-being.

Paying attention to these Hard Truths lets you take that important step forward. It lets you separate what you can change from what you probably cannot. Once you start applying your energy in a positive, effective manner, you will start to see your job satisfaction rise.

The Hard Truths might have left you a bit discouraged. That was not the intent. Far from it. Instead, it was meant to acknowledge and give voice to the things that you intuitively know: that some parts of Lean don't feel so great for you.

Knowing what these obstacles are, and where they are located, helps you steer clear of them. This allows you to spend your time on the good things that Lean has to offer you. And Lean *does* have a lot to offer you. Opportunities abound, once you decide not to let Lean's shortcomings hold you back.

CHAPTER 6

Whaddaya Mean I Gotta Be Lean?

UP UNTIL NOW, YOU HAVE BEEN DILIGENTLY building your knowledge base. Hopefully, you have a handle on what Lean is, why your company needs to be Lean, and why Lean is good for your business and its customers.

But the most important question remains: what about you? Where do you, as an individual employee, fit into this picture? What about the "I" in the *Whaddaya Mean I Gotta Be Lean?* Isn't that really the heart of the matter?

The single biggest challenge the front line faces is that for all of the good things Lean does for the company, Lean can be difficult for you personally. Why is Lean so hard? Because frontline employees (1) have the least amount of control over the situation, (2) are the ones who have to shoulder the biggest burden, and (3) endure the most significant changes. It is no wonder that your job satisfaction can take a bit hit.

But, don't despair—there is good news for you! Despite all the hurdles that you face, a lot of employees who hate Lean in the beginning later join the ranks of its biggest supporters. If you are a Lean opponent, believe it or not, *you* have a good chance to become a Lean advocate. Right now, it is probably hard to imagine that happening. Once you are well-versed in Lean though, you will start seeing some of its very real benefits—benefits for *you and your team*, and not just the drawbacks you may be struggling alone with now.

In fact, down the road when the dust has started to settle, if your boss were to suddenly suggest going back to pre-Lean ways, you would likely fight harder against that change than you ever did about going Lean in the first place. As impossible as that sounds, it happens all the time.

That level of dedication to Lean is hard to picture for anyone who has yet to see the rewards. Believing that Lean will make things better for you is a leap of faith, because you have not yet seen the proof. You only know what you are dealing with right now. What makes it even more challenging is that:

Lean stirs up emotions in a way that almost no other business decision can.

On the surface, Lean seems ordinary. Bosses give instructions to people every day. People are always expected to be productive and provide quality work on time. Why, then, are the emotions surrounding Lean so strong and so frequently negative? Because you pay a steep upfront admission price for Lean. It can make you feel worse before you start to feel better.

Let's take a closer look at why a Lean implementation feels more difficult than the previous changes you have gone through at work. Everyone's experience is different. You may be one of the lucky ones and the following list may not resonate with you. Alternatively, you may be struggling with Lean on several fronts. Regardless of where you fall on the spectrum, the goal is to help identify what a lot of employees may be going through—things that a lot of managers simply don't recognize or, if they do, don't know what to do about it.

Do you remember when we talked about the importance of you learning how your company thinks? Well the same applies here for your managers who are reading this as well. Just like you needed to learn what is important to your company, now your bosses need to pay particular attention to learn how a lot of you might be feeling about this transition. "Perceptions matter more than reality" applies here, too. What you perceive about Lean has a big impact on your manager and your company. If you understand your boss's viewpoint, and she understands where you are coming from, it makes it easier to create a win-win situation.

Let's take a closer look at some of the common Lean struggles for the front line:

- ***Lean can take all of your energy.*** Being Lean means your job will continually change. There are always opportunities to be Leaner. There are no rest stops and no final destination. The progress that you make today will have to be improved upon tomorrow. It seems like you are sprinting a twenty-six mile marathon. Working at that pace can be exhausting.

- ***Lean can make you feel unappreciated.*** Chances are, you were already feeling overworked and stressed out before Lean was introduced. When the bosses start talking about continuous improvement it appears as if they are saying you weren't working very hard to begin with. The subtext that you may hear is that it is "time to stop slacking off," which is pretty demoralizing. Not only does past performance seem to come into question, once you actually meet your new targets the bar will be raised. It doesn't take much to get discouraged and think that no matter how hard you work, it will never be enough to satisfy your boss, so, why bother?

- ***Lean can be invasive.*** Lean is rarely contained to one spot. It spreads horizontally throughout different departments and vertically into every crevice of your work area. It can even get into your personal workspace by dictating how you have to arrange your cubicle—that's if you even still have one to call your own. All aspects of your work will be touched by Lean at some point. It can seem like you can't escape it.

- ***Lean can be controlling.*** Work instructions tell you what to do, how to do it, and when to do it. You follow step-by-step procedures which can lead you to the opinion that you are being micromanaged. Most adults prefer making their own decisions and experienced employees resent being told how to do every last detail of their job.
- ***Lean can change the value of skills and experience.*** Seniority, and the experience that comes with it, seem less valuable in Lean. Why? Lean changes things so quickly, that process experience quickly becomes obsolete. Furthermore, as processes are standardized, it makes it easier for other people to come in and do your job. You might come to believe that you are replaceable. Finally, the skills needed to thrive under Lean, like problem prevention, replace skills that were formerly respected and needed, like "firefighting." Switching to a continuous improvement culture starts all employees over at square one.
- ***Lean can make your team's success and failures more public.*** You don't mind being acknowledged for a job well done, but don't like seeing a chart on a wall that shows your work group falling short of its targets. People worry about being embarrassed if they don't measure up.
- ***Lean can make you feel isolated from the upper ranks.*** You may think that the managers and executives just don't get it anymore. You probably also worry that you can't ask questions or vocalize your concerns, for fear of getting labeled as "resistant to change." Instead, you bite your tongue and continue to simmer as you resent your boss and worry about your future.
- ***Lean can make you like your job less.*** It can be easy to feel alone and overwhelmed, especially at the beginning of your Lean journey. You may believe you are caught in the middle—you can't quit because of all the bills you have to pay, but are unable to figure out how you can stay and survive these sweeping changes. It can be hard to see a how things will work out.

- ***Lean can decrease the things you value at work.*** When waste is reduced, those little things that make your job more enjoyable often go away, too. Having those five-minute chats in the mailroom or having a little downtime between phone calls may have helped you get through the day. Now, the time and opportunities to rest are gone. You are angry that the company took those simple pleasures away.

Now, each of these viewpoints looks at things in a pessimistic way. These are the worst-case interpretations. But think back to the discussion about optimistic people doing better with change. A half-full employee might view each of those items in a more positive way. For example, "Lean can be controlling" could become "Lean can minimize errors by reducing variability." Rather than "Lean can be invasive," you could think, "Lean can help in every area."

This switch from negative to positive thought doesn't come easily. In fact, Lean advocates frequently make one critical mistake in the area of employee relations. They try to convince resistant employees that feeling bad about Lean is wrong. Bear in mind, this is not just bosses who do this. If you support Lean and try to bring your coworkers along, you might be guilty of the same thing. Let's just acknowledge one simple fact:

Lean has some unintended side effects that can dramatically reduce job satisfaction.

When the front line transitions to Lean there are real problems that create bad feelings that *must* be addressed. You, your manager, and your company will never be fully successful at Lean unless all parties deal with that fact.

The take and give

One reason bad feelings are so prominent early in the transition is that Lean "takes" before it "gives." Interestingly, many employees forget that they had mixed feelings about their jobs even *before* they started down the Lean path. Most people, prior to Lean, have some aspects they like about their job, and some that they don't. At the beginning of Lean, though, many people experience an increase in the negative parts of their jobs, and a dip in the positive ones. Little by little, though, frontline employees in Lean companies start to like more things about their jobs. In many cases, as shown in the accompanying graph, they end up liking their job even more than they did before Lean.

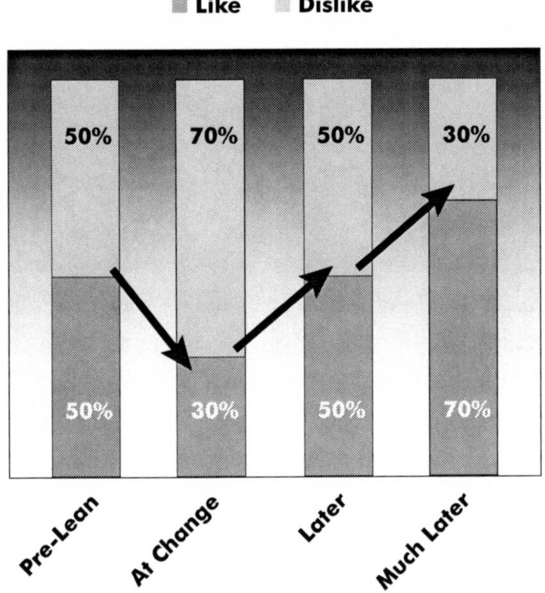

Most people have mixed feelings about their jobs.

Let's take a look at the three main causes for these initial difficulties when transitioning to Lean.

First of all, most people are reluctant to accept change. Think about how you might react if your favorite coffee shop changed its signature blend. Or if your grocery store switched to a different bakery and stopped carrying a type of bagel that you love. You might have negative feelings about the change *before you even tried the new products.*

In the beginning, it can be hard to adjust to something new.

Second, some of the initial changes in Lean come from automating and removing simple tasks. That leaves the more difficult, more stressful work to fill your day. Eventually, Lean addresses and improves these high-stress parts of a job, but in the meantime, satisfaction suffers.

Some of the easiest (and possibly most enjoyable) aspects of a job may go by the wayside.

The third cause of early difficulties with Lean has to do with survival instinct. If you are scuba diving and find a treasure chest just as a shark starts circling you, where do you focus your attention? Intuitively, you'll deal with the danger as your highest priority. Do you really think you could enjoy counting those gold coins if a hammerhead was gnawing on your leg?

Perceived danger must be dealt with before rewards can be enjoyed.

The biggest Lean threat that people consistently worry about is that they will lose their job. They find it hard to believe that productivity gains won't lead to lower headcounts through layoffs (unlikely, if their managers have their act together). They also might worry that they will get fired if they are not completely in favor of Lean from the start (unlikely, if you have your act together).

So, how do people deal with threats? Since the beginning of time, the gray matter of the human brain has been wired to identify and deal with danger. If risks can't be identified and dealt with, the brain (and the person it is attached to) doesn't last very long.

When people are placed in peril, they generally respond with one of the "three Fs"—fight, flight, or freeze. In a Lean environment, the ones who fight get labeled as resistant to change. The ones who take flight, or leave, lose out on security and probably some benefits. The majority of employees just freeze and try to wait to see what will happen.

Fortunately, Lean doesn't *have* to be a threat. It is all about perception, right? It can, instead, be an opportunity—an opening for redefining your job in a way that increases your satisfaction.

The trick to managing your perception is to step back and look at how you go about forming your opinions of the events unfolding around you. Those opinions inevitably cause emotions (fear) that drive your behaviors (freezing).

A wonderful thing about being human is that you are aware that you are thinking and can choose to consciously control your thoughts. And that gives you the power to do something about how you view your situation.

Have hope

This power to modify your thoughts should give you hope that you can change how Lean affects you—and hope that you can improve your job satisfaction.

In the following chapters, you will see, in detail, how this can happen. For now, just know that (1) you *can* influence how Lean affects your satisfaction, and (2) when you believe your situation *can* get better, you can accomplish amazing things.

As you learn how to shape your thoughts, you will experience a significant transformation. For example, you will shift from believing that things will always be the way they are now, to the belief that you can alter your environment to help meet your needs. That means *you* can control your own job satisfaction. That power is both liberating and invigorating.

One of the most difficult things for people to tolerate is chronic stress with no end in sight. When you create a light at the end of your tunnel, you will notice a change in your attitude when you get up for work each morning.

To get there, though, it is critical to understand how you get from A to Z, or in this case, from the EVENT to the RESULT.

Traveling from EVENTS to RESULTS

Whether or not you pay attention to your internal state, how you feel and what you think always shape your final destination. Sometimes you blitz through the thinking and feeling process without realizing it. In other cases, progress is excruciatingly slow. You travel this route countless times each day, but chances are you have never given the stops along the actual trail much thought. Imagine this path as a chain. Each link of the chain brings you closer to your RESULT. Let's start with a brief overview of the **How-You-Think Links**.

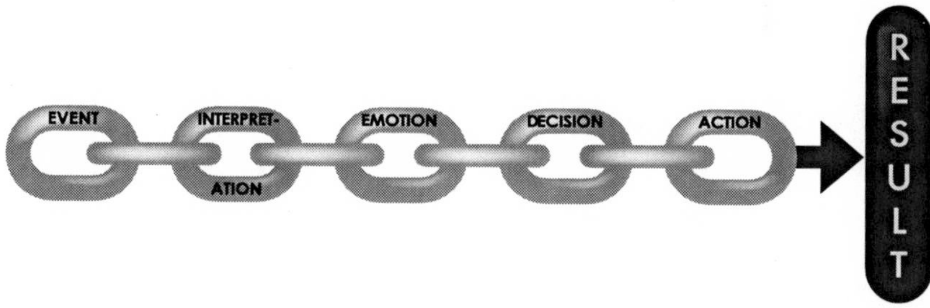

The How-You-Think Links

- **EVENT.** Someone does something or says something. Something happens. The EVENT link contains the objective facts that would be viewed and recorded the same way by everyone witnessing the incident. A person speaking "too loudly" (subjective opinion) is not an EVENT. Your coworker talking at eighty-three decibels (objective fact) is an EVENT.

- **INTERPRETATION.** This is the link where the subjective meaning gets applied to the EVENT. The INTERPRETATION link is where those eighty-three decibels become "too loud." It all depends on how *you* look at it.

- **EMOTION.** EMOTIONS are the inevitable byproduct of INTERPRETATIONS. Some feelings are weak, and some are intense. They can sometimes even be hidden, but feelings are always there. In this example, "too loud" could trigger anger.

- **Decision.** In this link, you weigh your options and make a DECISION about how to act on your EMOTION. In regard to your anger about the loud talking, you could choose to leave the area, put in earplugs, or confront the noise maker.
- **Action.** Once you make a DECISION, you must the take ACTION. Sometimes things go according to plan, and sometimes they don't. But always, there's going to be a . . .
- **Result.** RESULTS are the consequences of your ACTIONS. You confront your noisy coworker and call her disruptive. She reacts by telling you that you are critical and that you are not a team player— just as one of the VPs is walking by. That might not be the RESULT that you wanted, but it is still an outcome of how you advanced through the earlier links.

It is important to keep in mind that you can jump backward to revisit a link, but you cannot skip ahead. It is impossible to jump from INTERPRETATION to ACTION without experiencing at least a fleeting EMOTION or making a DECISION about what to do. Now let's take a look at each link in more depth.

What's happening?

The **EVENT** is the initial incident—it's what happens that gets the proverbial ball rolling.

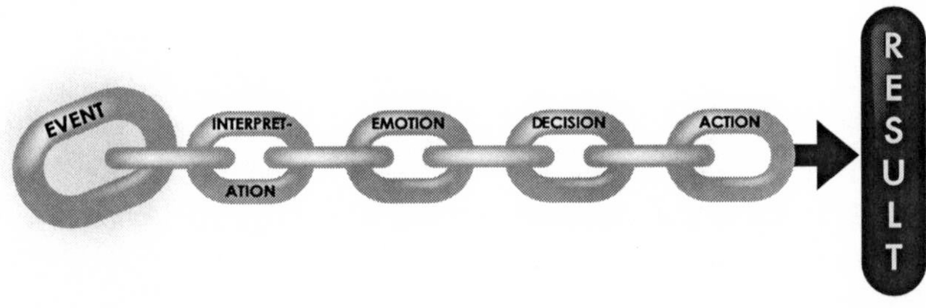

The Event Link

An EVENT is some sort of activity or situation that affects you. A big storm is brewing on the weekend that you planned to go camping. You are assigned to a new project team.

Let's look at an example of how the EVENT link works. Consider all the conditions surrounding a traffic light changing from green to red:

- ***Traffic patterns.***
- ***Your speed and the type of vehicle you are driving.***
- ***Visibility, weather, and road conditions.***
- ***The presence of a police officer.***

The list can go on and on. In fact, you probably take in a lot more information than you realize. One thing in common to all these conditions is that they can be measured objectively. The number of cars on the road is countable, and your distance from the corner when the light changes could be determined with a tape measure. Your speed, clocked in miles per hour, is the same, no matter who is watching you.

What about an EVENT at work? Perhaps you show up late. The EVENT may be surrounded by several conditions. Again, note that each of the items in this list is measurable, and would appear identical to anyone watching the situation unfold.

- ***The time your alarm clock went off.***
- ***The amount of time it took you to drive to work.***
- ***The time showing on the wall clock when you arrived.***
- ***The tone, pitch, and tempo of how your boss speaks to you.***

Notice that this list lacks any opinion or INTERPRETATION of the EVENT. For example, you don't see "Your boss sounds mad!" in that list. An EVENT is simply the facts of the case.

To complicate matters, some obstacles can get in the way of gathering up all the details about an EVENT:

- ***Limited information.*** Your access to some of the conditions may be limited. This just means that you don't know everything about the EVENT. You may not see that police car waiting behind a building. Regarding Lean, you may not be privy to the knowledge that your company is on the verge of bankruptcy, or that a competitor just started its own Lean program and is making huge strides in undercutting your company's prices.

- ***Misinformation.*** People, on occasion, will try to deceive you. Fortunately, these cases are the exception, rather than the rule. Unfortunately, there is no neon sign that points out when someone is trying to pull the wool over your eyes. The most common form of misinformation is the intentional withholding of important pieces of evidence. Perhaps a coworker really wants a particular practice put in place. He may "forget" to tell you about a problem that he noticed during a test.
- ***Incorrect facts.*** Sometimes you get the facts wrong. You believe you were going twenty-seven miles per hour. The radar gun says otherwise.
- ***Memory.*** You won't recall everything perfectly. You may forget the due date your boss gave you for a project, for example.

Fear not, though—despite obstacles, you can take some steps to adjust the EVENT link. You will learn more about these as you read about the strategies later in the book. For now, just know that nothing is set in stone. You can change things. You can improve your job satisfaction.

How do you INTERPRET the world around you?

So, an EVENT takes place and the next question is what does it mean to you? You form that answer in the second link of the chain, the **INTERPRETATION** of the EVENT. Your INTERPRETATION of an EVENT is unique—it is the meaning *you* apply to the given situation.

The INTERPRETATION Link

Unlike the EVENT link, where conditions can change in an instant, your INTERPRETATIONS come from contributing factors that were formed over a long period of time. Your parents probably started shaping your values about the time you got out of diapers. Since then, you have been bombarded with messages from everywhere—bosses, coworkers, siblings, spouses, teachers, drill sergeants, clergy, the media. Some of these messages stick with you, further shaping how you INTERPRET EVENTS.

The following list includes some of the most common factors that influence your INTERPRETATIONS:

- ***Your values and beliefs.***
- ***Your character.***
- ***Your priorities.***
- ***Your experience and life lessons.***
- ***Your knowledge and education.***
- ***Your relationships.***
- ***Your mood.***
- ***Your attitude.***
- ***Social pressures.***
- ***The media: TV, magazines, etc.***

Let's look at just how these contributors affect your INTERPRETATION. Remember that noise example mentioned earlier? That was an EVENT. You heard an eighty-three decibel sound. All the experiences that you have had in your life up until that moment shape how *you* view that incident. If you grew up in a three-room house with nine siblings, you may have a very high tolerance for noise—a jetliner might not disturb you. On the other hand, if you were raised by soft-spoken monks in the Himalayas, mice nibbling on a piece of cheese might give you a headache.

Notice the difference in perspective? The INTERPRETATION step is where you apply the meaning to an EVENT. It is where you try to determine if the coworker is yelling at eighty-three decibels out of anger, or just to get your attention. It is where you try to figure out if an e-mail message from your boss had hidden meaning in it. It is where you make judgments about peoples' actions.

Your INTERPRETATION of an EVENT is the most important link in the chain because it sets the course you will follow to reach the RESULT.

For example, in a Lean project, discussions can get heated. When they do, you INTERPRET all the facts—body language (arms were crossed), tone of voice (very high pitched), the time of day (7:04 p.m.)—and come up with a judgment. You decide if the excitable person had a point, or if they crossed a line. You should keep several things in mind about this link:

- ***INTERPRETATIONS can vary for the same person at different times.*** Your moods change, right? A teasing jab can appear funny to you when you are happy, but it might seem more of a mean attack when your mood is foul.
- ***INTERPRETATIONS shift over time.*** While this can be done intentionally as a strategy to improve your job satisfaction, INTERPRETATIONS also evolve naturally. Frequently, an employee's view of an

executive will change after spending a week on a *kaizen* with her. That senior leader will seem more human, and will be given more benefit of the doubt when she makes an unpopular decision.

- ***Interpretations depend on relationships.*** A close friend can bump against your arm and spill a drink in your lap. You are upset, but you shrug it off as an obvious accident. On the other hand, if a drunk bumps into you at a bar, an angry glare and harsh words from either of you could escalate to an outright fight.
- ***Interpretations aren't always right or wrong.*** Interpretations are individual opinions. You might *think* you are right, but so might the person you are disagreeing with. Politics is a prime topic where people have strongly opposing views. Let's look at a less controversial example, though. You like chocolate ice cream. Your spouse prefers vanilla. Who's right?
- ***Interpretation fills in the blanks.*** If you don't have all the information, your brain automatically completes the picture. Sometimes this is useful. Imagine that you are a caveman who had never before seen a saber-toothed tiger. You have previously and painfully learned that sharp teeth in the mouth of any animal can hurt you. As a result, seeing the bared teeth of the pre-historic tiger sounds the danger bell in your head. This happens even if the animal as a whole is unfamiliar. Imagine how this might alter your view of Lean. You don't know much about the new system, but you have seen other, similar "animals" come and go over the years and those experiences were unpleasant. So, Lean gets classified in the same way.
- ***Interpretations come from how you weigh evidence.*** One of the reasons that interpretations vary is that people assign different values to the same pieces of evidence. When reviewing a dining experience you may hold the quality of the food in high regard, your dining partner may place service at the top of the list. When you each mentally score the shared experience, the

outcome can be far different. Lean provides a lot of evidence to evaluate, increasing the likelihood that you, your boss, your coworkers, and your customers will come to different conclusions about EVENTS.

Since the way that people INTERPRET information is influenced by so many long-standing factors, Lean sometimes struggles to get off the ground. Frustration reigns when your INTERPRETATIONS differ from those of the people around you. This can be a problem between managers and employees even without a Lean transition muddying the waters. For example, is a fifty-hour work week long or short? Fifty hours may not seem long at all to a manager trying to hit her targets at the end of the quarter. But, it might seem impossibly long for a frontline employee who has several other pressing responsibilities outside of work.

With Lean, the opportunities for misaligned INTERPRETATIONS can be even greater. What happens when a manager thinks you have an obligation to fill down time with additional work? What about when you disagree on whether a target is reasonable, or if a new process really is "better"? Same EVENTS, different INTERPRETATION.

On a positive note, though, there are many ways that you can modify your INTERPRETATIONS to be more successful in a Lean environment.

Yes, we have to discuss your EMOTIONS

The feelings you develop in the INTERPRETATION link trigger an **EMOTION.**

The EMOTION Link

When your boss tells you to report on the progress of a project, you have a new EVENT link on your hands. You might INTERPRET that EVENT as an opportunity to show off all the great things you've done with the project and then feel excitement. Or, you might worry about all the things that have gone wrong (and still could) and be consumed with fear and apprehension. If you are convinced that your boss knows how much you hate public speaking, you might even become angry.

As you can see, how you INTERPRET the EVENT triggers different EMOTIONS. Those feelings might vary depending on the time of the day—say, if you are told about a new project first thing Monday morning versus learning about it on your way out the door on Friday afternoon.

Before we get too deep into this subject, let's take a moment to look at a common misconception about the word "feelings." You will hear, "I don't *feel* like this will work." But, the correct statement is, "I don't *think* that will work." People frequently confuse thoughts with feelings but, surprisingly, only a few core EMOTIONS really exist. Irritated, mad, and furious may describe the *degree* of a feeling—but they are all variations of the core EMOTION of anger.

- ***The positive core EMOTIONS are:***
  - Love
  - Happiness
  - Excitement

- ***The negative core EMOTIONS are:***
  - Anger
  - Hurt
  - Sadness
  - Guilt
  - Fear

EMOTIONS are usually accompanied by physical responses. Think back to a time when you felt strongly about something. If you were angry or excited, you probably felt your breathing quicken or your heart rate climb a few beats per minute. Fear might have made your palms sweat, your mouth go dry, or your stomach churn. Other possible physiological responses include goose bumps, fidgeting, twitching, shivering, rising blood pressure, nausea, and even the sensation of warmth.

EMOTIONS have several factors that contribute to their formation. Your health and well-being can be contributors. If you have a bad headache or you are experiencing chronic pain, you had better believe those conditions will factor into how you feel in a given situation. In the same regard, environment plays a role. Having to check out an unusual sound coming from the dark, spooky attic on a stormy night brings out different feelings than grabbing a cup of hot chocolate and snuggling in front of a cozy fireplace to watch the first winter snowfall.

EMOTIONS are also contagious. Happy people tend to lift the spirits of people around them. Miserable people tend to drag others down.

Your current EMOTION not only affects other people, but it also sets the stage for how you will INTERPRET the next EVENT that comes along. Negative EMOTIONS are a fertile breeding ground for *more* negative feelings; the same holds true on the other end of the spectrum. When you are already happy, you are more likely to INTERPRET an EVENT in a positive way. If you are already feeling hurt, it isn't a big leap to anger.

For some of you, as soon as we started talking about your feelings, your eyes may have started to glaze over and you might have tuned out. Generally, the idea that EMOTIONS can play a role in business is just not very well accepted. Some years back, the character played by Tom Hanks had this line in *A League of Their Own* (1992): "Are you crying? . . . There's no crying in baseball!"[38] The sentiment could easily be modified to "There are no feelings in business!" This usually summarizes the beliefs of managers and many frontline employees: Feelings, bad. Logic, good.

---

[38] (Marshall, 1992)

Where does this view on EMOTIONS come from? Well, it is a side effect of testosterone. Like it or not, until the recent past, men have dominated the business world. Many masculine perspectives persist.

Why is it critical to understand the relationship between EMOTIONS and Lean? The EMOTION link determines the *manner* in which you approach a DECISION. The behaviors you choose, and ultimately your RESULTS, are heavily influenced by how you are feeling at the time of your DECISION. Positive EMOTIONS breed cooperation; negative EMOTIONS drive confrontational actions. The more aware you are of your feelings, and the more able you are to change them, the better you will be able to shape the process to get the RESULTS you want. When navigating through the EMOTION link, keep some of these following pitfalls in mind:

- ***EMOTIONS can change rapidly.*** You don't experience multiple EMOTIONS at exactly the same time. Rather, you flip back and forth between them. Most often, these feelings are related. You may alternate between being excited and scared about an upcoming river rafting trip or between sadness and anger when a friend moves away. In Lean, the EMOTIONS might bounce from optimism (excitement) about a change, to worry (fear) that it won't work, to anger at the boss. This moving EMOTIONAL target makes DECISIONS difficult. You may have trouble making a choice when your feelings continuously alter your DECISION-making criteria.

- ***Employees hide their EMOTIONS.*** To make things a little more challenging, employees conceal their EMOTIONS—sometimes unwittingly, sometimes on purpose. "I'm not mad!" is a surprisingly common phrase in *kaizens,* even when it is clear that the person is furious. What most people don't realize, though, is that even when an EMOTION is masked, it still creeps into the process of making DECISIONS.

- ***Emotions are confusing.*** You might not completely understand what you are feeling in a given situation. This most commonly happens when strong negative EMOTIONS mask painful ones. You might cover guilt or sadness with anger. Obviously, this makes DECISION making even more challenging than normal.

Decisions, decisions

So, after you INTERPRET an EVENT and experience the following EMOTION, what's next? At some point it becomes time to make a **DECISION**. You look at all your options, and you choose one.

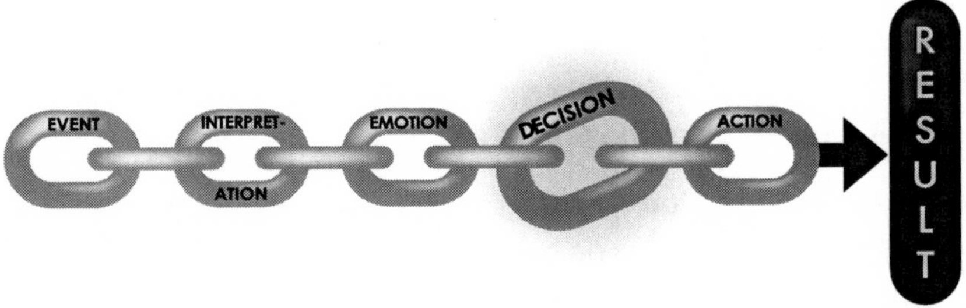

The Decision Link

Sometimes, you might make a snap DECISION without putting a lot of thought into it: choosing between french fries or a salad, for example. Other times, you might deliberate for an extended period of time.

How about the output of the DECISION link? It might be a complicated, multi-page plan, or it might be a simple "Yes" or "No." Sometimes, the DECISION even ends up being to do nothing; but when you think about it, you are still *choosing* to do nothing.

Generally, important DECISIONS take a long time to make. The exception? When EMOTIONS are strong, they bias the DECISION-making process, and make it shorter than it should be. Have you ever done something in the heat of the moment that you regretted at a later time? That's because your EMOTIONS will alter your ability to choose the best course of ACTION, if you let them. Obviously, DECISIONS made out of anger will be much different than DECISIONS made when you are happy.

As we discussed earlier, the INTERPRETATION link is the most important link in the chain because it sets the stage for your RESULTS. The DECISION link, though, is your safety net! It should be the link that gives you the greatest hope, because, as you will read many times in this book, you have the power to choose. And the more you know about why you INTERPRET things in a particular way and why you feel the EMOTIONS that you do, the better you can select a choice that gives you good RESULTS.

The more that you understand about the process the better your outcomes are. Several factors contribute to the DECISION link including:

- ***Skill.*** DECISION-making is a form of problem solving. Problem solving is a process. You can learn problem-solving skills that will help you achieve the RESULTS you want.
- ***Insight.*** Being able to foresee the outcome of a DECISION improves your odds of success.
- ***Time.*** Some DECISIONS are needed right away. Others can wait for a while. Often, a little extra time can help improve an outcome.
- ***Routine.*** Practice makes perfect. Every time you use a structured DECISION-making method, your skills get better and the process becomes more natural.
- ***Experience.*** When you have seen a similar situation before, it is easier to come up with a good solution.
- ***Support.*** Nobody says you have to make DECISIONS alone. Other people can help you come up with solutions—former teachers, mentors, family members, friends, coworkers, clergy, bartenders, self-help columnists, and, yes, even your boss.

Think of the DECISION-making process like a funnel. When you start the process, you fill it with all of your options. The funnel quickly narrows down those options until only one comes out the other end—the choice you will ACT on in the next link. So what are the obstacles that narrow down this funnel?

- ***Habits.*** Unlike routines, in which the *process* is automatic, with habits, the *choices* are automatic. Habits occur when people skip the DECISION-making process and leap immediately to a choice that they regularly use. Some habits are good—like brushing your teeth every night. It would waste a lot of time if you went through a lengthy process every night to DECIDE if tooth decay was a battle worth fighting. Unfortunately, habits that hinder are more common. Many people mindlessly flop in front of the TV after dinner, limiting their choices of what they could be doing with their time. When habits dictate your choices, you might overlook potentially better options. If you always order the same meal at a restaurant, you might miss out on a new dish that you would really enjoy. At work, your habit might be that you get defensive when someone brings a problem to your attention. Habits tend to come from an over-reliance on past experiences in the DECISION-making process.

- ***Gut responses.*** While intuition can be very valuable as part of DECISION-making, it can hurt you if you let it become the *whole* DECISION-making process.

- ***Poor advice.*** Many DECISIONS get derailed by bad advice. The biggest culprit? People who don't have to share the costs of bad DECISIONS with you, or even worse, people who have their own agendas. Remember, everyone's satisfaction is different. Before taking advice, make sure that the advisor is both competent and vested in you getting a good outcome.

- ***Limited exposure.*** Many ideas spring forth from previous experiences. If you never leave your daily routine, you have less of that worldly exposure to call upon when reviewing your options.

- ***Shortsightedness.*** You have to be able to envision outcomes, much like a good chess player does. He looks several moves down the road and considers the odds that the game will play out a certain way. Sometimes, when the rewards are high, a chess player's DECISION will even call for the sacrifice of a game piece. In your DECISION, you may have to sacrifice time, energy, or something else important to you, in order to achieve the RESULTS you want. Many DECISIONS are made by predicting outcomes. Will you make it through the light before it turns red? If you try, what are the chances that you'll get a ticket or get into an accident? If you are unable to envision outcomes, DECISIONS—especially difficult ones—are much, much harder to make.

- ***Indecision.*** Sometimes, try as you might to expand your options, no easy solutions jump out at you. Consider your choices surrounding taxes. You can choose to pay your taxes, or you can choose the unpleasant alternatives: incarceration and financial penalties. Neither is appealing, but you *do* have that choice. DECISIONS are hardest when there is no obvious winner. Often, you will be faced with a buffet of unappetizing options.
- ***Self-imposed limitations.*** Many people often latch onto one of the first options they think of, even if it is a bad one, and stop looking further. Maybe you are shopping, and don't see a shirt you like. You might settle for one of the few lackluster garments in front of you. Or, you might try to identify more choices. Maybe you ask a clerk if there are more shirts in the back. You might think about wearing a sweater instead. In a Lean environment, you have more flexibility to try new options than you realize. Be creative, and don't settle.

A call to ACTION

Once you make your DECISION, the next step is **ACTION**.

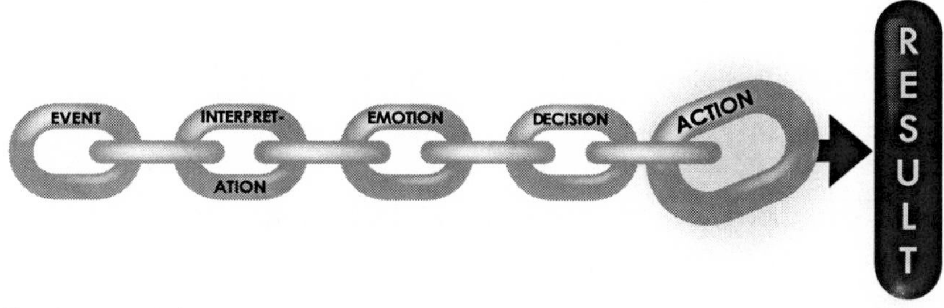

The ACTION Link

Apart from some of the physical responses that tag along with the EMOTION link, the ACTION link is the most visible part of the process. This is where people can finally see what you are doing in response to the initial EVENT.

Sometimes an ACTION is simple. You might decide to hang up a phone when someone is yelling at you on the other end. Sometimes an ACTION is complicated and time consuming, such as following through on the DECISION to return to college. The ACTION link is where the rubber meets the road in your quest for satisfaction. As with the other links, many factors influence the ACTION link:

- ***Abilities.*** Abilities come from natural talent, training, and practice. If you are playing golf, once you DECIDE to try to clear a water hazard, your abilities take over. The RESULT you want, a ball on the other side of the obstacle, depends on how well you perform your ACTION—swinging the club. In Lean, your abilities will also determine your level of success. For example, your skill with a Pareto chart[39] will play a role in how good your RESULTS are.

- ***Luck.*** People like to think they are in control of what goes on around them. Although you can never completely remove the effect of chance on your ACTIONS, you can greatly improve your odds of a desirable outcome. Locking your car doors reduces the odds that your belongings will be stolen—it doesn't guarantee it, though. Your car might just be in the wrong place at the wrong time. But successful people try to create their own luck. Basically, this just means that they identify and account for risk, which stacks the odds in their favor.

- ***Commitment.*** Commitment is the choice to stand by your DECISION and stick with a plan through its completion. The threshold

[39] **Pareto Charts** are bar charts that are sequenced to show the biggest categories first. The name comes from an Italian economist who first identified the 80/20 rule: eighty percent of the outcome is determined by twenty percent of the causes.

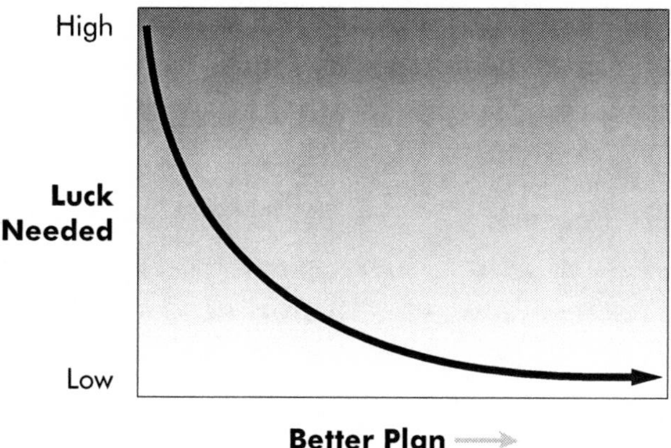

The better your plan, the less you have to rely on luck for good RESULTS.

for overcoming difficulties is different for every person. Some sports fans leave the stands once their team gets behind, while others stay until the bitter end—each group of fans has a different level of dedication to its team.

- ***Determination.*** If commitment is how long you stay with a plan, determination is how much effort and energy you put into it. A determined person will allocate whatever resources are necessary to get the task done.
- ***Teamwork.*** Working well with others is critical for some ACTIONS. Not every task can be completed independently. Teamwork includes a whole set of sub-skills: coordination, communication, negotiating, and consensus building, to name a few.

The following obstacles can hinder your progress through the ACTION link:

- ***A poor plan.*** No ACTION can be successful when the plan starts off on the wrong foot. The more detailed and specific the plan is, the more effective ACTIONS will be.
- ***Overestimating abilities.*** Some employees do not have a good idea of how they will perform, and they bite off more

than they can chew. The biggest problem generally comes from planning too much work for the time available. It is not uncommon for many people to think they will get more done than they really can.

- ***Competing agendas.*** Other people might have agendas that don't mesh well with yours. This frequently comes from competition for scarce resources, usually time or space. Two competing plans generally don't work well together.
- ***Assumptions.*** Taking details for granted derails many plans. Some assumptions cause plans to fail simply because the planner did not confirm a fact, like the availability of tools or resources. When something that was supposed to be in place, isn't, the plan falls apart.

Get the RESULTS you want

So, by now, you should have some insight into how the chain plays a role in your day-to-day experiences. But, understanding the How-You-Think Links is not really your goal in reading this book. What really matters to you is how you can use your knowledge of the links to improve your satisfaction in your job and, consequently, in all areas of your life. In the end, it's the **RESULTS** that count.

As you learn how to shape your outcomes, beware of the pitfalls that can hamper your progress:

- ***You focus on the process rather than the RESULTS.*** This is like a carpenter spending years learning the ins and outs of woodworking, but never putting it to use to make a cabinet. Knowing all about how you think and make DECISIONS is important, but only as a means to an end. What is more important is using the process to get somewhere you want to go.
- ***You aren't sure what you really want.*** You may get exactly the outcome that you planned and then realize that you still are not happy. The question some people fail to ask is not what the ACTION will bring, but whether that RESULT is what they really want.

- ***You think about the short term RESULTS instead of the big picture.*** You get what you want now, but miss out on bigger rewards later. Taking vacations every year may be fun, but those trips may be taking the place of buying that dream home you have always wanted.

In the words of Stephen Covey, author of the *The 7 Habits of Highly Effective People,* truly effective people "begin with the end in mind."[40] For the purposes of being satisfied in a Lean workplace, that means you have to think long and hard about the end RESULT you need to be fulfilled at work and happy in your life; then you have to tailor your chain around that end.

Connecting the chain to Lean

Bosses recognize that Lean will introduce immense changes at your workplace. Most will anticipate the impact on employees and try to assist with the transition. When a Lean company is firing on all cylinders, the pace of even small changes picks up dramatically, and hardly a day will go by when everything stays exactly the same. A higher frequency of changes—or, EVENTS—means more opportunities for negative INTERPRETATIONS, EMOTIONS, DECISIONS, ACTIONS, and RESULTS than ever before.

The chain gives you a tool to use when these changes come around. You can step back and think about what is happening. You can determine which link you are on, and figure out how you can get back on track if things are not going in the direction you would like. Let's take a look at how this chain might work in a Lean situation.

- ***EVENT.*** Imagine that, as usual, you've finished placing orders with the company's suppliers before heading off to your team's morning meeting. There, your boss reviews the daily plan and hands out some special instructions. At the end of the meeting,

[40] (Covey, 1989)

he mentions he wants to form a project team to improve the department's productivity. He announces that the team will be doing a 5S project in a few weeks. The goal will be to standardize the desks of all the people on the team. Unfortunately, he presented the information at the end of the meeting, without allocating time for the team's responses or questions.

- ***Interpretation.*** You have a lot of unanswered questions and immediately start trying to fill in the blanks yourself. Why is there a push to increase productivity? You wonder if something is going on that you don't know about. You question if the team is facing a budget crunch . . . or, is this push for productivity to reduce the team's head count? Will you lose your personal space? Do your pictures have to come down? In the absence of information, your brain does the best it can to come up with answers. You also apply intent to your boss's actions . . . In particular, why wasn't time left for questions? Was that intentional or an oversight? Does your boss just not care about how invasive this major change is? You see more work for you and your teammates on the horizon and suspect that you will not have much say about personal effects on your desk.

- ***Emotion.*** Almost immediately, your EMOTIONS take hold. You alternate between anger and fear—angry at your boss for how he approached the issue, and fearful that this change is an indicator of even bigger things to come.

- ***Decision.*** You have several options. You can talk to your boss about the problem. You can do nothing. You can get on the project team and try to guide the outcome toward a RESULT that is acceptable to you. You can spend time in the lunchroom complaining. You can go to the gym and try to do some yoga. You can even choose to combine some of these options. Let's imagine that you do, indeed, settle on talking to your boss about how he handled the announcement and request a spot on the project team.

- ***Action.*** Rather than plan a time to talk to your boss when he won't be rushed, you approach him as he is getting ready for another meeting. Since you are still angry, the conversation with your boss does not go so well. As a RESULT, he probably isn't going to put you on the project team.
- ***Result.*** Now, you have this issue looming over you. You are still mad at your boss, who is now likely frustrated with you, as well. You probably lost your chance to be on the project team. A RESULT, yes, but not exactly the one you wanted.

The next step

Here's the thing about the chain. People use it whether they know about it or not. They always go through the links, and the chain always ties into some RESULT.

What is not a given is the ability people have to influence how they progress through the chain. In the previous example, your boss did not have to end up irritated with you. You can learn to get positive RESULTS by paying attention to what is happening at each stage of the process. You can use some tricks and techniques to get better RESULTS. This next chapter shows you how.

CHAPTER 7
Strategies for satisfaction

Mastery

GREAT NEWS! IN THIS CHAPTER, YOU WILL LEARN how to minimize the impact of many hurdles that Lean might put in the way of your job satisfaction. You will learn some general tactics that you can use to close that satisfaction gap and take charge of your fulfillment at work. The following chapters will give you some specific strategies for dealing with the various problems you might encounter as you progress on your Lean journey. Master these methods, and you'll have a good chance at loving your job even more than you did before Lean came along.

Change the process

You have the power to change any situation and make your life better *if you choose to.* Every process can be made better, whether it is at work, at home, or even a thought process in your mind. A continuous improvement culture can work for you, as well as for the company.

Shaping your future starts with understanding how to control the How-You-Think Links. And the best part about the chain? You can modify a RESULT by intervening at any one of the five links. You can use the knowledge of the chain to play to your strengths or to minimize the impact of your weaknesses.

Each change you make, big or small, will affect your RESULTS. And the RESULTS will inform you about the wisdom of the changes you make. If you get good RESULTS, it will confirm that your new process works. If your RESULTS are less than desirable, you will likely discard the changes and try a new tactic.

There is one final piece to add to the chain: the **feedback loop.** Every time you get the RESULTS that you want, you reinforce the methods you used to get them. The way you currently progress through the chain is a product of this feedback loop. You kept the things that worked, and stopped doing the things that didn't.

As you become a Lean advocate, the definition of good RESULTS changes for you. If you use the same old methods, you will be unlikely to get what you want. So, you'll try a new way of INTERPRETING what it means to be measured, or you'll add some tools to your DECISION-making process, and you'll see better, Leaner RESULTS. Your new behaviors will stick, because they get you what you want.

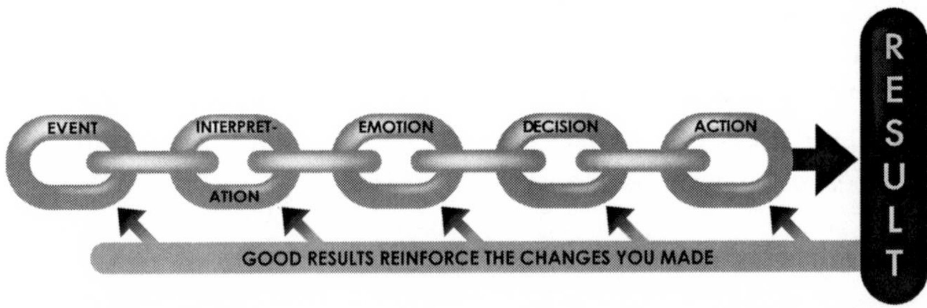

The Feedback Loop

The following sections give an overview of the methods you can use to improve the way you progress through each link in your chain. They are intended to lay the foundation for your efforts to improve your satisfaction. This groundwork will provide you with a better understanding of how and why the strategies in the following chapters will work.

So, where should you start? A general rule of thumb is that the further upstream (closer to the EVENT) that you can influence the chain, the better your RESULT will be. Why? Problems get magnified as you move through the chain. Prevent or change an EVENT that you don't like, and you don't even have to modify anything else in the chain. But, if you let your anger influence your DECISIONS about how to interact with a police officer after you run that red light, the degree of difficulty goes up.

It is much easier to intervene at the upstream links than it is to change the downstream links.

Modify the EVENTS

While it is impossible to go back into the past and alter something that has already happened, you can influence future EVENTS. You do this by modifying the environment in which you operate—the who, how, what, and where of a situation. Some things that you can do:

- ***Influence those around you.*** This includes not only your boss, but also your coworkers, friends, and family members. When the important people in your life change their behavior, the EVENTS that affect you tend to be more positive. This intervention starts with open and effective communication.
- ***Fix a work process.*** Some processes cause frustration, whether it is from a sore back or dissatisfied customers. When you fix processes, you have fewer negative EVENTS that require your energy and attention.
- ***Change policies.*** If you and enough other people ask for a change and convince the top brass that it is good for the company, you may be able to arrange a change in policy.
- ***Alter your environment.*** Poor lighting can give you a headache—an EVENT you need to deal with. You may not have the absolute

authority in every situation, but you probably can get a lot of help from your boss in improving your workspace. Again, this is easier if you can convince her that it is not only good for you, but also benefits the company.

Adjust your INTERPRETATION

Remember, INTERPRETATIONS are the most important link because they have the biggest impact on your RESULTS. You have the potential to create change if you:

- ***Review your values and beliefs.*** Your values are basically the underlying rules that guide how you behave in certain situations. Since you can hold two (or more) opposing values simultaneously, this can create a dilemma. Consider the employee who has a strong work ethic but also believes it is important to spend time with his family. Those two conflicting values would pose a challenge at quitting time if tasks were yet to be done.

  A fundamental part of INTERPRETATION is to be honest with yourself. Review your true values and make sure you understand what is really important to you. You need to come to terms with how your values fit into your company's culture.

  In order to make your life easier, you might think about changing your values. This is an extremely difficult task, however, because your values are so deeply rooted. Generally, values change in only one of two ways. The first is when you experience a major life change that immediately alters much of what you believe. You may start to value family more as you have children or you may commit to a fitness routine after a serious health scare. The second way values can be altered is when you make a make a conscious decision to change.

  Changing values is not an overnight project—it is hard go cold turkey and immediately stop thought patterns that you have had for years. It is practically impossible to simply decide to have a new value system. More likely, you will only be able to change your beliefs by committing to a series of new behaviors.

For instance, you can't just *say* education is important to you. You have to choose behaviors that support that value, such as enrolling in college courses or starting a self-study program. At first, those behaviors take effort, but after a while, as values start to shift, the behaviors will come more easily.

It would be a big leap to suddenly adopt Lean values, especially if you struggle with any of its side effects. Instead, you can alter your behaviors in ways that support Lean, and that simultaneously get you more of what you want. Over time, your choices will become more and more automatic as they lead to better RESULTS. Before long, your values start to shift.

- ***Think consciously.*** The most common cause of a bad RESULT is an erroneous INTERPRETATION. Let's say that you had a friend stand you up when you were supposed to meet somewhere. With a hasty and erroneous INTERPRETATION, your first thoughts might lead to an EMOTION of anger. However, if you can pull back and actually look at the situation, you might INTERPRET the absence differently.

When you pay attention to what you are thinking, you gain clarity. Step back and remove yourself from the situation for a moment. You might find alternate INTERPRETATIONS about the tardiness—ones that are not malicious or disrespectful. Perhaps you consider that your friend got stuck in traffic, got held up in a long meeting, or worse, had an accident. You might even consider that the mistake was yours. Perhaps you got the date or time wrong.

This might lead to a different ACTION—perhaps calling to get more information, rather than leaving a nasty message on his voicemail. The goal is to avoid racing down a path that leads to a negative EMOTIONAL response and a destructive RESULT.

Avoid passing quick judgment, and you may save yourself a lot of bad RESULTS. Obviously, in Lean, you can do the same. When you start to feel an EMOTION forming, back up a link to your INTERPRETATION and take a moment to look at *all* the facts, and not just the ones that support your hasty conclusion. Spend some time considering alternative explanations for the initial EVENT.

- ***Educate yourself.*** Specific knowledge is critical to making correct INTERPRETATIONS. The first way to learn about a topic is to research basic information. With a search engine, you have a tremendous resource—the Internet—at your fingertips.

  A second way to learn about a subject is to gain experience. You may form a negative INTERPRETATION if you don't know why a driver in front of you is slowing down—that is, until you follow him into a sharp curve with poor visibility at the edge of a steep drop off. The next time you travel down that stretch of road, you probably won't react the same way to the driver in front of you. Experience teaches valuable lessons.

- ***Observe.*** The more you study people, the better you will be at INTERPRETATION. Observing is very similar to collecting facts but focuses more on nonverbal cues. Do your boss's ACTIONS match her words? Watching carefully, in many cases, will tell you far more than simply listening to what she says. Crossed arms, a body turned away from you, scowls—these are all tell-tale signs that someone is upset.

- ***Remove your filters.*** Every day, you are bombarded with sensory input that your mind has to deal with. To keep from being overloaded, your mind has developed a set of **filters**. Filters are simply mental shortcuts that immediately process a piece of information, streamlining INTERPRETATION.

  Stop right now, close your eyes, and just listen for a minute. How many sounds can you identify? You may hear a fan whirring in the background from a refrigerator, a noise from the street, or a TV show that a family member is watching. You had probably tuned out all these distraction until you really gave them your attention. These sorts of filters, in general, are helpful because you could easily be overwhelmed if you had to INTERPRET every bit of input all the time.

Be careful that your filters do not keep out data that you should be using to form a more complete, and more correct, INTERPRETATION. It takes dedicated, conscious effort to step back and try to take in that extra information. More often than not you will be glad you did.

- ***Outsource.*** Find someone you trust to bounce the facts off. Perhaps a coworker heard your boss talking to you. See if she INTERPRETED that EVENT the same way you did. While you thought the boss was demeaning, a coworker might have seen the exchange as reasonable constructive criticism.

Alter your EMOTIONS

Imagine being in a dentist's chair, about to have your tooth drilled, and you hear these reassuring words: "Now, just relax . . ." Relaxing is never simple when you are facing a challenge, is it? Instead, your EMOTIONS take over as you hear that high-pitched whine of the drill. There are a few tricks you can learn that will help you manage your EMOTIONS and reduce undesirable RESULTS:

- ***Identify your "root" EMOTION.*** Make sure you know what EMOTION you are really dealing with. Is that really anger you are feeling? Or, is the anger a cover EMOTION for fear? Knowing what you are feeling is an important step in figuring out what to do about it. Here's a hint if you ever catch yourself saying, "I am *not* mad!" There is a really good chance that you are.

- ***Control your physical response.*** Reducing the intensity of the physical response that accompanies an EMOTION can help you manage your chain. If you are afraid of public speaking, it wouldn't be uncommon for you to have a fast heartbeat and rapid, shallow breathing. Taking a few deep breaths can sometimes help lessen the physiological reaction and subsequently reduce your fear.

- ***Break the cycle.*** EMOTIONS feed on repetition. Most emotional responses are usually short lived. When someone steps on your foot in a crowded room, your immediate burst of anger will, usually, quickly subside. On the other hand, if you dwell on an insult or a problem over and over in your mind, you re-live the same feelings again and again. And each time you revisit the situation, you feed and grow the negative EMOTION. Distraction or separating yourself from the situation can sometimes break the cycle and let the EMOTION dissipate rather than fester and get stronger. After you cool off, you can return in a better state of mind.

- ***Improve your well-being.*** Being physically and emotionally healthy helps you deal with the stress of negative feelings. Try to actively manage your physical fitness and emotional well-being. Avoid unhealthy behavior, such as poor eating habits or surrounding yourself with people that sabotage your goals. Take part in activities that restore your energy and enthusiasm. The more of this reserve you have, the less negative feelings will impact you. Having these energy stores is especially important during periods of prolonged stress, like during the transition to Lean.

- ***Avoidance.*** Strong, continuous, negative EMOTIONS take a toll on you. Sometimes, you just can't seem to shake the bad feelings. If all else fails, leave the situation. This strategy is most useful when the emotional costs are greater than the benefits, and when you have exhausted all your other, less drastic, options.

- ***Write it down.*** Most people don't have the time or the desire to write a journal. For many, it is just a little too "touchy-feely" to be an effective technique to manage EMOTIONS. But for some people, writing down thoughts seems to help relieve stress and reduce the intensity of negative EMOTIONS. After you write, it doesn't even matter if you destroy the pages—it is the *process* of the writing that helps you sort things out. In the spirit of continuous improvement, why not try it for a few days and see how you feel?

Make better DECISIONS

If you were unable to modify the upstream links, the DECISION-making process is yet another place where you can improve your chance to get the RESULTS you want.

The early links—especially INTERPRETATION, heavily influence how much effort you will have to put into the DECISION link.

You can do several things to become a more effective DECISION-maker:

- ***Improve your DECISION-making skills.*** Read about problem-solving methods and DECISION-making strategies and find a process that works for you. The best DECISION-making strategies take into account what is important to you, the likelihood of getting the RESULTS you want, and the potential downfalls if you make a wrong DECISION.
- ***Practice making DECISIONS.*** Practice using your DECISION-making strategies over and over in simple situations until the process becomes habit. Try this out on a low-risk DECISION you normally make out of habit every day, like choosing a restaurant for lunch, or deciding what to wear. This is the equivalent of doing a daily workout to improve your DECISION-making "muscles." The repetition improves your ability to make good DECISIONS when you encounter more difficult problems.
- ***Recruit help.*** Find other people to help you. Mentors, family members, friends, and professionals like lawyers or accountants can give you information that might help you make the best DECISION possible. Choose your help wisely, though—make sure that they are willing and able to help you and that they are

vested in your favorable RESULTS. That means they have to listen to what *you* want, not act automatically on what they think is best for you.

- ***Write it out.*** One way of taking EMOTION out of your DECISIONS is to write out your DECISION-making steps. Having the words in black and white makes sure you don't forget anything important and helps you think critically about the initial EVENT. One other benefit—writing out your process puts the situation and options neatly on paper and lets you share your strategies and DECISIONS with others.
- ***Defer your DECISION.*** Pause before you act—you don't have to make all DECISIONS instantly. Sometimes waiting a bit lets you gather additional information and look at the situation from alternate viewpoints, preventing negative consequences for making a DECISION in the heat of a moment. The break can be short—maybe just a few breaths, but enough time to rethink whether you really want to give your manager a piece of your mind.
- ***Test your DECISION.*** Sometimes, you can ease your way into a choice. Thinking of moving to a different state? Maybe taking a long trip, or spending a summer at the potential new locale will help you make a better DECISION before committing to a permanent change. Having a party catered? Dine out at the caterer's restaurant before you fork over the cash for the big bash. Trying to DECIDE if Lean is for you? Join a project in another work area to see what it is like.
- ***Trial and error.*** Trial and error is a method of problem solving in which you just keep trying different options until you get one that works. If one doesn't turn out like you want it to, you just try the next one. Looking for a lost sock is normally a trial-and-error process. You just keep eliminating places to look.

  This method doesn't work well with everything. The DECISION to get a tattoo is not easily reversible. Fortunately, with Lean, you generally have the option to try something else if your first pass through the DECISION link does not go so well. For example, if you move the benches in your work area, and the change doesn't work out, just keep trying new locations until you find one that works.

You can't completely control your environment, but you can make your own DECISIONS. Try this exercise to convince yourself you are the one in charge. Whenever you think "I have to . . ." or "I had to . . ." or something similar, change the wording to "I choose to . . ." or "I decided to . . ."

Sure, someone might ask you to do something or tell you to do a task, but ultimately, you choose whether or not you will do it. You follow the chain, calculating the costs and the benefits and the consequences of a variety of ACTIONS, and you DECIDE what ACTION is in your best interest.

When you get up in the morning, most people think, "I have to go to work." Well, that is not exactly true. You do "have" to go if you want a certain RESULT—in this case, a paycheck. However, you could also choose to go back to bed, get on a different shift, or buy a smaller house that wouldn't require such a high-stress job to pay the bills. True, you may not like those outcomes, but realize that you are choosing to go to work because it gives you the most of what you want. Rather than looking at your job like a prison when things get tough, think instead, "I choose to go to work because I do not want to be homeless."

Moving from thoughts to ACTIONS

Once you make a DECISION, you then have to translate it into ACTION. In some cases, an ACTION may take seconds, or less, to complete. Signing a contract is an example of this—all the work was done during the DECISION-making process. More often than not, the ACTION link is where the real, hard work begins, though. If paint starts peeling off your house, the DECISION to repaint it yourself might be easy; but the actual conversion of that DECISION into a bright and shiny home will take some time and effort.

You have several ways in which you can modify the ACTION link to increase your odds of success:

- ***Take luck out of the equation.*** Luck straddles the boundary between the DECISION link and the ACTION link. In the DECISION link, you consider how to avoid random problems. In the ACTION link, you have to actually keep chance from throwing a monkey wrench into your plan.

  Perhaps getting to work on time is challenging for you. In the DECISION link, you would come up with a plan to limit the chance of bad luck making you late. This might include using an alarm with a battery backup, DECIDING on your clothing the night before, planning time to make breakfast at home rather stopping by the sometimes-busy local drive through, and selecting the most consistent route to your workplace.

  In the ACTION link, you actually check your alarm clock to make sure it is set properly, iron your clothes, cook your own oatmeal, and drive to work. By making DECISIONS and doing the ACTIONS you decided on, you reduce your chance of tardinesss.

- ***Broaden your skills.*** The more skills you have, the more success you will find. If you don't have the right skills, you have two choices. You can settle for whatever RESULTS you can scrape together, or you can get the right skills by taking some formal classes, reading, or finding a mentor.

- ***Repetition.*** Once you learn something, you have to use it. If you haven't ridden a bicycle in years, you might find you are a little wobbly. Repetition keeps you from losing the talents you worked hard to get and keeps your skills from deteriorating.

Get the RESULTS you want

To understand how to be successful, you might first take a step back and think about why people fail.

Remember, everyone has a personal limit on what they can accomplish. For instance, not everyone can run a four-minute mile, even if they train correctly. Most bodies just aren't built to do what only a few world-class athletes can. You probably would not argue that everyone could run that fast, if they just tried a little harder. Yet, a common expression is, "You can do anything you put your mind to."

This expression is false. Just as people have a range of physical abilities, they also vary in mental skills. Some are more intelligent than others. Some are more insightful. Some tell better jokes. The fact is that natural abilities vary. That doesn't mean, though, that people are not successful if they don't perform as well as others. Contrary to what many people think, failure is not falling short of what someone else can do. Failure is when you don't live up to your own potential. The good news: that potential is probably much greater than you think it is.

Think about the power of this. If you decide you want to run faster, would you set a target of that elusive four-minute mile? Not likely. Nor would success be defined by running faster than your neighbor. You only fail if you don't live up to the potential you can reach with hard work.

So, what else keeps you from reaching your peak performance? Basically, you can hold yourself back in one of three ways:

- ***You don't know how to make a change.*** In many cases, you just don't have the right information about what you need to do to change. Maybe you want to be more environmentally correct, but you don't know whether you should choose paper or plastic bags at the supermarket. This is generally the easiest obstacle to overcome. Once you educate yourself on a subject, you know what to do. Many of the strategies that you will soon be reading target this lack of information.
- ***You don't believe in yourself.*** You start the chain without really believing you will come up with a solution that will get you good

RESULTS. With that kind of attitude, success is often elusive. Good RESULTS stem from a strong, positive outlook.

Obviously, you would be foolish to be overconfident. Common sense dictates that you should avoid challenging an NBA® all-star to a game of basketball. But, the flip side is that most people underestimate what they can accomplish. Time and time again, people surprise themselves. They end up doing well at something they didn't believe they could do before they tried it. Using the strategies in this book will help grow your self-confidence. As your skills improve and you see success, you will be willing, slowly but surely, to try more and more things.

- ***The change isn't really a priority to you.*** You speak louder with your ACTIONS than you do with your words. You may say that something is a priority, but if you don't devote time or effort to the endeavor, your words are just lip service. An example: a friend may say that learning to play an instrument is important to him; but day after day, he talks about the shows he watched on TV the previous evening. Until he actually buys an instrument and starts playing it, instead of watching bad reruns, his priority is clearly not learning to play an instrument.

This lack of priority is perhaps the hardest performance inhibitor to deal with. Why? Because, nothing is inherently wrong with wanting one thing over another. The problem, from a satisfaction standpoint, comes from the mismatch in priorities like when you and your boss don't agree on continuous improvement. If you don't like Lean it doesn't make you a bad person. It will, however, make it hard for you to thrive in a Lean company.

Starting the journey (Note: This is important!)

At the end of this book, you will have the tools to make a DECISION about what you are going to do with the hand you have been dealt. Imagine yourself aboard one of those ancient ships on which everyone has a long oar sticking out the side. After rowing steadily for as long as you can remember, you hear your leaders announce a change of course—to "Lean Island." What are your options? You could paddle backward, against the rest of the crew, and try to stay where you are. You could pull your oar out of the water, and just go along for the ride. Or, you can do what your bosses want and row toward the destination they have chosen.

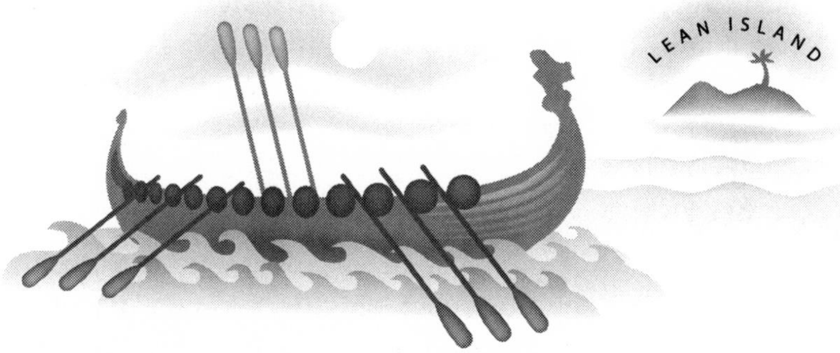

What will you choose to do?

While debating your DECISION to resist, not participate, or give Lean a shot, you have two realities to face, as well. The first is that:

Conflict makes everything more difficult.

In sports, when team members squabble and point fingers, winning becomes much tougher. It is also much harder to have fun.

The second reality is that, in your managers' eyes:

Resistance is regarded as poor performance.

You may have been a shining star before Lean, but if continuous improvement makes you noticeably surly, or not very cooperative, your career could be quickly derailed.

So, as you move down the Lean path, you have your choice to make. You may not have much say in a lot of things about Lean, but you can always control how you respond to the changes.

Attitude is everything.

If you approach Lean with the idea that you are going to give it a try and you then stay open to the ideas, concepts, and culture that it brings, you will be much more likely to have success and to enjoy your job. If you fight Lean, your negative emotion will cloud everything you do at work. Pretty soon, your resentment will bubble over and be displayed to your customers, your coworkers, and your boss. It will likely come home with you and affect your family as well.

Strategy preview

We live in a society of quick fixes. But unfortunately, you can't wave a magic wand and improve your job satisfaction in an instant. The path to increased satisfaction takes more work than that. The good news is that you don't need to make sweeping life changes to be more fulfilled. The key is taking small, *sustainable*, baby steps. When you repeatedly chose specific, proactive behaviors, they will eventually form good habits. The benefits will add up over time and will gradually shift the way you start to think, and feel, about Lean.

Strategies can often be strengthened by understanding *why* the advice works. For example, a tennis partner might tell you that drinking ice water will help increase your fitness. But, knowing why might make you more inclined to do it than just hearing his advice. He tells you that your body has to use energy to get the water up to 98.6 degrees, and so drinking it actually makes you expend a few calories. If you understand the principle behind a recommendation, you can apply the idea to your specific situation—in this case, maybe you could switch from hot tea (a drink that you love) to iced tea and get the same benefit as drinking ice water.

The following chapters really are the heart of this book. They will examine problems you are likely to encounter at some point or another, and discuss how the issues could affect you at work. They will reveal practical and easy to implement strategies that you can use to reduce conflict, diminish the negative effects of Lean on your job satisfaction, and find a way to be content in a Lean environment.

Some of these strategies will work for your personality and situation, while others will not. Some are more effective early in your Lean journey, and others will help you later on. Some will be most applicable to the shop floor; others will work best in the office. Pick and choose whatever works best for you.

Also, it should go without saying, but choose strategies that match your boss and your company. Just like you, your leaders have their own personalities and their own challenges that they are struggling with. Use good judgment to make sure that the strategies you choose do not ruffle feathers.

Most bosses will like that you are trying new ways to improve your satisfaction, especially when those strategies align with what they want. You might even consider including your boss in your DECISION-making process. (Show them this book so they understand what you are trying to achieve.) Most managers will appreciate your problem-solving efforts and your willingness to give Lean a chance. Remember, when your manager is happy, it increases the likelihood that you will be, too.

So, have you made your DECISION about rowing? If you are feeling brave enough to dip your oar into the water, look through the following strategies and see how you can make it a win-win for you and your boss as you all head toward "Lean Island" together.

CHAPTER 8

Thriving in a continuous improvement culture

YOU WILL FREQUENTLY HEAR THE TERM "continuous improvement culture" mentioned in Lean circles. A continuous improvement culture is a shared mindset based on the belief that the long-term success of an organization comes from shareholders, executives, managers, *and* employees constantly reviewing and improving what they do. For most people, making the leap to that type of environment is a challenge.

So, what does it mean to be in a continuous improvement culture? First and foremost, it means changing your responsibility from "doing your job" to "doing your job better." Being good at your job isn't enough in the Lean environment; you have to be better than you were yesterday.

An essential element to succeeding in a continuous improvement culture is the belief that:

Your job is important.

Many people sell themselves short by looking only at what they do on a very small scale; they don't recognize the greater good they provide. Your job is important or you would not be paid to do it. A trash collector can view his job as emptying garbage cans, or he can think of himself as making a city beautiful and livable. When thinking about your job, reframe the work. Don't look at your work in terms of the movements and chores you do—look at the value you bring to the world.

Look at the big picture. A bank teller doesn't just count money. She helps people finance their dreams. Police officers have a motto: *"Protect and Serve."* They don't just write traffic citations. Refocusing on the big picture and viewing your job with pride will make it easier for you to commit energy toward improving the aspects of it that you don't like. What do you do in your job that makes the world a better place? Write it down and put it someplace where it will remind you every day of your contributions.

If you struggle with a continuous improvement culture, the following strategies might help you make the transition more easily.

Strategies: Transitioning to continuous improvement values

Problem: You don't know where the company is headed.

How this affects you: Imagine boarding a plane and hearing the pilot ask, "Does anyone know where we are going today?" These words, from someone who is supposed to be in charge, would instill fear. Most people like to think that their boss has a clear destination in mind.

Action to take: Ask your manager about the company's objectives, and what your team's role will be. Consider requesting a copy of your group's value stream map. This will give you a sense of where your process fits into the scheme of things.

Why this works: These actions help in several ways. First, learning your team's objectives lets you see how committed your leadership is to Lean. Most likely, they do have a plan, even if they haven't yet formalized it, or communicated it to your team. Second, seeing that there is a plan raises your confidence in your boss—you know he is not just "winging it." Through some gentle questions, you might even make the plan better by seeing something that is missing. Third, just the act of asking about the company's strategy pegs you as someone who is interested in Lean.

Anxiety diminishes when employees think that their leaders are on top of things and are not just going through the motions. The bonus? If you ask to see the value stream map, and the boss doesn't have one, your question will spur him to action. You are actually doing him a favor. Giving him an incentive to map a value stream and build a strategy will make him a more effective leader.

Problem: You don't know why you have to do a particular task.

How this affects you: It is easier to do something when you know *why* you have to do it. When you don't understand the reason or don't see how it helps the company, you may find yourself angry that you are wasting your time.

Action to take: In the 1984 movie *The Karate Kid*, a young man learns martial arts from a wise, but eccentric mentor.[41] The instructor has the teenager painting fences and waxing cars, all with very precise movements. The boy finally gets fed up with his teacher and demands to know why he has to perform these mundane tasks. In response, the mentor throws several punches and kicks at the boy, who blocks them all by using the same motions he'd learned during those chores. The work had a purpose, but the boy never knew what it was during the training process. That lack of knowledge created hard feelings between him and his mentor, until the purpose of the chores was revealed.

When a task seems like a waste of time, ask your boss how it links to the group's goals. She'll either reconsider the assignment, explain that it's just one of those things that has to get

---

[41] (Avildsen, 1984)

done, or clarify how she thinks it will help the team achieve its objectives. When you ask, use good judgment and make sure you present yourself and your question in a positive way. Don't come across like you are giving her a hard time or like you are trying to avoid work.

Why this works: Knowing the objectives helps you understand your role in the scheme of things. It is important to believe that you are part of something worthwhile. Assignments seem like less of a burden when you know how valuable they are to the big picture.

Problem: Continuous improvement, by definition, is never finished.

How this affects you: Many people thrive on a sense of completion, and they struggle with the idea that something is never-ending. How much would you enjoy the Olympic Games if they went on forever and never had clear winners?

Action to take: Pick small milestones that you can shoot for along the way.

Why this works: Sometimes, it is easier to look at *only* the next task you have to do—rather than all the projects you know are looming beyond the horizon. Joggers understand this. One strategy they use when running up a big hill is to pick a point a little ways ahead and run to it, then pick another point and run to it, and so on. In much the same way, you can break a daunting goal into a series of smaller targets that are more manageable. A series of two or three percent gains somehow seems easier to achieve than a ten percent improvement. These bite-sized chunks of work keep you moving forward without feeling overwhelmed.

Problem: Leaders abandon Lean when the road gets bumpy.

How this affects you: It is discouraging and confusing to see your leaders cast Lean methods aside when setbacks are encountered. Lean principles are hard to support if they are only followed sporadically by those above you in the company. Watching your boss bend or ignore rules can inspire anger and resentment. You probably don't think it is fair that you have to consistently follow Lean policies, but your leaders don't.

Action to take: The boss tells you to expedite a customer order, disregarding a standard process, or he tells you to stop using the *andon* light because the response team is complaining about the frequency of its use. If your manager asks you to do something non-Lean once new practices have been established in your area, confirm that the boss is asking you to set the policy aside in this situation. Obviously, you have to know the rules to recognize when something slips outside the proper routine. When you talk to your boss, be direct, but respectful. Ask something like, "Just to make sure I understand you correctly, are you asking me to do this process differently than my Standard Work says to?" That kind of question makes him think about what he is asking.

Lean might be new to him as well. Perhaps the request is just an oversight. If he still decides to skirt the process, at least try to make sure that the original problem gets logged for resolution.

Why this works: Your goal is to gently point out to your manager that you are being asked to work outside a Lean process. Most managers don't want to derail Lean; they are just stressed about deadlines or pressures from their own bosses. Use common sense in your approach and don't make your manager think you are throwing up a roadblock. You don't want to appear like you are making his life harder. Instead, help him figure out why it was difficult to utilize Lean in this situation. Assist him in determining how this problem can be avoided in the future. Bonus: if you offer a solution when you approach him with the problem, your boss will probably be much more receptive to your comments.

Problem: A part of your job is harder than it should be.

How this affects you: You start fuming whenever you have to do a particular task and you avoid it until it absolutely has to be done.

In some cases, the task might be physically uncomfortable, like having to press a tight part into place with your thumb; or it might be dangerous, like having to install a heavy part above your head. It could also be something upsetting, like having to tell a demanding customer about yet another delay in the shipment of his product.

Action to take: Ask for a project to fix the problem. If it is small, you might get some time freed up to work on it or even some assistance. If it is a big issue, you might get a *kaizen* to resolve it. You have a better chance of getting a project if you can talk about it in a way that emphasizes what is important to the company: bottom-line results, higher productivity, fewer defects, and of course, safety. Be specific.

Why this works: Solving problems helps you and your employer. Managers understand that team members who initiate a project are more vested in the results than if a project is mandated from above. Creating solutions in this manner marks you as someone who demonstrates initiative.

Problem: Your coworkers are reluctant to help you out when you need support.

How this affects you: This is an ongoing problem in office environments where people have their own piles of work, rather than a shared workload, like on an assembly line. Instead of operating as a team where everyone contributes to a group effort, individuals in the office are only responsible for their own slice of the workload. As customer demand fluctuates, employees alternate from being on top of things to being swamped. This type of environment makes people less likely to assist others—after all, their own workload could dramatically increase at any time.

Action to take: As workloads rise and fall, like they periodically do, offer to help others when you can. If you help with someone else's peaks during your lulls, you are more likely to get help during your peaks. Also, be receptive when someone asks that your workload be changed because of a project, or when someone asks you to volunteer for a *kaizen* event.

Why this works: Workload balance is hard to find—some degree of inequity usually exists. Because of constant process improvement, this inequity will move around so that at some point, nearly everyone ends up needing help. Most people don't like working with coworkers who always take but never give, so make sure you help others out when you have the chance. A reputation for being a "taker" is hard to overcome.

Problem: You worry that the bar is set too high.

How this affects you: Stress rises when a job seems impossible. You may worry because you just don't see how things can possibly turn out right, or you may be angry because of the load your boss is putting on you.

Action to take: Avoid saying "can't" at all costs! It is a positively negative word. When you get the urge to say "can't," think of why you believe that it can't work. It is most likely because you don't know something—not because it really can't be done. Some *kaizen* teams even go so far as to set up a "Can't Jar," where naysayers have to drop a quarter in every time they say this particular four-letter word.

Why this works: Repeatedly, people on continuous improvement projects spend their time arguing about why something can't be done rather than just trying to do it. In reality, people say "can't" when they really mean "won't." In Lean, it is okay to fail on occasion, but it is not okay to avoid trying new processes. There are many clichés about positive attitudes, but one that is worth remembering is, "If you say you can do something, there's a chance you will succeed. If you say you can't, your failure is guaranteed." Being too negative also has a

The "Can't" Jar

chance of getting you labeled as a Lean resistor, which tends to strain your relationship with your boss.

Problem: You don't participate in problem solving because you don't like conflict.

How this affects you: Employees are vested in the outcomes of projects, so conflict tends to happen. And, if you are the type of person that doesn't like to argue, this can be a challenge. One reason some people steer clear of conflict is the concern it will damage relationships if they disagree with friends or coworkers. As a result, they simply avoid participating in the continuous improvement process altogether, or they participate but avoid voicing dissenting opinions. In either case, they lose their say in the solution. If this scenario applies to you, you'll end up getting stuck trying the idea of whoever can talk the loudest. Without a voice in the process, change is hard to tolerate, and it increases the likelihood that you will not be content at work.

Action to take: Try to find an ally that can stand in for you in discussions. Feed that person your ideas, and then let her be the one out in front. Another option is to talk to the person you disagree with in private. This can make the conversation less stressful, since it is not being observed by the whole project team. Finally, give the team leader an anonymous note with your comments or ideas.

Why this works: In all these methods, you are reducing or eliminating the strain of potential disagreement. This lets you focus on communicating ideas rather than worrying about the stress of their delivery.

Problem: Quality problems and production issues from other areas show up in your workstation.

How this affects you: You are already working hard, so it doesn't take much to get overwhelmed and discouraged when additional problems end up in your lap. As Lean gets going, your leaders will place an increasing emphasis on highlighting quality issues and correcting problems. Your boss will expect you to help solve whatever difficulties you discover, even if you didn't cause the defect. That extra work makes your job harder and hurts your relationship with upstream coworkers.

Action to take: The real solution starts from a general attitude that quality is everyone's responsibility. Many major problems can trace their way to small, correctible errors upstream. It can be tempting to take the easy way out and pass on poor quality, especially if it didn't originate in your area. Instead, follow the *andon* process. Call for help to get problems fixed.

If you do provide a quick fix on something, make sure you notify whoever is manning the station at the source of the problem. If defects persist, record them and become a bulldog to get the issues resolved. Stand-up meetings at the start of a workday provide you a great opportunity to keep attention on the problem.

Why this works: Most quality problems magnify as they move downstream. If something makes it to the end of a production line, a defect that could have taken minutes to fix in your station might now take hours for someone else. Obviously, the longer something takes to fix, the greater the cost. If the problem makes it to a customer, it could add even more cost for time on the phone with a service tech, or for warranty claims. Worse yet, the company's reputation could be tarnished and future sales might be lost.

It is also harder to prevent future problems when defects make it to the end of the process. As time passes, it becomes increasingly difficult to link the defect with the error. When a problem is immediately identified, the source of the error is much easier to discover.

Problem: Your ideas don't seem to get used by your leaders.

How this affects you: Your leaders don't seem to think your comments or suggestions are very important. Your boss or *kaizen* team leader hears you out, but your ideas are not put in place. When they are discarded, you are worried that you are not viewed as a valuable team member. It also makes you less likely to offer ideas in the future.

Action to take: Everyone has an idea about how to fix one thing or another. Go to any local watering hole, and you can hear dozens of ways to fix the legal system, end unemployment, and bring prosperity to the country. Coming up with ideas is not usually a problem. It's making sure they are practical that is not so easy.

Even if you present a workable idea to a manager, he still might not use it. Your boss has some additional hurdles to overcome—prioritizing the good ideas, making a plan, and finding the resources to actually implement them.

Your satisfaction will increase if you find a way to get more of your suggestions used. To do this, make them stand out. Your first order of business is to make sure you've done your homework. The more fleshed out an idea is, the more likely it is to be considered. Give examples of where a similar idea has been used in another department. Calculate how much the idea would cost to put in place and how much it will save, or what other benefits it might offer. Make sure you use specifics. General ideas just add to a boss's workload. Specifics make his job easier. Which of these descriptions sounds easier for your boss to follow up on?

- We shouldn't use glue to seal the product's case.
- Several customers have complained about glue that has seeped out and hardened along the seams of their product's case. This has increased our customer complaints by three percent over the past two months. We should consider using a hinge and a screw to secure the case, like we do on the WidgetMax 3000. Tooling said it would only take a few hours to modify the mold, and the screw is only a few cents.

When presenting ideas, put your thoughts into terms that the boss understands. Speaking in a common language with your leaders makes them have faith in what you are saying. Mention the Lean tools you think will be needed—for example ***poka yokes*** (mistake-proofing devices, like the switch in your microwave that shuts off the unit when the door opens) or Pareto charts. Talk about how the idea adds value to the process. This shows that you have put a little effort into thinking about the issue.

Above all, continue to offer suggestions, even if the majority are discarded. And don't be afraid to ask for feedback about why they weren't implemented. Use that feedback to make future proposals more likely to be put in place.

Why this works: Making sure your ideas are linked to company goals is a good way to improve the odds that they will be used. Believe it or not, it is fairly easy to do this. Most companies have a cost-reduction goal and some sort of customer satisfaction target. Many, if not most, of your ideas will affect one or both of these. Leaders are always under pressure to meet their goals, so, they are usually receptive to any ideas that help them "make their numbers." As mentioned previously, when your idea helps your boss, she tends to be more satisfied in her job. Remember what that means? Satisfied bosses tend to make satisfied employees.

Spending time preparing your idea also helps you preserve your satisfaction in another way. It keeps you from using ideas as veiled complaints. If you come up with a "suggestion" that lacks evidence and corrective actions, there's a good chance you are just venting about something that is bothering you. Most managers don't view these types of "suggestions" as helpful or appreciated. While managers certainly want to know if something is wrong, they prefer that you are straightforward with them. Dressing a complaint up like an idea just makes them think you are trying to pull something over on them.

Remember, having your bosses listen to you does not always mean that they will do what you want. So, be ready for (and expect) your boss to say "no" to you.

If she does say no, realize that managers get lots of ideas and suggestions every day and that they simply do not have enough time, money, or resources to get them all done. Maybe she just doesn't think your idea is the highest priority on the long laundry list of what needs doing. Or maybe, she thinks a better way can be found to do what you are asking. Perhaps a different solution is already in the works. Your manager also probably has access to much more information than you do, so she can see more obstacles that might derail your suggestion. More often than not, the reason your boss rejects your idea is not personal. In fact, most people in charge also see a lot of their own ideas land in the circular file. They probably are not treating your ideas much differently than they treat their own.

Strategies: Communicating more effectively

Problem: Your eyes glaze over when leaders start throwing around new terms and Japanese words.

How this affects you: If you don't speak the same Lean language that your boss does, you might not understand what is going on or how to participate in a Lean conversation. This can make your satisfaction (and maybe even your self-esteem) plummet.

Action to take: Learn about Lean terms and how to apply them to your situation. You don't need to be an expert on the terminology, but you should have a working knowledge if you want to participate effectively in continuous improvement.

Why this works: Being able to understand conversations and then sounding intelligent when you speak up makes people listen to you. "This isn't working" is not as powerful as, "Can you get someone to do a run chart to see if parts quality is getting worse?" Your boss will be much more likely to listen and act on your concerns and suggestions if you show that you have taken the time and effort to learn about Lean.

Problem: You see problems that need fixing, but your boss just thinks you like complaining.

How this affects you: You want to discuss problems with your manager without worrying about repercussions. If you think your boss views your concerns as complaints, you might feel annoyed that you are not being listened to. Worse, you might become worried that you are going to be labeled as a troublemaker. In either case, you won't be able to rally any support to fix the problem you are trying to address.

Action to take: Try to find the root cause of a problem before you approach your boss. If you do not have time to do detailed research, at least be able to provide a starting point that shows you are interested in identifying the problem. Then, offer a couple of possible solutions to jumpstart the problem-solving process. As an example, consider this simple sentence: "We are out of parts, again." Do you recognize this as a complaint? Now, weigh that against this fact and solution-packed sentence: "Can we get a *kaizen* to speed up re-ordering? Every time parts have been late this month, the *kanban* card sat in the collection point too long."

Why this works: In Lean transitions, many bosses hear far more grumbles than they want to. They would much rather hear about someone who takes a stab at figuring out the root cause of an issue and shows some initiative to start working on a solution. If you put in even a little bit of such effort, your boss will be much more receptive to your comments and concerns. Make his life easier by helping him troubleshoot and come up with a solution. Otherwise, you are just relaying a problem that needs to be fixed and adding something else to his ever-growing to-do lists.

Problem: You don't think a problem is getting the resources it needs to fix it.

How this affects you: You have identified a difficulty, but you can't seem to convince your boss how serious the situation is. You're not only aggravated by the ongoing problem, but you are also concerned by the lack of support and resources.

Action to take: Make sure you talk with your boss in specific terms. Do not generalize or give wide, sweeping statements—those rarely get much attention at all. Consider which of the following you think a manager will listen to more: "Customers hate the new policy," or "Since the new policy started, FakeCo Construction and five other customers have cancelled their accounts." If you can't find actual examples to back up your claim, you should probably question your original statement. Linking your examples to the company's quality, delivery, and cost goals makes them carry more weight. If FakeCo left because of on-time delivery (OTD) issues, use the actual delivery history, or bring in a stack of e-mail complaints when trying to convince your boss of the need for resources.

Why this works: Examples make people pay attention because they turn an abstract issue into something that can be defined. Once a problem can be described in detail, the solution finding can begin.

Problem: You find it hard to get your boss to come to the same conclusions as you do.

How this affects you: You look at the "facts of a case," and come to one conclusion. You boss examines the same information and comes to an entirely different one. You try to convince him, but he just doesn't agree with what you are trying to say and you end up frustrated.

Action to take: First, ask specific questions and make precise comments. General queries and assumptions tend to reduce your credibility and are often considered "loaded," which can put a listener on the defensive. A telltale sign that you are doing this: you use all-encompassing words like "always" and "everyone." These terms make bosses suspicious and skeptical, and paint you as an exaggerator.

Second, avoid assumptions—given an incomplete set of data, your boss may not form the same conclusions you do. If you open with conjecture, your boss is unlikely to agree with you, no matter how much you try to convince him. "Our customers will never order online, so we should . . ." starts with an assumption that may or may not be true. It is clear that you are starting with an agenda—to avoid doing online sales. Your boss might have a different take on the matter. If the facts support your position, you won't need to use assumptions.

Finally, your boss has to evaluate all the evidence to form his own opinion. If you understand how he thinks, you can make sure you anticipate the questions he will ask and have good information ready from the start. Some bosses, once they say "No," are unlikely to change their minds. Take advantage of that first opportunity to anticipate all his possible questions. If you do that, you'll be more likely to convince him you are drawing the best conclusion.

Why this works: Clear, direct communication goes a long way toward preventing conflict. Remember the How-You-Think Links? Are you presenting information in a way that will help your boss interpret an event the same way as you?

Problem: One of the bigwigs asks how things are going, and you're not sure how, or if, you should respond.

How this affects you: Senior leaders like to walk around (**go to *gemba***) and talk to employees. They want to find out what is happening down in the trenches. For some employees, these situations can be stressful, because they worry that saying what is really on their minds will get them, a coworker, or their boss in hot water. Anxiety may be costing these frontline workers a prime opportunity to get assistance on a persistent problem.

Action to take: This is a fine line to walk. First, think of the reason the executive is there in the first place: he is sincerely interested in finding out how the operation is running and how workers are doing. But employees generally tend to be uncomfortable when executives are around and just want "the suit" to leave. To hasten that retreat, subordinates rarely ask questions, voice concerns, or make any comment at all. This means that any comments you choose to make will stand out. You can often make very important points with great payoffs. The big bosses, if they agree with your comments, will not only be impressed with you for taking a little risk, but they can almost always get things done more quickly than anyone else.

Now, here are some tips for talking to executives. Limit how much you say—control the *quantity*. Don't bring up a laundry list of problems—you'll only come across as disgruntled. Be concise. If you are long-winded, the executive's mind will wander onto something else. They always have lots going on. If it feels too stressful being the one to talk, recruit the outspoken person on your team who will say just about anything to anyone (every team has one). Ask him to voice your concerns for you.

Another rule of thumb is to never surprise your own, immediate boss and jump over her head. Make sure that whatever you say, it is something you have already tried to get fixed. Unhappy bosses make for unhappy employees, so phrase your comments in a way that doesn't incriminate your manager. Also, since relationships are important to your satisfaction, try to avoid blaming coworkers. They won't like having fingers pointed at them, especially in front of an executive.

An example: instead of saying that your manager hasn't gotten a necessary improvement project started, say that your boss and the team have been working hard to meet productivity requirements and haven't been able to spare the resources to take on additional tasks. Ask if the executive can help. In this way, you've reframed a problem. You demonstrate that your boss and your team have been industrious and are interested in improvements. You've proposed a course of action rather than just offering criticism, and you requested assistance to meet business goals.

If your boss *is* a problem, and you know he will take issue with you bringing something up publicly, think twice about airing concerns in front of an executive. Instead, try using the anonymous approach. It tends to be less effective, but will likely insulate you from your boss's displeasure.

Why this works: Executives have lots of clout. When they want something done, that project will often jump to the front of the line.

Problem: You need to air grievances with your manager.

How this affects you: Your boss's decisions have had a big impact on your job. You want him to understand how they are affecting you.

Action to take: Don't ambush your boss in the hallway with complaints when he is running off to an important meeting. Instead, ask to schedule a private time to discuss your concerns. Once that request is granted, plan ahead and be prepared with no more than two or three specific points that you want to address. Blasting your boss with a series of grievances will likely put him on the defensive and make him tune out.

During your planning phase, consider whether you just want your manager to know how you feel or if you want to present a specific action you would like him to take to resolve a problem. (Remember—don't complain. Pure complaints seldom bring any resolution.) When you present problems and offer solutions to your boss, include supporting data. Speak your manager's language in terms of workplace satisfaction, continuous improvement, safety, quality, and customer needs. Help him help you.

During the meeting, discuss your biggest concern first. If you don't prioritize what is most important to you, you may run out of time—or your boss's attention. Be careful to make sure that you are actually addressing the problem that is really bothering you. Sometimes, people tend to use a more acceptable, more presentable problem to cover for the one that is really getting under their skin. They expect one solution to resolve both.

For instance, let's say you are upset because you no longer have reason to visit the mailroom to retrieve mail and therefore have less contact with your friends throughout the day. Rather than address the real issue—the fact that you miss the social interaction with your coworkers along the way—you decide to present a more acceptable side of the problem. You tell your boss that your legs get cramped from the increased number of hours at your desk. Unfortunately, the resolution might actually solve only the cramping problem—perhaps a more ergonomically correct office. Your boss would believe, incorrectly, that your issue had been resolved, even though you are still unhappy.

Why this works: A big part of discussing grievances is the development of trust. Employees have to be able to believe in their leaders. They have to think the boss will be compassionate about the issues under consideration. Bosses have to be able to take their employees comments at face value. Once trust develops in both directions, problems and their solutions become easier to discuss.

Problem: You hear something different from what your boss has said.

How this affects you: You find yourself in hot water when you thought you were doing the right thing.

Action to take: Remove the filters from your brain. People have a knack for selectively hearing what they want to. When you do this it can change the meaning of what a manager has said because crucial information gets left out. How do you learn to listen more carefully? One good method is to repeat back what you think you heard. When the boss tells you something, don't just say, "Okay." Instead, repeat what you heard him tell you. This is called a **brief back.** Say, "So, you want me to . . ." If your brief back is not what the boss meant, the boss will let you know right then, and you won't have wasted a lot of effort on the wrong thing.

Why this works: You know immediately that your interpretation of your boss's message is correct. Instead of just thinking that you have it right, you are confirming it and saving yourself the hassle of a misunderstanding. In addition, your boss has an opportunity to see right then and there that you received his message correctly.

Problem: Your boss doesn't always follow up on promises.

How this affects you: You are expected to do what you say. When your boss agrees to something, it is only fair, then, that she should have to deliver on her word as well. Relationships with bosses and trust in managers are big components of job satisfaction. Broken promises erode this relationship and cause resentment.

Action to take: Keep your boss honest. She may tell you something in passing but then never follow up on it. When she said it, she no doubt meant it; however, on the way back to her desk, she may have had a dozen other problems brought to her attention. As she dealt with pressing matters, your task unintentionally got pushed to the back of her mind. Help her out. First of all, when she says she'll do something, ask her when—bosses give you deadlines, so isn't turnabout fair play? Second, put your understanding in writing by sending a thank you (reminder) e-mail: "I appreciate your offer to help look into training projects for me. I look forward to hearing which ones I can choose from next week." Follow up again if you don't hear back.

Why this works: You help your managers stay on top of things. If they know you are going to hold them accountable for what they say, they are more likely to follow through. Your follow-up will frequently spur the boss to action. She doesn't like looking as if she is not getting things done any more than you do, so she'll find the time to close out the issue. An additional benefit to following up is that it shows the boss you pay attention when she speaks.

Oh, one cautionary note: make sure that your reminders don't become "pesky." Don't send daily countdown notes—"Only four more days to go!" An initial reminder, and then a single coordination follow-up shortly before the due date are usually acceptable.

Problem: You have no say in your company.

How this affects you: You probably spend more waking hours at work than anywhere else. As a consequence, you want some control in how things are going but you don't think you have a voice.

Action to take: Join a committee. Many companies have some type of employee group that gets team members in front of executives. It may be a Lean-specific group, or it may be for general company issues. Either way, it provides employees with a chance to discuss problems. If you don't feel comfortable being on a committee yourself, talk to the committee's representative from the front line. Give her some ideas about what's bothering you, and offer suggestions for making your work environment better.

Why this works: Committees enable frontline employees to meet executives and vice versa. As the groups get to know each other a little better, employees and senior leaders tend to have more open and effective communication.

Another benefit is that the executives get a balanced, first-hand understanding of how things are *really* going in the trenches. It is surprising how often upper management is insulated from the day-to-day problems that face their employees. If they don't know about your concerns, you rob them of the opportunity to help fix them.

Problem: You don't know what to expect with all this Lean stuff.

How this affects you: When you are in the dark about something, your stress level increases and work becomes less enjoyable. This apprehension often continues to build as the change gets closer and closer.

Action to take: If you really want to find out what a pending change will mean to you, talk to coworkers who have already been through it. If you are about to join your first *kaizen*, find someone who recently finished one. Ask specific questions about the things that concern you. Some questions you might ask include: "How was the facilitator?" "How are the changes working out?" "What got harder?" "What got easier?"

Why this works: Colleagues who have gone Lean (or gotten Leaner) will probably give you a different perspective on the transition than your bosses do. Peers are easier to relate to and often more believable. For many people, the anticipation of a change can be worse than the actual change itself.

Problem: You can't get your manager to understand how much a broken machine, dilapidated computer, or missing tool is costing the company.

How this affects you: Perhaps you have to struggle with a finicky machine or a slow computer, and your day is full of frustration. You know how much time you are wasting, but you can't seem to make your boss see it.

Action to take: Speak with your manager in terms of profit, making it clear what the company gets in return for investing in tools that support a better process. If you don't know exact figures, give the details that you do know. You can probably figure out things like how many minutes *you* waste working with a slow computer, how often the maintenance team comes around to fix a dilapidated machine, or how often a defective tool damages a part. Then, let your boss calculate the actual costs. Make sure you use the word "profit" in the conversation—it steers your boss toward thinking about the bottom line.

Why this works: Managers understand costs, so saying that your computer is old and slow might not make an impact. Instead, explain that Joe, who just got a new computer, is now able to process nine percent more orders in a day. That is information that makes managers take notice. If they see that replacing twenty old computers in the department can avoid having to hire a new person, you have a fighting chance of getting the checkbook opened and seeing less of that hourglass on your computer screen.

Talking about profit makes the solution a win-win for you and your boss. You get what you need, and the boss improves the bottom line.

Problem: You just don't believe what your boss tells you about Lean's capabilities.

How this affects you: If you think your leaders are setting unrealistic expectations about how much Lean can deliver, you may believe you are wasting your time.

Action to take: Ask your boss if you can attend another team's report out from an improvement project. **Report outs** (which are also occasionally called **sunset reports**) are short summaries (ten minutes or so) of a team's accomplishments. Project teams normally present report outs on the Friday of a *kaizen* week.

Why this works: Watching another group's report out helps you understand the *kaizen* process a little better. This can be especially beneficial if you have not been in an improvement event before. More importantly, it lets you see actual results that Lean achieved elsewhere in *your* company. A big difference exists between hearing about something and actually seeing your coworkers talk about their accomplishments. Don't forget to go up to the team members after the presentation and ask them about their personal experiences with the *kaizen*.

Strategies: Improving relationships with peers

Problem: You see and hear (and maybe even make) lots of complaints.

How this affects you: Complaints can come from you, your coworkers, and your friends (who may or may not also be coworkers). Complaining seems like it is a method of venting frustration, but it is really just a way that people deal with their perception that they are helpless. People who complain frequently are stuck talking about problems rather than finding solutions. Why? They don't realize that there are strategies for dealing with the problem that they are complaining about.

Why are complaints a problem? They are contagious. They spread like wildfire, expanding out of control and often growing more intense as time passes, even if nothing new happens to fuel them. As those around you become increasingly negative and cynical, your day becomes less fun, which can lead to even more complaints. Remember, relationships can be one of the biggest sources of satisfaction at work. But constant complaints can put a strain on those relationships, even if you agree with the complainers.

Action to take: To stem the tide of complaints, the best starting point is you. Train your mind to recognize when you are complaining. You'll probably be surprised how readily you complain without even thinking about it. You may not even realize that what you are doing is, in fact, complaining. "Gas prices are too high." "It's too hot out today." "This porridge is too hot." "This porridge is too cold." When you start to pay attention to your complaints, you'll realize how often you do it.

Let's take a moment to define the word **"complaint."** For the purpose of this book, a complaint is a negative commentary without any proposed solution. Compare, "Gas prices are too high!" with, "Gas prices are so high—would you like to carpool?" See the difference?

So, how do you recognize when you are complaining? Sometimes, all it takes is to think about what you say. You can set a "watch for complaints" reminder on your calendar or leave yourself a note someplace where you frequently pass by. The goal is to develop your ability to identify complaints before they come out of your mouth.

In the process of recognizing spoken complaints, you should also monitor your body language—eye rolling, tightening of the mouth, huffing, cocking your head to the side—all might accompany a complaint. Once you learn to recognize these behaviors, estimate how often it happens each day. Then actually count and record the number. Chances are, the real number will be much higher than you think. Being aware of how often you do it is usually enough to help your effort to reduce it.

Once you start getting your mindset under control, start thinking about your relationships, specifically with people that you talk to about work. In your effort to control your fault-finding behavior, surround yourself with positive, optimistic people. Eat lunch with people who talk about things other than problems at work. Limit phone calls and e-mails that center on how bad your work is.

After work, be wary of groups that meet following a tough day—these gatherings tend to become complaint fests. Consider staying for just a short time or not going at all if you suspect it will be a negative experience. If you have to be around other people who want to get things off their chests, try to exert some influence over the topic by changing the subject to something the whole group enjoys. Or decide not to participate in the conversation—maybe read a book or listen to music. That way you can still be around your friends, but you won't need to engage in the negativity.

When you are off-duty, you can choose who you spend time with. At work, avoiding complaints can be very difficult—you can't just get up and walk away from a bad situation.

The best option is to ignore negative comments. If you don't engage and just let the comments go, over time, the complainers will realize you are not interested in hearing yet another reason why Lean bothers them. Eventually, they will move on to other topics or other listeners.

Another subtle approach is to try redirecting your coworkers' discussions to another topic. You might choose to listen briefly to a complaint about work, but then fairly quickly steer the conversation to another topic. This technique allows your associates to vent, albeit briefly. This time can be a small price to pay for future peace.

If subtle approaches don't succeed, you can redirect discussions more directly, by flat out asking the speaker to cut back on his or her complaining. Sometimes, people in work groups think that everyone shares their opinions and wants to hear about their viewpoints. Let them know that is not the case, but try to avoid engaging in an argument with them about it.

If you think your coworker is just struggling with a specific, one-time issue and not just sprinkling around pessimism, you could use your skills to eliminate the problem together. Remove the source, and you remove the complaint.

If things still don't improve, talk to your boss, or leave an anonymous comment. Knowing about "negativity problems" or morale issues will inspire many bosses to visit their teams more often. If bosses frequent the work area, complaining tends to decrease. Leaders will also be more likely to see problems as they happen, which makes your boss more likely to act on the issues.

When you do have a choice at work, take advantage of it. Choose to sit with positive people at meetings. Pick project partners who are encouraging and supportive, rather than negative.

A final, and more extreme option, is to ask for a transfer. Find a work group that is more positive about Lean, and try to join them. Working around positive people is far more enjoyable, and better for your job satisfaction, than working around a group of complainers.

Why this works: Reducing your number of complaints does a few things for you. First, it saves energy—complaining takes a lot of work! Second, it frees up brainpower to use for problem solving. Third, it makes you more fun to be around. If you are considered to be a complainer, you will eventually find that people start avoiding you! Reducing complaints also helps your company because Lean efforts work best when the complainers are a minority. Widespread unrest is a warning sign of big problems.

You may wonder, though, why worry about complaints when you are away from your job? Well, off-duty time is critical for you to unwind, recharge, and recover from stress and pressure. When your time off is filled with bad feelings about work, you have no time to reset.

It is easy to complain and blame others. But have you ever seen a self-help book recommending that you complain your way to a better life? Why not? Because it just doesn't work. Instead, spend your energy on changing what *will* improve your satisfaction.

Strategies: Using the tools

Problem: Your manager doesn't seem to really understand the Lean tools, and your team is not getting good outcomes.

How this affects you: You are putting a great deal of effort into helping to get Lean rolled out, but your job doesn't seem to be getting any easier or better.

Action to take: This can be disheartening, but keep in mind that your manager may be just as new at Lean as you are—and she has to learn a lot more than you do.

If you are really concerned, you can step up and help by learning specific tools that will support your manager and your team. For example, become an expert at 5S techniques. You'll find plenty of reading material available on the subject, and it is something that you can work on in your own area.

Why this works: Most good managers will be receptive to assistance, especially when they are swamped. In addition to reducing workload, having a knowledgeable team helps keep managers from making mistakes. Need an example? Managers like to add data collection to a process. If you become an expert on **check sheets** (a tool used to collect data), you make sure that the data is useful and accurate, plus, you can make sure that it is done in a way that minimizes the burden on your team.

Problem: Demand picked way up, but staffing isn't going to be adjusted.

How this affects you: Demand has picked up more quickly than expected. You feel overloaded, but management isn't going to add a new team member to pick up the extra work.

Action to take: Staffing plans and budgets go hand in hand, and they are usually done far in advance. Managers generally consider two things when preparing them: the demand forecast, and projected productivity growth.

Most Lean organizations set an improvement target each year—let's say ten percent. If demand is expected to grow by ten percent, it's a wash, and headcount stays the same. If demand growth is projected to exceed ten percent, the budget would likely include a few extra people on the staff.

If the demand growth is below ten percent, though, you'll eventually end up with fewer people on the team than when you started. Don't worry—Lean leaders understand that they can't lay people off and still get them to work hard at improvements. This reduction will come in the form of attrition—retirements, transfers, or resignations. Really good Lean leaders will also try to keep a buffer of temporary workers on their teams. This gives them even more flexibility to match team size with demand.

So, what happens when things don't go according to plan?

Generally, on large teams, adding a person only changes capacity by a small amount. On a twenty person manufacturing team, a twenty-first person only adds five percent to the capacity. If demand goes up by five percent more than expected, the extra person makes sense.

So, what's the problem? Well, there are really two issues. The first is that sometimes, even if demand rises, executives and senior managers may be reluctant to hire more people. They may be concerned that the demand increase is temporary or may have other reasons for not wanting to hire more staff.

The second problem occurs when a team is small. Let's look at a four person team that experiences the same five percent demand growth. If your boss adds a person, capacity increases by twenty-five percent—five times as much as your team needs! You'd be hard pressed to get a manger that would choose twenty percent overstaffed instead of five percent understaffed.

Okay, that's a lot of background information, but it is important to know why your team won't be hiring anyone else. It lets you move on to other, more creative, options.

Know Lean fundamentals—especially Standard Work. Sit down with your boss and ask him to help you come up with a specific plan to get your work done in the face of increasing demand. Use your Standard Work Sheet during the discussion. The numbers have to add up for Lean to work effectively. If Standard Work says eight people are needed to build a product at the current cycle time and the revised *takt* time[42], but only six people are assigned, there is a problem that needs an action plan to resolve.

Be persistent. Ask direct questions. Use Lean terms. Ask what the new *takt* time is at the new demand. (Remember, *takt* time is the required pace of production—how frequently your company must product products to meet customer demand.) It will be shorter than the old *takt* time. Ask for updated Standard Work Sheets so you can see what you are supposed to do to meet that new *takt* time. Remind your boss of the risk to quality when you don't follow Standard Work exactly. The goal here is to gain acknowledgement from your boss that there is a problem meeting demand.

Now, this is where you have to cooperate if you want a good outcome. Many bosses look to overtime as an initial solution. Be willing to work it, without complaint, as long as your boss is putting effort at other solutions as well.

---

[42] The basic math is that the total cycle time for all the stations, divide by *takt* time tells you how many operators are needed for a perfectly balanced line.

What other solutions? *Kaizen* is always a good option. Your boss should be trying to get resources to do more projects. He could also try to balance work with upstream and downstream groups that have some extra capacity. Your manager might hire some part-time help to do clean-up or daily maintenance to pull some work off your plate.

Finally, creative staffing options can be used. Maybe an employee can be shared by two teams that both need an extra half of a person.

Don't just keep asking your boss to hire someone. Be open to alternatives, and suggest ideas. Lean is all about trying out new approaches to see if they will work. The point is to work *with* your manager here. If you are just making life difficult for him, it won't help your situation. Your goal should be to help find solutions, not assign blame.

Why this works: Managers want productivity gains. When growth justifies it, they would hire more people if they could. Most often, they just can't get the funding from their own bosses. When you keep the pressure up (respectfully so, of course), they will try to find a Lean way to get things done properly. Good bosses look at Standard Work like a contract. Employees have to hit the target; bosses can't expect more speed whenever they want it.

Problem: You don't like getting checked up on.

How this affects you: You think that your boss shows a lack of trust when he audits your progress. Plus, it can be annoying to have to answer all those questions.

Action to take: Familiarize yourself with the **Plan-Do-Check-Act (PDCA) cycle,** and try not to get worked up about the "check" part. (The PDCA cycle is sometimes called the **Deming Cycle.**) When you start a project, get it in your mind that someone will be coming around to follow up on changes to the process. In fact, you can even put it on your calendar, so it doesn't seem like such a surprise when it happens.

To ensure that the check is as painless as possible, make sure to finish any leftover assignments before their deadlines, or at least let your boss know as early as possible that you are running behind. Audits are much harder on you when you don't give your manager fair warning about problems in advance.

Let's say that, as a follow-up task, you were supposed to label (5S) the new shadow board (a pegboard that has outlines of the tool shapes). If that part of the project doesn't get done and the first time your boss hears about it is on the day of an audit, you should probably expect some mild discomfort as you try to explain your role in the delay.

Unpleasantly surprising your boss is not such a great idea, especially if she has to explain to *her* boss why tasks were not completed. If, on the other hand, she knows a week ahead of time that your team has not gotten to a task because it was building extra products, you will likely get some support or a reprieve.

Why this works: If you think of audits as checking up on you, you take the process too personally, and your satisfaction suffers. If you look at it as part of the overall method of improvement and remember that the scrutiny is on the results, rather than on you, the follow-up checks become less uncomfortable.

Problem: You aren't sure what to do when a problem halts production.

How this affects you: Computers go down. Conveyors jam. A quality problem pops up. In any case, employees face one of three choices when production comes to a halt. You can stand around. You can try to get production going again. Or you can work on an improvement project. The choice can be frustrating. What you might want to do (take a break) doesn't match what you need to do to hit your targets, or what your boss (who will be around) wants you to do. You might even feel angry, since stoppages often cause unexpected overtime.

Action to take: Obviously, the priority will be to resolve issues and get production up and running again. So, if the problem is in your area or if you have skills that might help solve the problem, offer to help. You might want to offer assistance even if you don't have the right skills; having an extra set of hands can be useful.

In some cases, you won't have a choice about what to do—your boss will have let you know in advance what you should be doing when production stops. He will have a standing project list for the team.

If things are under control and you don't have specific guidance from your boss, resist the urge to stand around, chat, or take a mini-break. As nice as it may seem when you are tired, it will serve you better in the long-run to do an individual project in the downtime instead. If being social is *really* important to you, find a partner to work with on a project. You'll have a little more relaxed pace to catch up with a coworker while getting something done.

The time to figure out what to do is not when the alarm bells start going off on a conveyor belt or when the accounting program's server crashes. Instead, have one big project and several smaller projects lined up in advance—this includes having a plan, as well as having the right materials and tools available. Start on a short project, but if you hear production will be down for a while, switch to the big one.

Remember that some tools are in short supply. When production stops, everyone may want many of the same items. Knowing what you need in advance, and where the items are, gives you a leg up on getting to the tools first.

Resist the urge to do time-filling projects such as re-taping marked areas on the floor. People want to look busy, and some (leaders included) don't want to put any extra thought into contingency planning. Replacing tape is an easy idea to come up with and it looks like productive work, even if it isn't accomplishing anything. If taping or re-taping really needs to be done—to outline a new layout, or to replace an area where the tape is so worn it is no longer clearly marked—by all means, do it. Otherwise, it is just sucking resources that could be making real improvements. Ask yourself what impact the project you are doing will have on any quality, delivery, and cost metrics.

Why this works: This is one of those times when being Lean makes things a little harder in the short-run, but better in the long-run. A little bit of planning not only prevents wasted time—it makes your work area better for you down the road. Plus, this forethought has a bonus for you. Your boss will notice, and you will score points, especially if you are finding projects that deliver solid gains. You get extra credit for working on a project that can make her life easier!

Problem: You think you have an answer, but other people discover evidence that contradicts your theory.

How this affects you: You complete a thorough investigation, only to be surprised, and a little embarrassed, when someone presents opposing data or a conflicting interpretation of the facts.

Action to take: Take a step back and think about whether you ever see evidence that contradicts what you want. It is easy to see only what supports your theory while discounting any data that opposes your viewpoint.

Try to find as many pieces of information as you can to support *and* oppose your views. You may not be able to find any opposition data; sometimes your theory will be right on the money. In most cases, though, you will find plenty of information that can contradict your theory. If you have trouble seeing both sides, find someone who can collect opposing evidence for you. This works best when that person is not vested in a specific outcome.

Why this works: This problem is more common for opinions than it is for facts. Obviously, the square footage of a work area is hard to dispute. However, if you are discussing the best place for a task to be done or whether working four ten-hour days is better than working five days a week, you should be able to uncover abundant evidence to support both sides of the argument. Since the filters you use during your interpretation come from years of conditioning, changing them takes a while. This strategy helps you compensate when you know the filters are there.

Problem: You don't think a Lean tool will work in your area.

How this affects you: You are trying to solve a problem, but you don't think the Lean tools your boss wants you to use are the right ones for the job.

Action to take: Not all Lean tools or techniques work well in all places or for all processes. Before you discard anything, though, consider if it could be modified for your work area. Experiment a little. Be flexible. Take the best of what the tool has to offer and make it work for your situation. A partial benefit from a modified technique is better than no improvement at all.

This challenge usually presents itself in the office environment. For instance, *takt* time can be difficult to put in place in an administrative setting. Office workers usually perform several different processes throughout the day, and each process has significant variation—phone calls vary in length due to the "human factor," loan applications might require different levels of documentation depending on credit reports, and customer purchase orders each have different formats.

Instead of trying to rigidly apply Lean tools, find a compromise that gets most of what the tool is supposed to do, but without the limitations. In the office, trying to pace a process to *takt* time would frustrate a team. They would probably never be on track due to the variation. An office team, instead, might try to put in a few "checkpoints" throughout the day to account for the variation. Instead of having one credit check done at 8:04 and two done at 8:08 and three done at 8:12, your team would know that it should have thirty done by 10:00. This compensates for variation, but provides frequent indicators of whether the team is on track to meet its customers' needs. More importantly, the team knows to take action if it is not!

Why this works: This works because some progress is better than no progress. It is easy to dismiss a tool when it is not a perfect fit—it is harder to apply the *spirit* of continuous improvement to the *process* of continuous improvement itself. Problem solving in your area tags you as a supporter of Lean. Once you gain that reputation with your boss, you will get a lot more flexibility in how you implement Lean in your area.

Problem: You see a repetitive problem.

How this affects you: You see the same problem coming up over and over and over again, and your frustration grows because you have to repeatedly deal with the same error.

Action to take: As Lean takes hold, you will probably begin to have morning stand-up meetings to address the issues of the upcoming day. If you make the effort to record problems in your area, these meetings provide a great opportunity to highlight these issues so your leader can deal with the problems.

Numbers don't lie. The root cause of a problem becomes apparent when data is collected. What's the point? Well, people are reluctant to "rat out" their coworkers. They are also resistant to working harder because someone else is not pulling his own weight.

The good news is that you don't have to be the one seperating the two issues—that's your boss's job. All you have to do is log when there is a problem that affects your production. You never have to say, "Joe gave me a bad part." You just note that a part had a burr on it that kept it from fitting properly.

Why this works: Knowing what is wrong is one of the keys to making improvements. Data collection helps pinpoint patterns and abnormal conditions that make it easier to find and implement solutions.

Strategies: Upgrading your personal performance

Problem: Your mission each day at work is to survive until quitting time.

How this affects you: Having nothing to look forward to can be depressing and can lead to a sense of dread. This chronic stress affects not only your well-being, but your health too.

Action to take: Set positive, achievable goals for yourself. Just getting through the day is technically a goal, but merely surviving doesn't really shout optimism. Try to replace "getting by" and "surviving" with goals that are more upbeat and specific—defining a number of projects you want to work on, completing a course or class or getting a qualification certificate, or earning a promotion because of your Lean skills.

Don't limit yourself to goals that only relate to advancement in the company. If you don't want to move up, think of other goals that sound appealing. Learn how to operate a new piece of equipment. Win an attendance award. Set a record for days without a defect from your area. Use your creativity to find something that makes your job more exciting. As you complete a goal, follow that success with a reward: celebrate!

If you don't want to move up in the company, it is helpful to know what your boss thinks about your decision. Why? Your manager probably has at least a little "type A" in his personality. These types of people are ambitious and want to climb the corporate ladder. He may not understand that you are not inspired by the prospect of longer hours and greater responsibility. You may find yourself falling short in his eyes if you don't see things the same way, or if you make different choices than he does. If you find yourself with a different set of goals than your boss, you will need to negotiate with him and try to figure out how you both can win so you both get what is important to you.

Why this works: Setting goals and celebrating your successes are two ways that you can take control of how Lean affects your life. Since you will be Lean, you might as well find a way to get something out of it. Creating your own milestones and rewarding yourself for your achievements gives you something to look forward to.

Problem: You don't know how you are going to be evaluated now that you are Lean.

How this affects you: Your work seems different every day. You worry that your company is changing the rules on you in the middle of the game.

Action to take: The first thing to do is get a clear understanding about your current position. A Lean job description will likely include something about problem solving. This means you will be asked to fix issues within your scope of responsibility rather than just report them like you may have done in the past. You should consider scheduling a time to talk with your boss to better understand how she will be rating your performance in a Lean environment.

In many companies, annual raises are closely linked to how well you do your job. If this is the case, it is important to know what you have to do to get the biggest raise. The first step is to recognize and accept the fact that your old job is gone and you have a new set of requirements. You risk a serious drop on your annual review if you can't get past this.

Why this works: Managers like seeing people take an interest in their own success. Simply asking about what you should be doing paints you in a very positive light. It creates a great impression, especially since so few employees ever initiate this conversation. The earlier you inquire about your concerns, the more say you will probably have in how your job gets defined. If you involve yourself in setting the requirements, you can encourage your boss to tailor the job to the things that you like and that you are good at.

Problem: You worry that Lean reduces your job security.

How this affects you: Worrying that you might be unemployed in the near future is very stressful. You know that in years past, productivity improvements have meant layoffs. Since Lean delivers even bigger gains, you likely have serious questions about job security.

Action to take: Stop resisting Lean. More people probably lose their jobs for fighting Lean than supporting it.

Why this works: A successful company knows it makes no sense to fire people who have worked hard to improve productivity. If a business decides to trim the ranks even *once,* why would workers ever engage in improvement efforts in the future? Who would work hard if the reward was a pink slip? Layoffs as a result of Lean are simply bad business. Employees will not engage in reducing waste if success means losing their jobs and not being able to put food on the table. Many companies explicitly state that nobody will get laid off due to process improvement efforts. Even if companies do make productivity gains faster than demand rises (i.e. they become overstaffed), they will likely avoid layoffs by just letting normal attrition reduce head count.

Here's a warning, though. Not embracing Lean *can* end up earning your walking papers. This doesn't mean you can't have normal concerns and struggles with the transition, but it does mean that you shouldn't bury your head in the sand or take up your sword against Lean efforts. When your job changes you will have to change with it. If the transition to Lean is required and you chose to avoid it or actively resist it, your value as an employee will go down. Compare this to a computer programmer who refuses to learn the latest programming languages. At some point, her skills will no longer be what the company needs.

Problem: You don't know how to be Lean.

How this affects you: Your job has changed, and you have no idea how to perform well with the new requirements. You are out of your element and feel more than a little insecure.

Action to take: Educate yourself on Lean. You can be passive and just absorb information as it comes along. Or, you can seek out opportunities to learn about it and get better at continuous improvement. Request some training on Lean. Ask your boss to recommend some Lean books. Find a mentor on your team who can help you out. Join a project. Ask your manager if you can help out with a problem. Be creative in how you gain Lean experience.

Don't neglect general skills that will help you with Lean. Having knowledge about computer programs like the Microsoft Office® suite (Excel® or Word®) will make your projects go much better. You can increase your value as an employee by building these sorts of skills. How can you learn? Take classes. Practice at home. Read a "how to" book. The nice thing? If you decide Lean isn't for you and eventually leave the company, these skills will transfer with you.[43]

Why this works: Expanding your knowledge and your skill set is likely to make you enjoy your job more. In Lean, being more competent makes your job less stressful. When you possess skills that are important to the company, you tend to increase your job security and your satisfaction as well.

Many people take a passive approach to this problem. They wait for training to come to them. Instead, take the option to be more proactive. Talk to your manager to help you come up with a plan to get the skills you need to be successful. One big plus for you: it shows your boss you are serious about becoming Lean. She will remember that when it comes time to decide about promotions and raises and choice assignments.

[43] Leaving is not recommended—Lean will follow you!

Problem: You can't seem to remember what you learn in Lean classes.

How this affects you: You want to do well, but you can't seem to retain information from the Lean classes. You know you will need to use the concepts later. You might worry that you will be put on the spot during an improvement event—you don't want to be embarrassed if you can't come up with an answer.

Action to take: Pay attention in class, especially before a *kaizen* or project. This advice sounds basic, but you'd be surprised by how many people do other things (reading, checking phone messages, writing grocery lists, talking to neighbors) during classes.

The more senses you use during learning, the better you tend to retain information. If you listen to the speaker while looking at slides, you use two senses. Taking notes, even if you are given a handout, engages yet another part of your brain. When you write down the main points it also gives you something to review after the class.

The absolute best way to keep ideas in your head, though, is to immediately use the concepts you learn. If you aren't on a project team, find some tasks where you can put your newfound knowledge to use. If you are having a hard time coming up with ideas for projects that need the skills that you have just learned, ask your manager for help.

Why this works: Satisfaction tends to be higher when you are able to do something well. Feeling like a fish out of water on a Lean project will make you uncomfortable and leave a bad taste in your mouth. If, on the other hand, you are able to use the lessons you were taught to improve a process, you will gain confidence and be viewed in higher regard.

Problem: You suspect you have started to get a bad reputation with your boss.

How this affects you: Life gets more difficult when your manager doesn't think you support the changes. You get fewer advancement opportunities and your job might even be at risk.

Action to take: Do you know if you've been labeled a **"concrete head?"** This term has somehow, despite the political incorrectness, survived translation from Japanese and is frequently used in Lean circles. It describes a person who has closed his mind and is not receptive to new ideas. Once you receive this label, it is very hard, although not impossible, to overcome. Some of the biggest Lean supporters were its strongest opponents in the beginning.

The best treatment for a bad reputation is prevention. Avoid looking as though you are not receptive to trying Lean. Manage misperceptions before any labeling happens. If you are past the possibility of prevention, ask your boss how you are doing, and be truly open to feedback. It doesn't really matter whether your manager is right or not. If he believes you are opposing Lean that is how he will treat you. After all, his opinion is the one that matters most when it comes to your job performance. After a discussion with your boss, do some soul searching. Consider if the issues he brings up have merit. If so, work on fixing your image. If you disagree, you will have to do a better job of marketing yourself to your boss or reconsider your fit for this team.

Why this works: This goes back to the Hard Truths about perceptions being reality. What your boss believes drives how he acts toward you. Being an obstacle is obviously not going to earn you his favor. But if you make an attempt to look at your standing in his eyes and make a genuine effort to change, you greatly raise your stock.

Problem: You constantly think about what is going on at work, even when you're not there.

How this affects you: You need some downtime away from everything that is going on, but you carry your worries home with you. This keeps you from being able to recharge and affects your personal relationships.

Action to take: Create a buffer zone that separates work and home. Being in your car doesn't really count—some commutes can be just as stressful as your workday, giving you no opportunity to transition. This boundary between work and home should be a positive place that allows you to shift gears—maybe meeting a friend at a coffee shop, going to the gym, or sitting on a bench at a park. After your transition is complete, put your time at home to positive use. Find a hobby. Spend time with family and friends. Find something that you enjoy to get your mind off the stress of the work day.

Why this works: Buffers give you the time and space to wind down from work before you go home. Work can be stressful at times, even when you love your job. It is important to have a place to restore yourself.

As people grow up, an interesting thing happens. Responsibilities take the place of fun. Many adults don't really have any regular hobbies to speak of, and they end up spending what little free time they have zoning out in front of the TV. Watching your favorite show *can* be good escapism, but it seldom leaves you feeling revitalized and ready to take on another day. Engaging activities give you a better break from thinking about stressors. They absorb your attention and help you add fuel to your tank.

CHAPTER 9

Set the standard in standardization

STANDARD WORK IS ONE OF THE FOUNDATIONS of any Lean program. As you may recall, Standard Work helps to stabilize a process and provide a basis for improvement.

Standard Work presents a particular challenge to your leaders. Each aspect of Standard Work can raise the satisfaction level for some employees and, at the same time, reduce it for others. For example:

- Standard Work can be viewed as restrictive, since you are required to follow it; or flexible, since you can change it if you find a better way to do a task.
- Standard Work can be thought of as dehumanizing, since you have to follow a strict schedule; or respectful, because it establishes a reasonable pace that can be maintained all day.
- Standard Work can be seen as diminishing job security, since you have to document all the secrets and tricks that only you know. On the other hand, you gain job security if you demonstrate that you can perform well in several areas, not just your own.

- Standard Work can make you think that your bosses only care about your productivity. Then again, it provides hard data for managers to get you more staff in your overworked department.
- Standard Work might reduce variety in a job, since it requires doing a process the same way every time. Alternatively, it might add variety. You could participate in a project outside your area since Standard Work makes it easier for other people to cover for you.
- Standard Work can make it seem like your day is micromanaged, since every step is detailed and you have little autonomy. On the other hand, you might feel liberated, since your boss doesn't look over your shoulder as much once the process is documented and stabilized.
- Standard Work tends to reduce the need for overtime. Some employees love this, while some hate losing the extra income.
- Though it is not the purpose of Standard Work, it does highlight personal skills. Prior to Standard Work, variations in ability could be attributed to using different processes. With Standard Work in place, differences in individual speed become more apparent. Some team members like this comparison, while others prefer a little more secrecy about how quick they are.
- Once it is in place, expect Standard Work to evolve as it drives more improvement. Ironically, once Standard Work is established, you will see more frequent alterations to the process, rather than fewer. (Remember, Standard Work provides a basis for improvement.) Some people like the constant change; others want to know exactly what they will be doing week to week and month to month.

The list could go on, but you get the point. Standard Work will affect job satisfaction for everyone in different ways. Because of that, the strategies you use to manage how you feel about using Standard Work might be different from what your coworkers use.

Despite how hard it can be to adjust to Standard Work, and for all the buttons it can push, it eventually tends to convert many employees over to being Lean supporters. For one thing, as procedures stabilize, work actually gets easier. The pace of production also gets more consistent and reasonable. In addition, your **internal suppliers** are also doing Standard Work. Internal suppliers are the groups, within your company, that give you the materials you need to do your job. The person cutting steel is an internal supplier to a welding team. A marketing team supplies promotional brochures to the sales team. When these suppliers use standardized processes, you get higher quality parts and better on-time delivery, which eliminates frustration for you. These benefits make it hard for many people to envision going back to their job before Lean.

The following strategies offer some tips on how to speed up the transition to being a Lean supporter, as well as ideas about how to benefit more from Standard Work once it is established in your area.

Strategies: Establishing Standard Work

Problem: Standard Work requires you to share your tricks and secrets.

How this affects you: You are reluctant to give up hard-earned knowledge. You worry that you will become less valuable if other people learn how to do your job. You wonder if that will increase the risk of losing your job.

Action to take: In order to preserve their value in the eyes of their company, some people hold back information. If this strikes a chord with you, change your strategy to focusing on new Lean skills rather than on hoarding current process knowledge. That switch can be achieved by becoming an expert at *kanbans,* or at using Microsoft Office programs. The more talents you have, the more secure you are in a Lean company.

Why this works: It might be true that having exclusive knowledge protects you, but the benefit is only short term. As the business around you becomes more and more Lean, your reluctance to share process information will become more apparent. Resisting instructions to document your process will put you at odds with your boss. If you are perceived to be hard to work with, your value as an employee hinges on your special skills. What happens if your job changes so your special skills are no longer required, or if your position gets eliminated? Your job security can vanish in an instant.

Problem: Stopwatches are everywhere.

How this affects you: You want to be viewed in a positive light, so working quickly seems like a good plan. But, you also know that your performance will become the new standard as soon as you are timed—maybe it would be better to pad the clock a little. You just don't know the best strategy to use.

Action to take: Work at your usual pace. Gaming the system always comes back to bite you.

Why this works: You only have three options. The first is the recommended action—work at your normal pace.

The second option is to work faster than average to impress the boss. You speed through the process and post a record time. Unfortunately, this is the equivalent of shooting yourself and your team in the foot! If you set the bar at an unsustainable rate, you will suffer while trying to keep up down the road.

The final option is to slow things down: take a little extra time and make the trials longer than normal. Employees generally have two reasons for deliberately performing tasks at a slower than normal pace. The first is simply to make life easier. A lower standard is easier to keep up with. The second is to build some wiggle room into a process for problems that are frequently encountered. The challenge is that if the pace is too slow, the numbers won't make sense. History shows how much a team was able to get done in the past. If the current times don't line up with past productivity, the boss will quickly figure out that someone was sandbagging during time studies. If you are that someone, imagine how hard it would be to find satisfaction when you lose your manager's trust.

Problem: Your team can't agree on who should be timed when developing Standard Work.

How this affects you: Who should be selected? If the team picks someone too fast or too slow, things can get difficult down the road.

Action to take: Do timing with an "average" person performing at a "normal" rate.

Why this works: Remember, it is the *process* that is being timed for Standard Work, not the *individual*. It is a subtle difference, but that difference goes a long way in taking the pressure off people to perform "well" for a time trial. Accuracy, not speed is the desired result of time trials.

For that reason, you and your team should make sure that the resulting time is repeatable by the whole team. Obviously, if a fast person is used, the rest of the team will have a difficult time keeping up the new pace. Using the slowest person would mean that most people would be standing around at the end of each production cycle. An "average" person will generally work at a pace that most team members can manage.

This concept applies to the office as well as the shop floor. One accounting administrator may have fast fingers and blitz through posting an expense in the books. A slower person would not want such a speedy standard, since it establishes productivity expectations.

Problem: You keep running into problems while trying to time for Standard Work.

How this affects you: You can't seem to get a "clean" time. After several cycles, only a couple of trials did not have a problem that delayed the process.

Action to take: Don't dismiss problems when taking times to establish Standard Work. Make a note of the issue and let the stopwatch keep running. Trying to subtract out "problem time" on the fly is too hard—the results just don't end up being accurate. Plus, if you write down the problem, you know what needs to get fixed to make Standard Work flow smoothly.

Setting a standard is difficult when there is a lot of variation. The best method is to start by resolving any problems that cause unpredictability in the process. The less variation you have when you start documenting, the smoother your task will go. Unfortunately, eliminating these issues is one of those easier-said-than-done tasks. After all, if the fixes were quick and simple, wouldn't they have already been done? Instead, your boss will need to make a choice. He will have to decide how to handle the problems.

Lean experts each seem to have their own way of managing problems and variations. If nothing else, this should tell you that your boss will be selecting from several less-than-perfect options. The most common options include the following:

- **Ignore the problems.** This means that the problem is not recorded on the Standard Work Sheet, even though it occurred during the timing. The logic here is that the issue is an aberration that would not take place during a "normal" run. Lean purists tend to push for this option. They would say that the problem should be worked on and removed, rather than enabled by including it in Standard Work. Problems that make it to the Standard Work Sheet are only visible to the operator doing the work. When a problem is treated as an exception, it becomes visible to leaders and engineers as well, which usually makes it get fixed quicker.

  If you don't document the issue on the Standard Work Sheet though, workers will exceed the *takt* time whenever the problem comes up. In that case, your boss must choose from two imperfect options:

- ***Take the hit and let production stop whenever the issue occurs.*** (Bad idea!)
- ***Develop a reaction plan that involves someone being available to help when problems come up.*** This might be an on-call engineer or a floater assigned to the area. This choice is better than the first option, but still is not great. It is wasteful because it throws resources at the problem, rather than eliminating the root cause.

- **Add in a little time.** Sometimes, your manager will try to average out the times and add a little buffer. What this really means is that if the work is done without a hitch, employees will be standing around for only a short time. When a problem arises, though, the buffer is not enough to cover the whole time it takes to resolve it. You end up with either too much spare time, or not enough. This method is used, though, because it has less production stoppage than the previous option, and less waiting time than the next one.
- **Add in enough time to address issues.** This option adds in a large time buffer—enough to handle the majority of problems. Some Lean leaders do this because it adds stability to the whole value stream. If one process constantly disrupts flow, it costs much less to throw a few labor hours at the problem than to let one problem continually stop a production line.

These options are really just different methods of paying for a problem. Each one manages the costs of the problem in a little different fashion. The real trick, regardless of which option your boss chooses, is to have a plan to permanently resolve issues. This is at the heart of Standard Work. Reduce variation, and then lock in the process. How can you standardize something that is different every time?

This means consistently tracking the issues and spending the time to collect data. If problems never make it onto a project list, they will never get fixed.

Why this works: Clear expectations on how to handle problems while recording Standard Work go a long way toward improving job satisfaction—not only while the document is created, but also as it is being used in production.

Another big plus for job satisfaction: having a resolution on the horizon. Not knowing how long you will have to deal with frustration tends to make you like your job less. When you identify issues while you are recording Standard Work it puts the problems on the radar screen for your manager. It also means that help should soon be on the way.

Problem: You unintentionally perform faster than usual when being timed.

How this affects you: The Hawthorne Effect is the subconscious tendency people have to improve productivity whenever a condition changes. (You'll find more about this in the next chapter.) Having an observer in the area can be one of those changes in conditions that usually results in the first few production cycles being faster than normal.

Action to take: Make sure you record several cycles whenever Standard Work is revised. Throw out the first couple of times and use the rest.

Why this works: Basically, you get used to being watched and eventually end up going back to your normal pace.

Problem: When you fall behind in your work, coworkers have no way to help you out.

How this affects you: Sometimes, Standard Work is set up in a way that makes it difficult for a coworker to step in and help out, even if he knows the process inside and out. This happens when the work is not organized in a way that two people can do it faster than one. Perhaps all the later steps build on earlier steps, limiting the work a helper can do. Maybe only one set of tools is available. Maybe space is limited at a workstation, which doesn't allow enough room for a second worker. Or perhaps the product is too small for a second set of hands. Basically, you are on your own when you fall behind.

Action to take: Build your Standard Work to support getting help when you need it:

- **Know your checkpoints.** Around the holidays it might take seven days for a present to arrive through the mail. If you haven't finished your shopping a week ahead of time, you are behind schedule. Use the same concept in your Standard Work to identify problems as early as possible. On the shop floor, you might know that when you start Step 4, you still have four minutes and eight seconds of work left to do. If the countdown clock on the wall show less than 4:08 remaining before the assembly line advances, and you haven't yet started Step 4, you are not going to make it. You should immediately use your *andon*. The earlier you call for help, the better the chance of avoiding a line stop.

- **Start with the hardest tasks first.** The hardest tasks are probably the most likely ones to have a delay. If you start with them first, you have the earliest warning if a problem comes up.

- **Do independent tasks last.** The sequence does not matter for some steps. Contemplate how you get ready for work in the morning. Let's say you wear contact lenses. You can't ask your spouse to put them in for you, can you? You are able, however, to ask your spouse to make you a cup of coffee. So, what sequence should you put in place to make sure you finish everything? If you start out by making coffee, then realize you are running late, you still have to get your lenses in on your own—late for work! Instead, if you put your lenses in first, then realize you are running late, you can ask your spouse to get the coffee started for you.

At work, identify the tasks in your area that could be done at any time by anyone who knows the process. Sequence these last on the Standard Work Combination Sheet. When you start falling behind, you can call for help and have someone pick up those tasks while you finish the other work.

Every station in your area should have these kinds of safety valves. If they don't, ask your boss to swap some steps around from other areas so workers at every station can receive assistance. Tasks such as installing trim work, marking serial numbers, applying decals, and attaching accessories tend to be easy processes that can be done in any sequence. Properly structured work lets a supervisor or floater come in any time and help.

- **Use checkpoints and cross-training to keep office processes on track.** Since office work is more independent than shop floor work, the methods of identifying problems and getting back on track will be a little different. An office checkpoint is most likely to be a quantity of work completed by a certain time. If you are behind, you would let your boss know, and he would shuffle some of your work to a coworker who might be ahead of schedule. Obviously, this requires cross-training. That coworker has to know what to do with the pile that lands on his desk.
- **Start the process with any sub-assemblies already assembled**. You can then build the "subs" for the next unit at the end of the current cycle. That lets a helper come in and build it for you if you need assistance.

Why this works: Your Standard Work should be designed to be able to handle problems. Just having a person or group designated to respond to *andon* signals is not enough. They must actually be able to do something when a problem pops up.

Problem: You and your boss don't agree on what you do, or how much you do, making it difficult to set a standard.

How this affects you: Offices pose an interesting challenge, since it is hard to tell exactly how much each person does. *You* know that you are working hard, but your manager may not see that. Take a look at an order entry team. Entering three big orders might require more work than ten small orders; however, if the *number* of orders is the only thing being measured, the ten would appear to be a bigger workload.

Or, someone may not enter any orders for a period of time while he is answering customer inquiries about order status. It may appear like he hasn't gotten anything done, if he has no complete orders during the measured period. If his boss does not understand the workload, she may not appreciate her team's entire contribution to the company.

Action to take: The first big step in defining what you do is to examine, and record, *all* the work you actually do each day. What are the duties you perform? How can they be categorized? Consider your phone calls. Are they incoming or outgoing? How much time do you spend on each phone call? What are the calls related to?

Once you have accurate information about all your duties, and how much time you spend doing each activity, you and your boss should make sure that you tally that work in a consistent way. Together, you should standardize how you take measurements and you should agree on how you count what you do.

Should you count the *number* of e-mails you answer, or should you only count the *tasks* the e-mails refer to? What's the difference? Let's say you are assigned to Accounts Receivable and one of your duties is to do credit checks on new customers. Your team averages ten new customers a day, but you also receive twenty e-mails from previous customers who have credit approvals pending. Do you count just the ten new credit checks that day, or do you account for the twenty e-mails you had to deal with as well?

Whatever you and your boss settle on for your standard, make sure the decision clarifies your role and your priorities—and that your ideas match your manager's. If you and your boss each have a different understanding of your work and different definitions of your success, you'll have a problem, especially when it comes time for your evaluations.

Why this works: Using this strategy—agreeing on definitions and measurements—makes your boss aware of what you accomplish each day, and makes you aware of what your boss thinks is important. When it comes time for your performance review, your boss will know the specifics of your job. That makes you more likely to get graded accurately than if she is thinking you are doing one thing and you are actually doing something else.

Problem: Demand varies widely in the office, making staffing difficult.

How this affects you: There are two types of demand that are relatively easy for managers to handle: seasonal variation in demand (like snow shovels in the winter or baseball gloves in springtime) and the gradual changes in demand that match economic upturns and downturns. Some customer demand cycles are far shorter, though. These peaks and valleys can happen inside of a month, a week, or even a single work shift (think about a coffee shop with its morning rush and afternoon lull). These cycles make it much harder for a manager to match personnel levels to demand. If he staffs the team for the busiest times, employees are idle during the slow parts of the day—not a profitable way to run a business. If he only hires enough people for the slow periods, employees get swamped during the rushes and can't keep up.

Action to take: Sit back and let your boss deal with this problem . . . after all, staffing is *his* responsibility, right? Bad idea. Proper staffing is critical to your satisfaction.

Help your boss figure out how to staff properly. The first step in accomplishing that is to help identify variations in demand. Since *you* do this every day and know the ins and outs of the daily workload, you are in the best position to give him an accurate picture of the trends. As you've read countless times already, use specific data.

Once you've identified the variations, the obvious next step is to come up with a way to meet the demand without creating waste. Be creative. The following list includes some possible ideas:

- ***Using part-timers or temps to add capacity at peak times.*** This means that you will have to help identify work (the easy stuff) that your team can hand off to rookies.
- ***Team up with other groups to share resources.*** The other group comes to help during your peak periods (their slow periods); your team supports their busy times during your slow periods. Your boss will have to negotiate this with the other team's leader, but you will have to commit to it and work with the other team on the details.
- ***Make use of leaders and support teams.*** Sometimes working supervisors or technical people can join teams when demand outpaces capacity. You boss will ask you to assist in setting up the process to make it easy for helpers to come and go.
- ***Shuffle the schedule around.*** Help your manager develop an unbalanced work schedule. Maybe a couple of people can put in extra hours a few days a week at peak times, but leave early on slow days.
- ***Be flexible about breaks and lunches.*** If your phone rings off the hook during your "normal" lunchtime, you may be asked to eat earlier or later in your shift (in accordance with employment laws, of course!)

Why this works: A big distinction between the office (and service) and the shop floor is in how well work "keeps." If a phone is not immediately answered, the call will likely be abandoned. Some customers will call back. Others will call a competitor who *will* answer the phone. The same holds true for people who walk into a fast food restaurant and see a long line. Some will stay, some will come back later, and some will go elsewhere.

Shop floor leaders have more options for managing demand cycles than office managers do. Production can generally be averaged out over a short period, small quantities from safety stock can be used to cover spikes, or teams can build more in overtime. Physical products also tend to have longer demand cycles than service and office work. Demand for fireworks peaks once or twice a year. Restaurant demand spikes every few hours. Call centers might see higher demand during lunch periods or early evening hours.

If you are resourceful and help find imaginative solutions that work for your boss and your customers, you are more likely to end up with a process that also improves your satisfaction.

Problem: You don't think Standard Work is effective in the office.

How this affects you: You just don't believe that the Lean experts you are working with *really* understand what goes on in your office. Their application of Standard Work doesn't fit your processes well—your office is much different than the shop floor. You never know from one moment to the next whether you will be answering a phone, responding to an e-mail, or entering data into a computer. Your sequence is often dictated by a customer rather than by your process.

Action to take: The first thing to do is accept that standardization *can* help you, even if Standard Work is not the right method of doing that. Standardization in the office should do several things:

- ***Identify who does what.***
- ***Define how many items (files, orders, applications, etc.) a person works on at one time.***
- ***Set a pace for evaluating progress and problems.***

- ***Establish a sequence.*** In the office, this may not be as linear as it is on the shop floor. It could, however, be documented on a flowchart that clearly defines how to react to any situation that comes up.

This closely mirrors the basics of Standard Work and offers many of the same benefits. To begin standardizing your work, document your processes on flowcharts that show the normal way you do your work. Next, compare your methods to those that other team members use. You might be surprised by how many different ways your team does the same work. Combine these methods to come up with a best practice for the whole team to use. Eventually, like on the shop floor, the whole team should be doing each task the same way.

Office workers deal with customers who might each have a different set of requirements—one client wants credit card billing, another wants shipments held until they are complete, and yet another wants an e-mail to tell them whenever you send a fax. Some variation even comes from within your own company—marketing groups are constantly coming up with new promotions that alter processes. That doesn't even take into account regulatory differences for various states and countries or inherent variations in how customers communicate. Some like the phone; others prefer e-mail. Some write short and sweet; some have the need to inquire about your grandchildren and the weather before getting on to business.

The office is much more people-centric than the shop floor. Preferences of customers play a big role. Once your company decides how responsive it wants to be to special requests, all that's left is documenting what you do. If company A likes products shipped to them overnight and company B wants an acknowledgment sent by e-mail when its order ships, then formalize those as processes. The point is that variation comes from customer choices. But even these variations in preferences can be documented into a process—an instruction on a flowchart could refer you to a supporting spreadsheet with customer shipping options.

Why this works: The fact is that most managers probably haven't had the time to dive into the nitty-gritty details of your process. They will be pleased to see a document that clearly describes all the different steps that you do. They will be amazed if this document covers all the nuances of your process and provides a basis for making improvements. Your boss won't have to badger you to adopt Standard Work (versus another form of standardization), and you won't feel like you are a square peg being thrust into a round hole. By creating a win-win, you help them meet their goals while keeping some of your autonomy in place.

Problem: Standard Work is not sticking.

How this affects you: Backsliding on Standard Work creates chaos in a work area.

Action to take: When Standard Work is put in place, follow it. If a problem arises, or if you simply don't like the details of Standard Work, go to your boss and ask to get involved in the company's procedure for getting it changed.

Why this works: If the team actively retreats from Standard Work, it can be because employees are overwhelmed by the new process, because they aren't committed to the change, or because that team's members hope that new methods will fail so they can go back to doing things the old way. In reality, if the attempt at Standard Work is unsuccessful, the group will face a higher level of scrutiny from the boss. This usually translates into the team having less input into the solution the next time around.

Standard Work won't go away just because of an unsuccessful first attempt. You are better off giving the new process a fair shake. In many cases, it will work if given half a chance. The good news, though, is that once you start following Standard Work all the time, the management response is different when your team misses targets. It stops being a people problem and starts being a process problem. That can often get you more resources and support instead of unwanted attention.

Strategies: Keeping autonomy and variety

Problem: You need help finding ideas for improvements.

How this affects you: Part of your job in Lean will be to constantly make things better. When you are new to Lean, coming up with ideas can be difficult. Over time, it will get easier. But in the beginning, it can seem as if there is a lot of pressure on you to find improvement opportunities.

Action to take: Use your Standard Work Combination Sheet to get your brain going. Find tasks with a lot of walking, waiting, or watching. Extremely long tasks are also prime targets for improvement. Once you find some good opportunities for projects, enlist an expert to help out—an engineer, your supervisor, or a Lean practitioner.

Why this works: Many resources are underutilized in a Lean company. A lot of professionals, most commonly engineers, have extensive backgrounds in Lean. Many of them are not only willing to help you with a project, but actually love when they get a chance to mentor someone who is excited about Lean. People with expertise are often eager to teach those who show an interest in learning.

Problem: You don't want to have to change how you do your process.

How this affects you: You've been doing a process *your* way for a long time. Now, you have to change how you do things as Standard Work gets established.

Action to take: When Standard Work is put in place, someone has to be the guinea pig. One of the operators will have to do the work while people watch her and furiously write down what she is doing and how long it takes. The downside? It is usually not all that fun to be observed like that. The upside? If you are the one under observation, then your process is the one that becomes the starting point for the standard.

Why this works: If you are brave enough to volunteer for some scrutiny, you could end up with many of your methods intact. Most people don't like being studied, so if you volunteer, you have a good chance of being selected. Your team will eventually have to settle on a single way of operating. Why not improve your satisfaction and have that way be your way?

Problem: You are having trouble getting improvements to stick—whatever you change gets changed back by someone else.

How this affects you: You have some great ideas. Unfortunately everyone else has their own ideas, too. Things get moved around whenever your coworkers rotate through the stations in your area. Even the night shift seems to want to do things their own way. Your frustration mounts as you compete with your coworkers.

Action to take: Obviously, the solution is to do what Standard Work says should be done. Usually the best thing to do when a conflict turns up is to open a channel of communication. Talk to whoever is doing things differently than you are, and see if you can come to an agreement on a single process. If it's not already in place, you could also ask your boss to implement formal Standard Work in your area.

If Standard Work is already established, figure out if one of you is not following it properly—that might be the reason for the changes to the workstation. If everyone *is* adhering to Standard Work, use 5S techniques to establish tool locations and lock in processes. Once locations are clearly defined, people seem much less likely to make changes to a workstation. Most people won't move a tool from a labeled location to an unlabeled one. If all else fails, let the stopwatch judge which arrangement is better.

Why this works: One of the really great things about Standard Work is that it sidesteps turf wars and helps eliminate conflict. Contrary to the expression, "time heals all wounds," the longer a disagreement goes unsettled, the harder it is to resolve. The more opportunities two people have to butt heads, the worse the relationship gets. Consequently, satisfaction drops. Use Standard Work as a tool to preserve some peace at work.

If members of a team have different opinions about which method (or tool location) should be adopted, the solution is simple. Time it one way; then time it the other way. Whichever way is faster wins, assuming no safety or quality problems pop up. Stopwatches do not argue or lie. Besides, how can you lose? You either get to do the process your way, or you learn a new way to do the process faster.

Problem: You don't know how to go about making changes to Standard Work.

How this affects you: It is a tough situation—you know what to do, but not *how* to get it done. Frequently, frontline employees can identify things that will make their jobs easier, but they don't know how to translate an idea they have into reality.

Action to take: Completing an improvement yourself should be your first choice. If that isn't possible or practical, the trick is to find the right allies. Most companies have a process in place for managing Standard Work. Ask your boss what it is. The answer will likely point to people who have the responsibility for keeping your team on track toward improvement goals. Generally, this will be your manager, who will delegate authority to your supervisor and any engineers who support you. Talking to them can usually get the ball rolling. They are the ones who:

- ***Are vested in your success.***
- ***Have the right skills.***

- ***Can get the appropriate resources.***
- ***Set project priorities.***

The people supporting your team often have their own improvement targets related to your work area. When you go to them with an idea that makes it easier for them to reach their goals, they will likely be very supportive. Best case, they will jump on the project and do it for you. Otherwise, they may end up providing support while you make the changes yourself.

Why this works: The spirit of Lean is to make ongoing changes to improve an area. The fact that you have identified a problem and are interested in finding a solution means that you are on the right path. When employees start taking action on their own, though, managers get really impressed. The leadership team wants to reinforce positive Lean behaviors (especially ones that make their own lives easier), so they will try to get the resources you need for improvement projects.

Problem: Doing the same job the same way every day bores you.

How this affects you: While some people love predictability, you are not one of them. You like variety to help make the hours pass by faster.

Action to take: Volunteer to get cross-trained to learn other jobs to add some more variety to your day. You can also offer to work on problems and join *kaizen* teams, or get on any continuous improvement committees that your company has. Another option is to attend training—that also gets you out of the office or shop, while helping you obtain the skills that you need to be invaluable in multiple roles.

Why this works: Adding variety to a job increases job satisfaction for some people. It gets you out of a rut. At first, it might be hard to move around, but after you adjust to the regular changes, you will start to look forward to rotating to new workstations. The same goes for *kaizen* events. At first, you won't know what to expect, but you will soon find you can quickly shift from your production job to your role on a project team. As you learn more, you will find your value to the company rising, which leads to increased job security and more satisfaction.

Problem: Your boss just took away all of your personal space.

How this affects you: Losing personal space causes a big hit to job satisfaction. This loss frequently comes hand in hand with the implementation of Standard Work. When a process gets set up, personal areas of a workstation often go away. Job rotation further removes personal ownership of space.

Action to take: Ask your boss to set up an area that you can call your own. It might be a locker or a drawer or even part of a bulletin board where you can put up pictures. While you probably won't be able to spread out like you used to, it can boost morale to have at least a little area where you can keep a few personal items.

Why this works: Your boss wants work areas to be functional but also wants her team to be happy. If you go to her with a compromise that doesn't hurt performance metrics, you both can win. She might not have even considered personal space when she was standardizing work areas. Not only can you get a little more of what you want, but proposing a solution rather than complaining about Lean will boost your reputation and standing with her as well.

Problem: You don't want anyone coming in and telling you how to arrange your workspace.

How this affects you: You still have some personal space left, but you are worried that you are going to be told how to arrange it. You like having your things the way you want them.

Action to take: Embrace 5S techniques: sort, simplify, straighten, standardize, and sustain. The more you keep your workspace in order, the less likely someone is to come in and tell you to change it. Your workspace needs to be neat and highly functional, with a non-disruptive level of personal items. If you use discretion in how much personalization you do in your workspace, you can frequently head off 5S ultimatums.

Why this works: Most people have seen a coworker's desk with dust all over it, knickknacks cluttering a shelf, and photos everywhere—plus work piled on every flat surface. At some point, a boss will surely come by and give specific directions on what to change. Those directions will be more restrictive than what would have been in place if that person had just de-cluttered her space on her own. The basic idea? Initiate 5S yourself and you will be more likely to get what you want than if management steps in and does it for you.

Strategies: Using Standard Work

Problem: Your boss is asking you to produce more than Standard Work says you should be able to do.

How this affects you: Standard Work is supposed to set a *sustainable* pace of work. It is frustrating to be asked to work faster than the document says you should.

Action to take: Standard Work is set up for a specific pace. When demand goes up, Standard Work should be adjusted to meet the new *takt* time. Sometimes, though, your boss might ask you to work faster than Standard Work says you should. Perhaps a machine was broken for a while and now your team needs to catch up to avoid late shipments. Or, maybe a big order came in that has to ship quickly. Regardless, the numbers just don't add up.

Managers sometimes forget that they can't just make employees work faster. Scrapping the standard pace generally causes quality problems and outpaces supply systems. Other than process improvement, managers should only increase production by (1) extending working hours through overtime, or (2) adding people. Some companies that are experts in Lean do this with different versions of Standard Work that staff for different *takt* times. When demand gets higher, a process might call for six people, but when it is lower, the process might call for four.

Your challenge is that your manager is going to be under pressure when he asks you to work faster. Overtime is an option, but if he is facing budget problems, he is probably trying to avoid that. Gently remind him of the training you received about Standard Work and see if he reconsiders the request to disregard the proper process.

This is one of those times you should exercise especially good judgment. Don't put yourself at risk by battling your manager about this. As unfair as it may be, a stressed-out manager trying to hit a target could easily view you as putting up roadblocks and making things harder on him. Instead, go along with your manager for the moment. When you return to the normal pace of your Standard Work, though, talk with your boss about the situation.

Discuss the problems that caused the delays in the first place. Offer to help solve those problems. You can also offer to help draw up additional versions of Standard Work for faster *takt* times, and offer to help with cross-training. This lets your manager adjust staffing quickly when demand spikes. Managers frequently run several different production teams, so they might have some flexibility to move people around.

If all else fails, try talking to a trusted person with more clout—an engineer, a human resources (HR) manager, or another manager that you have worked with in the past. Use the suggestion box if you can't find someone to talk to, or if you worry *at all* about repercussions from your manager. The point is to find a way to remind your manager about the proper usage of Standard Work without putting yourself at risk.

Why this works: Most managers want to do the right thing but react to the stress of a situation, just like anyone else. They often don't realize that their request to increase production over and above the normal Standard Work undercuts their credibility with the team and slows any progress they are making on Lean. They also might not recognize that trying to go faster than specified in Standard Work will *greatly* increase the chance for quality problems.

Problem: You have the urge to work ahead to prevent problems.

How this affects you: You want to work ahead to keep problems from affecting your production. Your boss, however, tells you not to produce before someone asks you to. You understand this in theory, but you don't want to end up having to stay late again if another problem causes delays.

Action to take: Instead of working ahead, try to identify the reasons you want to produce in advance. Then try to eliminate those reasons. If you are anticipating a specific problem, let your boss know about it so he can plan a project to resolve the issue. If nothing major is regularly delaying your work, look for little projects that can help stabilize the process. Many such projects can be done in the small chunks of time that become available when "Murphy" shows up. (You remember Murphy's Law, right? What can go wrong, will go wrong.) Organizing workspaces, revising Standard Work, tinkering with new tools and fixtures to make the job easier—lots of little projects exist if you use some ingenuity to find them.

Also, look at this from your boss's perspective. Why do you regularly have time to work ahead? If that extra time is available, your work is probably not balanced to the *takt* time. Talk to your boss about balancing your work better. Your boss probably doesn't realize that your job takes three minutes less than the Standard Work says it should. You are probably thinking, "Yeah, right! Like I am going to give up my extra free time!" You probably don't want to give it up, but think about how much it says about your character when you give time back to the team. Your boss will see that you really "get" Lean, and that you are a team player.

Besides, once cross-training and job rotation picks up steam, those three minutes won't be yours anymore, anyway.

Why this works: Working ahead makes your life easier in the short term but harder in the long run. Extra inventory hides problems. If these issues are hidden, nobody on your leadership team knows about them, and you will not get the resources you need to make your job more manageable over the long haul.

Problem: You have "workaround" processes that cover for problems.

How this affects you: "Workarounds," or **hidden factories**, mask problems, which means that they will never get fixed.

Action to take: Make sure you don't come to accept problems as a part of the process. For example, imagine that your Standard Work calls for a bushing (a bearing-like insert that reduces wear) to be pressed into a hole. Now, imagine that the hole often gets erroneously filled with paint during an earlier operation. While the layer of paint is not thick, it reduces the inside diameter of the hole just enough that the bushing will not fit. After repeated efforts to get the paint crew to design and implement a way to keep paint out of the hole, your team finally gives up. Instead, you add a step to your stage of the process—reaming the hole with a sander.

This new step makes a mess and increases the time for the process. In addition, had they known about it, the engineers would have cringed to know that their perfect holes were no longer perfect after you finished cleaning them out. Regardless, the process "solved" the problem, became accepted, and turned into a hidden factory. In some cases, bosses do not know about hidden factories; in others, they tolerate them.

A significant problem of hidden factories: they don't end up on the Standard Work Sheet, so the time they take is buried in another step. Since they are hidden, an outsider coming in would find no evidence that this step is a part of the process.

Two better options for dealing with a hidden factory would be to treat it as part of the normal process and add it to the documentation, or treat it as an abnormality and log the problem every time it occurs.

When presenting the issue to your boss, use an either-or question to find out how to handle the problem. Specifically ask, "Would you like this step added to Standard Work, or would you like me to use the *andon* process to handle it?" This approach frames the problem in a positive way that gets you what you want. It also gently reminds your boss that Lean is not magic—there is a price to pay for improvement.

Why this works: Most managers try to avoid telling you to do something that violates the spirit of Lean. In addition, good bosses won't dump a problem back on an employee without giving him the means to resolve it. The real problem with hidden factories is that they are not included in production goals. Basically, hidden factories steal time away from documented processes and make targets harder to hit—meaning you have to work harder. Hidden factories undermine the concept of Standard Work and tempt employees to cut corners. This strategy helps you team up with your leaders to solve problems.

Problem: You work slower than the rest of your team.

How this affects you: You want to perform well, but you just can't seem to keep up with the pace. You worry about losing your job.

Action to take: Figure out what the problem is. Most likely, you fall into one of two categories. The first is that you aren't following the process correctly. Often, a slow person is either adding unnecessary steps or not using proper techniques. Ask a faster employee to watch how you do the job and let you know what you are doing wrong. Most people prefer to start with a coworker watching them rather than their boss, for obvious reasons.

The more challenging problem is when you really are slower than other people. The simple fact is that some people are just quicker than others. If this was not true, imagine how boring a marathon would be. The whole mass of runners would never get spread out on the course. All the racers would finish in one big group, just like they started.

Teams usually have superstar workers and others who are "velocity-challenged." How can you tell if the issue lies in the process, or with your natural abilities? If you see several people having trouble keeping up, the variation in pace probably stems from the Standard Work. If the problem is with your speed, you will be the only one who can't produce within the allotted time. Assuming you are doing the process correctly, can you make yourself faster? For practical purposes, most people are stuck with their natural speed. If you constantly find yourself falling behind, consider whether you are simply in the wrong job. Certain types of work are not for everyone.

If you find this to be the case for you, you have two choices. The first is to just keep trying. Eventually, your boss will probably start to identify your speed as a problem and will attempt to help you improve your performance. The second is to go to your boss, or a trusted HR rep, and talk about the issue and your situation.

One word of warning here. Most bosses will prefer a proactive approach, but you have to judge whether your boss is "most bosses." Some bosses will not want to spend time helping you.

So, what do you do if your boss helps you go through an improvement plan, and you still are not able to speed up to the needed pace? You should probably begin building on other strengths that make you too valuable to let go—make yourself great at improving processes, be easy to work with, and find other ways to contribute to the corporate goals.

As a last resort, consider a transfer to a more appropriate position.

Why this works: When Standard Work gets established, it combines the best methods from several people. It normally turns out to be a faster process than any individual was doing before. Following a slower process than the rest of the team will make you, not surprisingly, slower than the rest of the team.

If you do find yourself in the wrong occupation, not only will you risk being fired, but you will probably not find job satisfaction. You will constantly be under scrutiny, and you will seldom feel successful. Prepare yourself for alternative jobs by building additional skills that play to your strengths. This readies you for when you decide to seek a job that can make you satisfied or for when your boss decides it is time for you to move on. Unfortunately, not everyone can do every job.

Problem: Someone on your team is not carrying his or her weight.

How this affects you: You don't want to work with a slacker, but you don't want to snitch on a coworker either. Doing more than your fair share of work and feeling trapped in a stressful situation significantly decreases your job satisfaction.

Action to take: Support Standard Work. Follow the process, even when an abnormal condition occurs. Generally, slackers only succeed in slacking when they are able to get other people to cover for them. If you just follow your Standard Work and record abnormalities according to your process, then the slacker will lose his place to hide. Your boss will follow the data and soon find the slacker on her own.

Why this works: Loafers are actually fairly common. Until Lean, they had some staying power, especially because the "good" ones figured out exactly how much effort they needed to put out to stay just below the radar. With a defined method and a predetermined rate, though, slackers have a hard time finding a place to conceal themselves in a Lean environment. If they don't keep up with the expected, reasonable pace, the boss immediately investigates the abnormal condition. Standard Work solves the problem of slackers for you.

One additional point on slackers: while most people don't want to see their coworkers get in trouble, they also don't want to work harder to make life easier for someone else. This is one of those cases where people hold opposing feelings. They are uncomfortable when they see a coworker squirm, but they like this aspect of fairness that Lean brings to their workplace.

Problem: A coworker hides the gains that he makes.

How this affects you: Most improvements should make their way to the Standard Work Sheet. Unfortunately, it's not uncommon for gains to be put into practice without being documented. Standard Work may say that a task takes eight minutes and thirty-six seconds, while in reality it only requires six minutes and eighteen seconds. The extra two minutes and change goes right into the pocket of the operator at that station. This happens most commonly when one person routinely works the same station and has improved the process little by little over time.

Not documenting that shorter time usually happens for one of two reasons. The first is the "time hoarder" just doesn't trust the response team and wants a little time in the bank to solve problems. The second is that people know more changes are always coming down the pike. They take comfort in preserving a little breathing room for themselves.

The issue comes down to the good of the individual versus the good of the team. If a single person hangs onto that extra time, the rest of the team has to work harder to come up with improvements to meet productivity targets. It is also disheartening for some people to be breaking a sweat with every production cycle while someone else is able to take it easy.

Action to take: Make sure that your Standard Work Sheet is up to date. When a process improvement changes the task, add that information to the sheet. If you see a coworker with extra time, take action. This doesn't mean you have to tell the boss or confront the person—both can be hard for people to do. Instead, ask your boss to start doing more job rotations. As other workers move through that position, they will be more likely than the "time hoarder" to comment about how quick the process is. You can also publicly ask the person how he got the gains that he made. In that way, you are being positive. You are highlighting his success instead of focusing on his negative behavior.

Why this works: As groups get more and more Lean, the bar gets higher and higher. It takes the effort of the whole team to meet its targets. If everyone kept information about their gains a secret, they would make their own lives easier, but the whole group would fall short of its goals.

Problem: You don't have time to keep your equipment in tip-top shape.

How this affects you: You are buried in a pile of your daily tasks, but your boss has given you a maintenance checklist for your equipment. Maintenance requirements are most common on the shop floor but could also be present for fax machines, printers, copiers, and the like.

Action to take: Treat maintenance tasks just like the rest of your job. This works best when the time is programmed into your day. When your boss gives you a maintenance checklist, use the principles of Lean to your advantage. Ask for your manager to time how long the maintenance checks take, and help set up a schedule. Make sure that the time is not double counted—it should count toward production or maintenance—but not both. That just means that if the boss says you do twenty minutes of maintenance on Monday morning, you should have twenty minutes less production on your daily target.

Why this works: Maintenance is critical to Standard Work. The normal production pace is set when tools and machines are working at their peaks. As tools and machines degrade, they slow down and the team has to work harder to keep up with demand. Computers also suffer from poor maintenance, as is the case when software clutters up the operating system and slows down your work.

When a piece of equipment breaks, the team has to stop production completely, which usually causes overtime. In many cases, these breakdowns are avoidable. Once you get to know your equipment, and scrutinize it through regular maintenance, you can predict failures in advance—say, when a machine gets a slight vibration or a motor starts to make a faint, unusual sound. This foresight allows maintenance and repairs to be done during scheduled shutdowns. If you get in the habit of maintaining tools and machines, you give Standard Work a better chance to be successful.

Problem: Your boss is constantly asking you to do tasks outside of Standard Work.

How this affects you: If your boss asks you to do these tasks *instead of* your regular work, they should have minimum impact on you. However, if these tasks are *in addition to* your regular Standard Work, she should either lower your target or assign your work to someone else. This happens less frequently on production lines than it does in situations where people work independently, like in welding shops or offices.

Action to take: Don't say, "No." Instead, ask your boss what part of your job takes priority. Say something like, "If I rearrange the filing system like you are asking, I won't get to the Jones account until tomorrow. Is that okay with you?" Make her understand how busy you are and that your workload is already demanding. Better yet, offer solutions. Tell her what it would take for you to do what she is asking of you.

On the other hand, if you really *do* have time, let your boss know it. If you build the sort of trust where you offer time when you have it, she will be more likely to believe you when you tell her you can't fit any extra projects in.

Why this works: Most bosses know that you have production to do, but they might suspect you can squeeze some extra time out of your day. Sometimes they are correct; when they are not, your knowledge of Standard Work can help you negotiate a solution that works for both of you.

Problem: Your boss can't easily get you help during temporary peak periods.

How this affects you: Many jobs have periods during which things get crazy. It might be an end-of-the-quarter push, a huge order that came in, or the rollout of a new product. Regardless, temporary increases in workload are very difficult to staff for, even if they are anticipated. Employees often end up getting worn out by the time things return to normal.

Action to take: First of all, don't keep asking your boss for extra people. Hiring a new person when the staff is needed year round is hard enough to justify. If the increased workload is not permanent, you won't convince your boss of the need for more people because she knows she won't be able to convince *her* boss of the necessity. Instead, consider temporary workers.

Many people believe that their jobs are just too complex to have a temporary worker step in with only limited training. But then, that's not exactly true; it's an overstatement. More accurately, *much* of a job would be too complex—almost every job has some aspects that are easy enough they could be completed by a quickly trained temporary employee.

Perhaps the temp would move between three small assembly lines, doing low-complexity packaging work at each one (with Standard Work, of course!). That would ease workloads on the permanent employees while not overwhelming the temporary worker with a complicated process. Which of the following requests for help will your boss likely listen to more closely? "We need another person," or, "If we add a temp to do the filing for the summer, we could cover the vacations that are planned without missing any deadlines."

Why this works: Your boss might agree with you that the workload is too much now, but she won't hire a permanent person—especially if she suspects the workload will return to normal down the road. No manager wants to hire someone that they will have to let go in a few months. For this reason, bosses like using temps because it increases the team's flexibility. There is also no cost, monetary or emotional, to letting them go when the demand spike subsides.

The disadvantage of using temps in this sort of role is that it takes a lot of up-front work to get ready for them. With good documentation, however, temps can be brought up to speed in short order, whenever they are needed. The foundation for success lies in having a good set of Standard Work documents prepared for the temps, as well as updated documents for the full-time employees.

Problem: A Lean office makes you more sedentary.

How this affects you: As your office gets streamlined, you leave your desk less frequently. As a result, you get uncomfortable and bored sitting for long stretches in your assigned position.

Action to take: Get creative. Do some brainstorming to find ways to be more active. Do mini-exercises while you are working. Take walks on your breaks rather than sitting in the lunchroom. Ask for an ergonomic evaluation of your station. Consider other alternatives. What about a stand-up desk and a higher chair that would let you switch between standing and sitting, or a small stair-stepper (exercise apparatus) under your desk that would keep your blood flowing? You can also volunteer to be cross-trained or ask to join a project that will require some physical activity.

Why this works: Keeping your body active keeps you healthier and helps keep stress at bay.

CHAPTER 10

Measure up in measurements

What's with all those stopwatches?

THE FIRST TIME SOMEONE PULLS OUT A STOPWATCH and stands over you with a clipboard, it can be a little unsettling. But, believe it or not, you will get used to it—by the hundredth time, you won't even notice!

Since measurements help determine a starting point and help provide a way to evaluate progress, they will become a big part of your life in a Lean company. Businesses that are serious about continuous improvement want to know what is working and what isn't. Once a target is set, the only way to know if a problem is getting better is to track the numbers. Leaders then compare this data to where the company started and how much progress it has made toward its goals.

Under the microscope

You might feel a little resentful as you realize that someone will be evaluating you on a regular basis. But when you step back and think about it, you'll find many examples of times throughout your life where you were measured. As an infant, you might have been given an APGAR score the moment you were born. (APGAR is an acronym standing for: Appearance, Pulse, Grimace, Activity, and Respiration.) This score gave an indication of your health in your first moments of life. One measurement was taken right away; another soon followed, to make sure that your first few minutes were progressing normally. These evaluations helped the medical team determine if any problems were present and, if so, what interventions were needed. As you grew, you were routinely weighed and measured at your pediatrician's office. Your height and weight were compared to your previous measurements, as well as to the averages for your age group.

Once you entered school, you started receiving letter grades. This was yet another form of evaluation where teachers decided if you were meeting their expectations and how you ranked in relation to your peers. If you were performing well, your parents may have chosen to reward you with praise or a special gift. If you were struggling, your parents may have enlisted the help of a tutor or offered incentives to spur your performance. Either way, grades helped your parents decide what action to take. While most kids would prefer to do without a report card, parents usually understand the reasons behind it.

What about the average adult, though? Do you get measured other than during your annual performance review? You better believe it. Your doctor uses data from your routine physical exams to advise you about what to do to improve your health. What about finances? Credit companies use all sorts of measurements about you to calculate your credit score. Your auto insurance company probably has ranked you as a safe driver or not, depending on how many speeding tickets or fender benders you have had. Your grocery store might use a discount card, which you swipe at the check-out, to record your purchases so they can offer effective incentives. Do you think they are tracking your shopping activity? You bet!

Still, despite having information routinely collected about you in your life outside of work, you may develop an uneasy feeling when you are measured on a regular basis on the job. Somehow it ends up feeling invasive.

If you are like most people, your job satisfaction will get dinged when you first get introduced to regular measurement. People usually don't like to be the center of this, or any type of attention. In fact, surveys show that the top fear of people in the U. S. is giving a public presentation.[44] People are even more afraid of it than death! Comedian Jerry Seinfeld has a routine about that. He jokes that most people would prefer lying in the casket to giving the eulogy.

Measurements are much like public speaking—all eyes are on you. Making mistakes in private is bad enough, but people fear making a mistake in public even more. There is a sense of shame that goes along with knowing that everyone will see if you screw up.

One of the challenges with a measurement culture is that many managers try to "logic" their team into being more comfortable with the constant evaluation. Using intellectual arguments seldom works to diminish or erase strong feelings. These types of conversations usually end on a sour note, with frustrated managers and resentful employees.

But if your manager is savvy, he will simply acknowledge that it might be hard for you to get used to being regularly measured at work. Instead of explaining what metrics will do for you, he'll point out to you each time something in your job gets better as a result of having processes measured. He will recognize that constant evaluation takes some getting used to.

Once people get comfortable with being measured, metrics become a very powerful tool. They highlight problems, and point you toward solutions. They provide a basis for improvement. They let you see if your *kaizen* efforts are successful. Measurements prevent you from spinning your wheels down an unproductive path.

With that in mind, here are some strategies to aid you in getting accustomed to working in a measurement-heavy environment,

---

[44] (DeNoon, 2006)

and in making the most out of measurements once they become an accepted part of your life.

Strategies: Setting up metrics

Problem: You don't know why something needs to be measured.

How this affects you: You've come to understand and accept the principles of measurements, but you don't know why something specific is being evaluated in your area. Not knowing the reasons makes you all the more frustrated about taking on yet another task that is going to waste time during your busy day.

Action to take: Ask your boss what goal a measurement is linked to and how long she anticipates tracking it.

Why this works: A manager's time, like yours, is in short supply. Managers don't usually waste time on busywork, so they will have a purpose for collecting data. Basically, they have three reasons for tracking performance:

- ***To fix a problem.*** When something changes for the worse, managers might put a temporary metric in place to identify and resolve the cause of the problem. An example: a manager might ask his team to track repair time if customers have started complaining that getting products back from the service department is taking longer than usual.

- ***To take advantage of an opportunity for improvement.*** Nothing has changed, but something should. These issues might be driven by a strategic initiative that cascades down to your work area. For instance, a goal to grow business in the Midwest might result in a salesperson being measured on new leads in Illinois.

  Managers have to be careful, though. If they come up with too many "opportunity" metrics, employees lose focus. That's just a fancy way of saying that when companies try to do too much, the balls that employees are juggling start to drop. These measurements, like the "problem" metrics, are usually temporary, lasting only until a target is reached.

- ***To prevent issues with a critical aspect of the business.*** Most companies monitor product quality, regardless of whether it is tied to a problem or a goal. They need to know if something is going on that could cause a critical problem. Early detection tends to prevent bigger problems in most cases. These measures are often ongoing and are most common in the make-or-break aspects of the business.

Problem: A measurement hasn't budged in ages.

How this affects you: You are frustrated and believe you are wasting your time collecting data that is showing the same results day in and day out.

Action to take: Talk to your boss. Arrange an appropriate time to review the group's metrics to see if the measures have outlived their usefulness. Use the numbers to your advantage—have your ducks in a row, and show how the process has been stable enough to deliver successful results over a sustained period of time.

For example, if a call center has met the goal on hold times (the length of time a customer is on hold before talking to a real, live human being) for the past two years, perhaps it is time to measure other processes. Certainly, the team has other problems that need monitoring instead.

Why this works: For whatever reason, metrics occasionally persist in your area for long periods of time. While new measures are easily added, old ones seldom get retired. After a while, nobody remembers how long the issue was supposed to be tracked and sometimes even the "why" is forgotten. The act of collecting measurements uses resources; their compilation and analysis should show a benefit. Once that purpose is gone, it is time to help your boss do some spring-cleaning and get rid of that metric.

Problem: Your boss has piles of spreadsheets that he has asked you to take a look at.

How this affects you: You have enough to do without the information overload that comes from reams of numbers. You might not even know where to start.

Action to take: Get some specific guidance from your boss. A common mistake, especially in managers who are trying to get on top of a new role, is that they try to put every existing piece of data to use. Knowing exactly what your manager wants to find will help you focus your search and reassures you that your boss isn't just "beating the bushes" to see what comes out.

Why this works: Many companies now have everything automated, cataloged, and available for the picking in computer databases. A moderately computer-literate manager can pull all sorts of reports off these systems. But the fact that more information is accessible doesn't mean it should all be retrieved. Data should have a purpose. When you ask for specific guidance, you ask your manager to step back and think about why he is asking you to look at all those numbers.

Problem: You have identified a problem that should be evaluated.

How this affects you: You repeatedly encounter a problem in your area, but it has not been addressed yet. You get tired of dealing with the same issue over and over.

Action to take: Don't just complain to your boss or tell her you need more help. All you need are facts and data to back up what you are saying. If the data does not exist, volunteer to collect it—the extra work will benefit you in the long run. The good news is that most bosses will be supportive of your efforts to collect information and will help you set up the metrics. Make sure you start the process of asking for a metric with an open mind, and realize that the solution may lie in changing your own process. Remember, also, that the goal is to fix a problem, not find the blame.

Why this works: The importance of a problem is more obvious to your boss when *you* are willing to fix it. If you are concerned enough to take the time to measure it, managers take notice. Once a specific problem is identified, chances are greater that your boss will allocate resources to make your life easier.

Problem: The metrics in your area seem to drive the wrong behavior.

How this affects you: Doing well on your metrics seems to make your job worse overall. You don't want to have to choose between hitting the numbers and doing the right thing.

Action to take: Take some time to review the measures in your department and what they mean. How well do they capture what you do, or more importantly, what you should be doing?

Consider a person working at a call center. The company probably wants the operator to be *both* efficient and effective. If only efficiency or speed (average call length) is measured, the operator will try to get the customer off the phone as quickly as possible. Obviously, this is not a good idea if the customer's problem is not resolved. An alternative is for the operator to strive for effectiveness in solving customer problems, which is measured by ratings on feedback surveys. Improving those ratings is fairly easy to do, but the call center's costs skyrocket as call length increases.

In either case, using only a single metric will make employees take actions that are not good for the future of the company—either they alienate customers who then take their business elsewhere; or costs rise, possibly to the point of unprofitability. Neither condition sets the stage for success—evidence that taking the wrong or incomplete measurements can be worse than taking no measurements at all. Metrics should drive neither undesirable nor unprofitable behavior.

If you think that working toward your current metrics takes you away from good results, talk to your boss. Asking to get rid of metrics will not be an option. Instead, suggest replacement metrics or additional metrics that you think will be better at driving the team toward success.

Why this works: Showing interest in how measurements are collected and used demonstrates to your boss that performance matters to you. You are showing that you want to do the right thing for the company, even if it means putting your process in the spotlight. Your boss will likely be impressed at the sacrifice you are willing to make.

Note that sometimes metrics seem to work against each other. In the call center example, you and your boss might come to the conclusion that both a call length and a satisfaction metric are needed to drive the right behavior. On the surface, it seems that spending time on customer satisfaction will hurt call length, and vice versa. Having both measures in place, though, drives innovative ideas that are less likely to improve one metric at the expense of the other.

Strategies: Using metrics

Problem: Leaders are always stopping by to check on your production board, but you don't even know what is on it.

How this affects you: Your team broadcasts its results in the form of a **production board,** often a piece of real estate on a wall where all the team's measures, status reports, plans, and ongoing projects are posted. The information on that board is used in making decisions that can play a huge role in what your job will be like in the future.

Action to take: Offer to be the one to keep the board up to date.

Why this works: Volunteering to work on the production board will provide a little variety in your job. In addition to trying something new, you will also learn a lot—both about Lean and about how your work area operates. Another plus is that having extra tasks like this brings you a step closer to managers and permits access to a little more information than you might otherwise have had. (Remember how important communication is to job satisfaction?) Last, but not least, you can make sure that the information you think is important is recorded accurately.

Problem: The information your boss (or a project team) needs in order to make a decision about a problem is not available.

How this affects you: People will periodically come into your area to gather data. The results of that data collection effort will then drive the outcome of a project. If your concerns are not recorded, they may not be addressed.

Action to take: Volunteer to help with these fact-finding missions. While this may seem like extra work, you will probably get some slack on your regular responsibilities during the information gathering period.

Why this works: Volunteering not only provides a little change of pace, but it is always nice to be in control of your own destiny. When you help collect the data yourself, you get a voice in the pending change. You can make sure that the information that you think is important is properly gathered.

Obviously, you must be accurate and fair, but much of the data collection process is subjective. Want an example? Phone calls in the service department have gotten longer, and a manager wants to gather data to find out why. During the review period, a customer on the phone tells you, "The on-hold recording got boring after a while." Is that a customer complaint about having to hold too long? Or, is it a comment on the recording itself? If you are the one collecting data, you can follow up and ask more detailed questions. You shouldn't be changing the meaning of the data—you are just using your knowledge of the process to make sure that the data shows a true picture of what is happening.

Problem: The data doesn't match how you think things are going.

How this affects you: Imagine that you are on the phone all day with customers, listening to complaints about late shipments, and yet your boss shows you a metric that says the company is delivering ninety-nine percent on time. When reality doesn't match what your leadership thinks is going on, you might be concerned that they won't allocate resources to fix the problems you are seeing.

Action to take: If your gut tells you that there is a discrepancy between what is really happening on the phone calls and what the metrics say is going on, follow up on your intuition. Learn *how* the measurements were taken so you can judge for yourself if they are accurate. On occasion, flaws do surface in the measurement system. Perhaps a computer is programmed incorrectly. Maybe a timer doesn't stop during lunches or breaks. Maybe someone forgets to write down problems. Sometimes a count is done differently by one person than it is by another. On occasion, data is double counted. In most cases, it doesn't take much investigating to figure out what is going on. If the inconsistency is not brought to your boss's attention, though, she will rely on the incorrect data.

Why this works: Who knows better than you how things are *really* going with your processes? Unless a metric is way off kilter, most people outside the immediate area won't question it. They simply won't have a reason to. You, on the other hand, see your process in action every day. That familiarity helps you recognize data collection problems.

That said, though, sometimes the data doesn't lie—once in a while, gut feelings are wrong. As an example, imagine a situation where excessive absences are causing an assembly line to have frequent line stops. You might share the common belief that this would also cause poor quality, but data would likely show the opposite to be true. Yes, the people filling in for the absent workers would have more errors, but their slow work is what causes the line stops. The rest of the assembly line would have time to double check their own work and the work done by those filling in for the absentees. That would actually reduce the total number of defects and improve quality.

Gut feelings are great early warning systems, but don't trust them blindly. Use real data before making decisions. Investigate whatever doesn't seem right to you.

Problem: You never see the results of data collection efforts.

How this affects you: Being the object of a data collection effort is difficult enough when you see the purpose behind it. It is even more challenging when you don't hear how the data turned out or if it resulted in any changes.

Action to take: Whenever you are asked to collect data, get in the habit of asking where and how the information is going to be used. It is important to believe that the energy you spend on an endeavor is worthwhile. The project overseer will also be on notice that you don't want your time wasted. Following up and asking about the data gives you an opportunity to make suggestions on how to improve the collection effort. After the project, ask what the results were.

Why this works: Whoever is collecting the data needs to be reminded that the exercise has a cost to it. If you are truly interested, your requests for information will be viewed as wanting to make the project successful. Plus, if you regularly ask good, insightful questions, your boss might even start asking for your opinion.

Problem: Important tasks that are not getting measured are not getting done.

How this affects you: You are working hard and meeting your targets. You have no time to do the work that *isn't* being measured and you worry that your manager will notice. For example, at a big warehouse-style retailer, one employee, John, approached another employee's cash register lane and commented on the pile of empty boxes that had accumulated nearby. The checker, Jane, said, "It's all about numbers, and taking out the garbage doesn't count." Jane was so engaged in doing well on measured tasks that she did not do the other jobs that still needed to be done. She was putting herself at risk because she didn't understand how to work under a measurement system.

Action to take: Do yourself a favor. Don't neglect an important part of your job just because it isn't measured. Employees that focus solely on rated tasks look good in the short term, but they suffer in the long run. What do you suppose coworkers think of you when they are forced to pick up your slack? What is your supervisor going to say about your performance if she needs to get involved? It is shortsighted to get overly focused only on work that is measured.

Take a look at whether you are alone in your struggle to get all of your work done or whether everyone in your group shares the same problem. In the retailer example, Jane was the only one having the problem and it was a coworker who called her on it. If this is the case for you, you are probably still being challenged by the whole concept of measurement. If, however, everyone is having the same problem, it is time for a talk with the boss. Group meetings are a good time to bring this up, since the whole team can confirm the problem. Just make sure you have the numbers to support your claim. And, don't let it be a rebellion—you just want to open a dialogue. At that meeting with your boss, there are several options you can suggest:

- ***Eliminate the unmeasured work in question.*** Don't spend time on wasteful or unimportant steps.
- ***Start measuring the unmeasured work.***
- ***Block off time to do the unmeasured work.*** This would effectively reduce the part of the day during which production is measured. Many manufacturers have a designated clean up time at the end of the day where no production is expected.
- ***Designate a single person, like a floater, to do these unmeasured tasks.*** This frees up the rest of the team to focus on the more important (i.e. measured) process work.

Bosses may also choose to audit the unmeasured work. This action will probably result in an overall drop in perceived performance because some of the recorded tasks have to give way to unmeasured tasks. This is not really a problem, though, if everyone on the team has the same drop.

Why this works: The danger with having measurement systems in place is that employees tend to complete whatever is evaluated first; then they finish their other tasks if time remains. Obviously, the metrics at the warehouse retailer didn't account for the time it took to keep boxes out of the way of customers leaving the store.

Most managers are pretty good judges of human behavior and understand that people will put more energy into activities that are graded than they will into activities that are not. Think back to when you were in school. Didn't someone always ask the teacher, "Is this going to be on the test?"

Managers are aware of the conflict that exists. They know that people want to do well, but don't have enough time to do everything. When you approach your boss with a concern that something important is not getting done, he usually will be responsive. Remember, you are trying to make sure that a potential problem is avoided. Frame it that way.

Problem: Your manager is not appreciating the team's hard work.

How this affects you: It is demoralizing to have your achievements barely recognized before the bar is set higher or another project is heaped onto your plate.

Action to take: First, look at your production board regularly and identify all the little successes. Get in the habit of being vocal about these small victories. When a metric closes in on a goal, bring it up during a morning meeting. Successes frequently go unnoticed, but when you highlight them, you remind the team that progress is being made. Announcing accomplishments also serves to notify the boss of the team's triumphs.

Most managers will take this as a cue to express some thanks for the team's efforts. If not, and if you have a good relationship with your boss, you might try a direct approach and tell her that she is not recognizing the team's efforts enough. Lobby for a reward for the team—a pizza party now and then goes a long way. It's not so much the actual food that is important, rather it's the time that a manager takes to let the team know they are important to the company.

When possible, take it to the next level. Many companies have recognition programs that encourage employees to nominate coworkers for commendations. Some companies have a newsletter that showcases individual and team accomplishments. Other companies recognize jobs well done by having workers vote for a Most Valuable Player style award recipient each month. Make sure to use recognition programs, if they exist.

Why this works: If you and your coworkers learn to celebrate small victories, your boss will probably take note as well. When someone on a sports team does well, high fives fly all around the playing field. When the whole team is successful, all the players rejoice with each other, even if the coach doesn't take part. Outside of work, people learn to give themselves and their friends a pat on the back—why not learn to do so at work?

The most frequent reason leaders don't stop to recognize their team's progress is because bosses have busy schedules and their own pressures to deal with. You probably won't get kudos for every little thing, but when a substantial accomplishment is pointed out in front of a manager, she almost certainly will comment. Once you encourage her to notice the good stuff, she will start doing it on her own.

A side note: everyone, including your manager, likes to feel appreciated once in awhile. Take a minute to think about all the things that your boss does for you and your team. There are probably times that she goes to bat for the group that you don't even know about. On occasion, offer specific praise to her as well. Not only is turnabout fair play, but when you are appreciative of her efforts it gives her encouragement to keep doing all those thankless tasks that benefit you and your team.

Problem: You think that no other team gets measured as much as yours does.

How this affects you: Job satisfaction can take a serious dive if you believe that you are being treated unfairly or that you have to work harder than other people in your company.

Action to take: Make sure you have the correct information. Spend time looking at other areas' production boards. Talk to coworkers in different departments. The goal is first to see if you really *are* getting measured more than others. In many cases, you just don't know what is happening in other areas.

Why this works: Inequity brings down job satisfaction so knowing that other employees are doing their fair share, too, helps ease this burden just a little bit.

Problem: Measurements are taken over a short period of time, and don't accurately reflect how your process normally operates.

How this affects you: Your boss just finished a data collection project and came up with some results that are far above the norm for your department. Now he is expecting that higher level of performance in the future.

Action to take: Before the project begins, talk with your boss about how long the data collection effort should be. You'll have more credibility at that point than if you approach him after the data has already been gathered. If processes are usually pretty stable, a small sample of data tends to match reality. If erratic conditions exist, though, you should push for a longer period of data collection to make sure the results reflect your situation. For instance, a short data collection effort at the post office at 2:30 in the afternoon might not tell the whole story. Use specific reasons to back up your request. Talk about cyclical demand or how suppliers are less reliable at the end of their quarters, or whatever else is happening to cause the inconsistencies.

Another reason to make observation periods longer is that people unintentionally change their pace when they are watched. Remember the **Hawthorne Effect**, described earlier? (It is the subconscious tendency people have to improve productivity whenever a condition changes.) To counter this, ask your boss to throw out results from the beginning of a testing period. Those numbers have a tendency to be different from "normal" conditions and set an incorrect standard. Jobs are hard enough without inaccurate measurements setting an unrealistic expectation.

Why this works: In the 1920s and 1930s, researchers conducted studies on worker behavior at the Hawthorne Works in Cicero, Illinois. While trying to determine the effect of lighting on productivity, researchers found very little correlation between the two factors. They noticed, however, that the introduction of change itself *did* have an effect on productivity. This happened even when the change was a *reduction* in lighting levels.[45] And so, the term "Hawthorne Effect" was coined.

In the practical application for Lean, this means that the act of being observed can cause a temporary spike in productivity. Those being observed probably won't even realize they are speeding up. As workers get used to the observation, they return to their normal pace. This means that measurements taken over short periods of time are questionable.

Problem: You have more than one boss and they measure different things.

How this affects you: It is not uncommon to have to answer to several people—some are official bosses, while others are those that you support with your work. For example, a planner might work for a materials manager but answer regularly to a manufacturing manager and even get direction from yet another manager running an office function, like order entry.

[45] (Davis, Aquilano, and Chase, 1999)

Having so many bosses, each with their own way of measuring your team's performance, can be a recipe for confusion and dissatisfaction.

Action to take: Engage your official boss—the one who writes your evaluations—as your ally. Explain what is happening. Write out a list and include details such as how often the measurements are taken and what happens when things get off track.

Ask your direct supervisor to prioritize your tasks. This will let you choose what to work on when you have competing directions. Stay out of the fight, though. If another boss gives you conflicting directions, refer them to your direct supervisor. Above all else, don't bad mouth any boss to any other one. They talk.

If there are several people in your area struggling with the same challenge, band together and request a *kaizen* to define and improve your jobs. Make sure that all of your bosses have a representative on the team so they will be onboard with the changes.

Why this works: Every boss has his or her own targets to hit. Sometimes, managers get so focused on their own teams' targets they forget to consider what is going on elsewhere in the company.

Problem: Bias is hard to keep out of a measurement.

How this affects you: If you are the one taking measurements, you run the risk of your preferences, or bias, affecting the outcome. If someone else is taking the measurements his preferences may alter the results as well.

Action to take: Whoever is collecting the data, whether it is you or someone else, should be neutral on how a problem is solved; the data collector can certainly be driven to get a resolution—he just shouldn't influence the data in a way that makes his preferred solution leap out over a *better* solution.

Data collectors should also understand the difference between opinion and fact. Opinions are beliefs that come from personal preferences and judgments. Facts are measurable and repeatable realities.

In some situations, opinions are okay. Perhaps blue is your favorite color. If you are painting a room in your home, it would be reasonable to expect you to use that opinion in making a decision on the room's paint color.

Imagine, though, that you work for an interior design company. Your team is told to paint a restaurant in a color that will help get the best sales. That decision should be based on well-studied facts surrounding the effect of color on consumer behavior. Use that information, rather than your personal preference for the color blue, to lead you toward a good choice for the client.

Data collectors also have to be careful not to nudge results toward a particular outcome. If you are asking a friend where she wants to go out for dinner, an unbiased question would be, "Where do you want to go for dinner?" One that lets your preference be known can influence your friend's response: "Do you want to go get pizza? Or, I guess if you don't want that, we *could* go somewhere else, even though I have wanted pepperoni all day." Can you see how such a question might sway your friend's response?

Even if you don't play a big role in data collection right now, you will eventually. As a company gets farther down the Lean path, data collection becomes more common and occurs closer to the front lines. You will probably get your first experience with a data collection plan during a *kaizen* week.

If you suspect that your personal preferences are playing a larger role than they should when you are collecting data, try some of these strategies to remove your bias:

- ***Have more than one person go over the results.*** This helps make sure that one single person doesn't make a decision that will alter the outcome of the project.

- ***Pay special attention to unintentional bias.*** This happens when a data collector is vested in an outcome and inadvertently pushes results in that direction. For example, *kaizen* teams tend to be overly optimistic and prefer to post impressive results.
- ***Pay special attention to intentional bias.*** Treat an *intentional* push of the data toward a preferred result as an ethics question rather than a bias issue. Think of this just like lying, since that is exactly what it is. It should go without saying, but make sure you are not intentionally *changing* the results of a measurement to suit your needs.
- ***Resist the urge to set limitations on the test.*** Obviously, measurements have to have a scope, but sometimes restrictions can change outcomes. As an example, you might decide to only collect data when the whole team is present so you don't miss customer deadlines, or you may suspend data collection when the team falls behind. In these cases, you are only measuring performance in the best conditions. Your results will look better than they should.
- ***Get someone with experience in data collection to help set up the methodology.*** Someone with expertise will save you time by helping you avoid common mistakes.

Why this works: These strategies help keep your personal preferences from inadvertently changing the outcome of a project.

Problem: You don't get the impression that the teams that support you are interested in getting better.

How this affects you: In a well-oiled production team, whether in the office or on the shop floor, you *will* be relying on other teams to support you—information technology (IT), materials, maintenance, the print shop, design engineering, tooling, accounting, etc. These groups all have many jobs, but sometimes it seems they don't think supporting you is one of them.

Action to take: Make a list of all the teams that support you, including internal suppliers, and how they help you. Now, think about all the ways their support is measured. If your company is like many, support won't be a primary role for these teams, so you won't see many measures in place.

Still, before you let your frustration get out of hand, remember that they do have their other, primary jobs to do as well. Design engineers are rolling out new products, as well as supporting your team with design changes. Manufacturing engineers have to figure out new tools and get ready for product releases, but they also have to respond to *andon* lights. Information technology folks have to update systems, manage backups, and keep the networks going—the act of writing programs for your improvement projects is extra work for them.

To measure how well these groups support your area, you will need the support of your boss. Suggest to her that you want to put some metrics in place, and ask her to coordinate those measurements with the other groups. If your manager is not overly responsive to your request, you could talk to a trusted HR rep, drop a note in the corporate suggestion box, or find that really bold coworker who will ask a question for you at a company meeting. The idea is to get the ball rolling on putting metrics in place for the support groups.

If the support teams, or internal suppliers, don't agree to measurements, it doesn't really matter. The great thing about suppliers is that you don't really need their permission to measure them. If the support group chooses not to track relevant data, your team will just have to do it. Work with your manager to post a metrics board for all the support groups that help you out, and track their performance. The data should be posted out in the open, so anyone who comes into the area can see it. A cautionary note: this should be done delicately and with your boss's permission, since it has the potential to inflame poor relationships. Just remember, though, the poor relationship is the reason for this tactic, not the cause of it. Posting metrics without an internal supplier's cooperation should be used as a last resort.

As an example, suppose your company has an escalation policy when an *andon* light is turned on. At some point, a manufacturing engineer would probably be required to respond. They are always busy somewhere, so you might get late response or no support at all. Regardless, try to remain positive, even as you are starting to track their performance. Instead of saying that the engineers are unresponsive, say that they are so busy they can't react in a timely manner. Don't go down the path of bad-mouthing the people you need on your side.

Why this works: Support teams get away with far worse service than any external vendor could. Imagine if your company hired a consultant who barely showed up or if a supplier frequently shipped late. Companies are far more forgiving of internal suppliers than they are of contractors that they hire.

Establishing metrics will likely clarify your expectations. Equally as important, though, they will transform an emotional issue ("You're not helping enough!") into a fact ("You have only been on time 37.2% of the time.") Most support groups take pride in their work. It doesn't take long for conditions to improve when support groups see their numbers (that paint them in an unflattering light) posted in public places. Once performance improves, your boss can use the posted metrics as an opportunity to recognize the support team's gains.

Posting metrics works for three reasons. First, it sends a message that you are serious about wanting good support. After all, you will be spending a lot of effort collecting and posting data. Second, it adds a little pressure—most people want to do well. Once metrics are posted (and remember, you are not doing anything to them that you are not doing to yourself), people are often moved to action. Finally, many groups are not used to daily measures. Sometimes they benefit from a little assistance in getting accustomed to it.

When support teams' managers see that your boss is serious about getting good support, they will start negotiating. And once measurements get a foothold, improvement soon follows.

CHAPTER 11

Be a pro at projects

THERE IS A BIG DIFFERENCE BETWEEN TALKING ABOUT Lean and actually committing resources to get better at Lean. Any leader can schedule a few classes and add some metrics to their organization. The real test of a manager's belief in Lean is if he puts his money where his mouth is. Lean has a cost. It takes time and energy and money to run projects. It pulls people out of their normal roles, making it harder to meet daily goals, at least during Lean's initial learning curve. When managers start accepting this cost and stop finding reasons *not* to do projects, Lean takes hold.

Projects clearly benefit the company. But they will have many effects on you, as well. You may see changes come from unexpected directions, even work areas that are far away from you—company operations are often so interconnected, it is difficult for any one area to make changes in isolation.

The good news for you, though, is that projects can increase your job satisfaction. They help you put your training and knowledge about Lean to work. It is one thing to hear about Lean theory. It is quite another to actually see the principles in action and to have a role in using them to improve your work area. Projects often convert "concrete heads" into Lean advocates. When these undertakings are done right, meaning that the goals are clearly spelled out and that the team has the authority to make changes, projects make you feel empowered. The project team gets to use its experience in the trenches to come up with a solution that works not only for the company, but for themselves as well.

Occasionally, leaders that are new to Lean will make a mistake and do a project the wrong way. "Wrong" means that the boss already knows what he plans to do and uses a project to force the team down that path. Pretending to allow a team to have a choice when the manager's mind is already made up is a grave error. This type of miscalculation is difficult to recover from, since trust is lost.

These are several different project types you will encounter in Lean:

- ***Garden-Variety Project.*** This type of project is generally an undertaking with established goals and a specific end, such as a construction project. These projects may be done by permanent teams that bounce from project to project, or they may be done by temporary recruits from somewhere else in the company. These projects may take all of someone's time or they may be assigned in addition to other, regular responsibilities. The scope can be huge, like building a new factory, or small, like rewriting a training manual. Big projects tend to originate at higher levels since they take up more resources.

- ***Kaizen, or Rapid Improvement Project. Kaizens*** are the projects that most often come to mind when people think of Lean. Other names include Rapid Improvement Workshop, Continuous Improvement Project, Lean event, or *Kaizen* blitz. *Kaizen* loosely translates to something like 'change for the better'. (In some organizations, it will be used as a generic term to mean any improvement. In others, it specifically means a weeklong, structured improvement project. Make sure you know how your company uses the term to prevent confusion.)

  Kaizens consist of a small team going after improvements on a specific process or in a single work area. These projects are structured and follow a well-defined methodology. They are usually a week long, a period that allows the overhaul of an area with dramatic results. At the beginning of the week, the team usually receives training, generally between half a day and a full day; then spends a day or so going over the area with a fine-toothed comb to come up with a plan. At the end of the *kaizen,* the team follows up the project with a report out. This presentation allows the team to communicate the changes it made to those employees that were not involved in the *kaizen,* but who will be affected by its outcome. That leaves about two full days and change to actually do the improvements. Often, the full days are *really* full. It is not uncommon to see teams working late into the night.

Kaizen teams should always try to keep their follow-up lists to a minimum. This is especially true on the shop floor. Teams often shut down production for a time while making changes. A long list means that getting things back up and running will be delayed, or that the operation will be hobbling along until everything is complete.

Office *kaizens* will often have bigger lists than shop floor *kaizens,* since it frequently takes longer to make changes there—especially when software is involved. Information technology has trouble making changes to computer programs overnight. Office *kaizens* also tend to impact customers more directly than shop floor events. Notifying customers of changes can delay implementation.

- ***Daily Improvement.*** A daily improvement is a "fix it now" task. It might be a supervisor telling someone on her team to mark out a location for a garbage can with tape. It might be color-coding types of files, or moving a fax machine closer to where it is most frequently used. These projects are often completed whenever time allows, such as when demand slows down temporarily or when a line-stop interferes with production. However, managers who allocate specific time for daily improvement show that they are truly committed to developing a continuous improvement culture.

Each of these different types of projects plays an important role in a Lean company. Big projects (the garden-variety type) are normally done to set up systems and processes that are too complicated to finish in a week. Examples might include the creation of a workshop stocked with tools and materials, where future teams can make improvements or development of a *kanban* system that will be rolled out companywide.

Kaizen projects are a staple of continuous improvement. Since the achievements made during a single *kaizen* week can be so remarkable, they provide the biggest "bang for the Lean buck." They do have some drawbacks, though. Primarily, they disrupt normal operations, making them impractical for frequent use in the same work area. They also require a great deal of prep work. In addition, many tweaks and adjustments often take place in the weeks and months that follow this type of project. Finally, *kaizens* are physically, mentally, and emotionally draining for those involved. Teams will need a recovery period after the stress of a demanding week. Unfortunately, especially in the office, there is usually no breather—there is a waiting pile of work instead.

Many people who are inexperienced at continuous improvement think that Lean and *kaizen* are one and the same. While *kaizens* are certainly important to Lean, they are just one part of an effective improvement strategy. Viewing them as the only option severely limits how well a company can implement Lean. Indeed, people with experience know that the real bread-and-butter projects of Lean—and the continuous improvement culture as a whole—is constant daily improvement. Big problems need big projects. But many processes have only small hiccups, which can be fixed in minutes if someone is creative and devotes the time to finding a solution. Perhaps you are frustrated that you spend too much time looking for files on your computer. It wouldn't take much time or many people to come up with a standard filing system that would reduce waste and increase job satisfaction.

You will be able to tell how sophisticated your leadership team is by how much emphasis they put on daily improvement versus *kaizen.* People who really understand continuous improvement recognize that world-class performance is not achieved by targeting an area a few times a year. Rather, it is constant attention and relentless, incremental improvements that transform an organization over time. Great leaders don't wait for time to become available; they make improvement a priority and make the time available.

This emphasis on daily improvement is a significant change for most employees. Remember, as you read earlier, employees are no longer just hired to get a job done, but, rather, to get it done better than they did it yesterday. Improvement becomes part of the job. That means that workers have to learn how to do projects well.

When people start doing continuous improvement, they can quickly become overwhelmed by the thought of having to come up with new ideas tomorrow, and the next day, and the next day. The common belief is that they will run out of ideas.

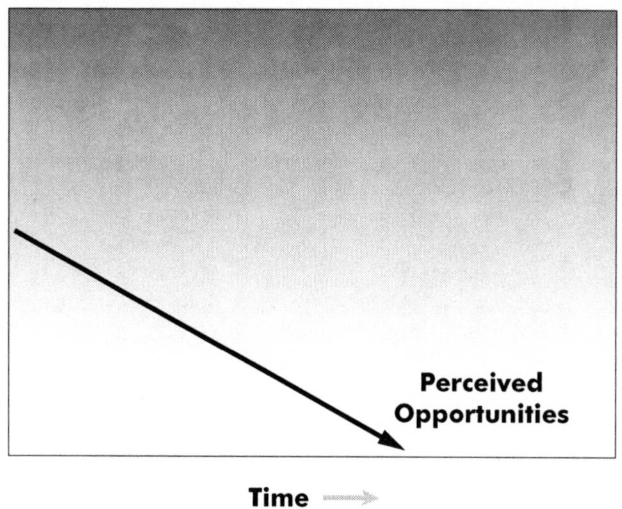

Perceived opportunities

It doesn't really end up working out like that. A company that is new to Lean has a lot of opportunities for improvement, but not much skill at implementing them. As managers and workers get better at Lean, they start putting all the easy improvements in place. Eventually, the original opportunities diminish. The thing is, though, the more projects a company does, the better they get at doing them. Finding projects that employees have the skills to complete gets easier.

The dashed line on the following chart ("Perceived Opportunities") shows the typical novice view about improvement—that all the opportunities will be found and fixed until the ideas run out. The "Real Opportunities" line shows what really happens. As the teams get more proficient, they find an increasing number of opportunities. This makes sense when you stop to think about it. If you are renovating your home, your choices are limited by the skills that you have. You may be able to hang a picture or paint a wall. But if you learn how to do carpentry, you've suddenly opened up a whole new range of improvement projects. You can design and install a built-in set of bookshelves. If you take some classes and develop some handiness at wiring, you can then replace light fixtures and add outlets. That's the way it is with Lean—as your expertise grows, your ability to take on more sophisticated tasks does, too.

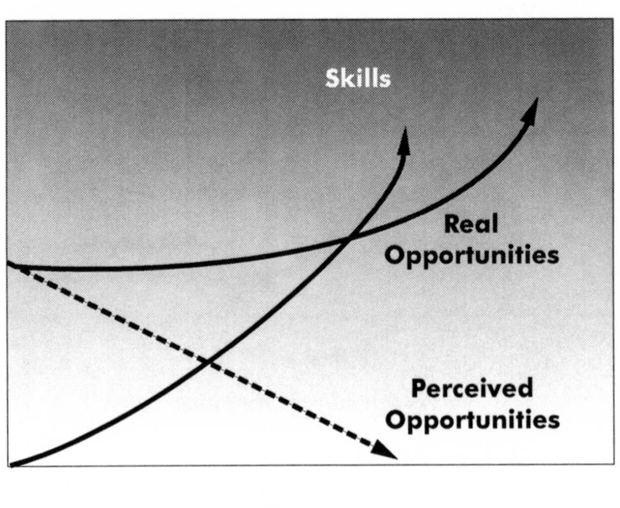

Time →

Real opportunities

Think of an apple tree, full of fruit. When you begin working with Lean, you start out picking all the low-hanging fruit off the tree. At the outset, you don't even consider the higher apples as possibilities—you just can't reach them. Then you learn to use a ladder. Suddenly, a whole new layer of fruit can end up in your bushels. Once you master that, you figure out how to use one of those pickers on the end of a stick—again, you can get more from the tree.

When you believe all the low-hanging fruit is picked, learn to "think taller."

And it isn't just about height—you can also learn to fertilize so the tree yields more apples. You can figure out how to keep the bugs off so the fruit isn't destroyed. The point is that people tend to limit themselves by what they know right now. They can't envision what they will be able to learn down the road.

All types of projects become much easier once you gain more skills. Just like anything, though, Lean takes practice and commitment.

As you can see on the second chart, when abilities get better at your company, new opportunities for improvement will start to outpace your team's ability to do them all.

Who's running the show?

Leaders play a critical role in the success of projects. In fact, they have two important tasks that can make or break Lean efforts. They must prioritize projects, and they have to make resources available.

Picking the right projects and completing them in the right order can have a huge impact in how well a team responds to Lean. Many Lean experts share a common strategy: get people a taste of success early on. That means that the initial projects should have high probabilities of turning out well.

As companies get more sophisticated in their Lean skills, managers can take a few chances. Consider a skier trying to improve her skills. A novice skier starts out on the easiest slopes and probably falls down a lot. Eventually, she will progress to bigger hills, but do you think she still falls down? Well, if she wants to improve, she will fall, especially if she pushes herself a little bit beyond her abilities. If she is content to stay on the bunny slopes, she will avoid some bumps and bruises, but she will also not get much better. That black diamond run with the commanding view from the top of the mountain will always be out of reach. If she wants a great reward, she has to try some new things that she hasn't done before.

Lean is the same way. If your boss only picks projects that she knows will work, she will miss out on a lot of probable wins. Your leader has to be a bit of a calculated risk taker. Remember—projects that are sure bets in Lean don't generally offer very big gains.

Just like life, continuous improvement has obstacles. Lean projects are not always going to work out perfectly. Lots of times, a project will start out as a great idea only to end up in the dumpster. If this doesn't happen to you eventually, the projects your bosses are selecting are probably not very challenging.

What should you expect of your leaders?

You have a lot of responsibilities in a Lean environment. Your bosses do, too. They include:

- ***Time to do projects.*** Reasonable leaders understand that they incur a cost for taking people from their daily jobs to work on improvement projects. They should adjust expectations when they change how employees spend their time. Asking employees to take on projects without adjusting their regular workload is a recipe for failure.

- ***Priorities that match the plan.*** Improvement doesn't happen by accident. Leaders must have a plan that outlines how their team is going to reach its goals. In a Lean journey, the basic question changes quickly from "What do I do?" to "What do I do first?" Opportunities will quickly outpace resources.

- ***Money to support projects.*** The old saying, "It takes money to make money," applies to Lean, just like it does to any other business undertaking. It can take some spending to reduce waste and improve the bottom line. Motivated employees who want to try out an idea can be frustrated and easily discouraged when their idea gets rejected because a manager denies an expense of a few hundred dollars. Good leaders make sure that budgets contain money to fund improvement projects. This probably means having a standing list of improvement ideas so they can make reasonable estimates during budget preparation.

- ***Training.*** Leaders should either train their team themselves, or they should get the team access to Lean training. They wouldn't ask their teams to do production work without proper instruction; they shouldn't ask them to make improvements without first learning about Lean.

- ***Mentorship.*** Leaders should be involved in projects. This might mean leading teams, coaching, or just being present to show support. The best Lean leaders help their teams learn how to make good Lean decisions on their own. A savvy manager knows that this strategy will not only help develop valuable skills for his employees, but it will also free up more time for himself—time that had been spent monitoring teams can be put to good use elsewhere.

- ***Authority.*** Some leaders might have a hard time letting go of power. But good ones will learn to trust their teams to make decisions on their own.

- ***Support.*** People will sometimes make bad decisions. The way a leader reacts will set the tone for his team's actions down the road. A good leader will use the mistake as an opportunity for the team to learn. Punishment will train the team not to take any risks or try anything new.

Will your boss meet these expectations? Not always—leaders are human, too. In some ways, bosses have it better than employees—more pay, more flexibility, and more autonomy. In other ways, their jobs are much harder. It is easy to forget, but your boss has a boss as well. She goes through exactly the same challenges with her boss that you do with her. She is learning about Lean (just like you are) and she will make mistakes. Try to cut her some slack. It makes the transition much easier when teams and leaders are working together rather than against each other.

Who's providing the horsepower?

Every project needs leadership to get the ball rolling. Most also need participation from a wide range of workers. Some projects are small and simple. Employees can handle these types from within their own work group. It doesn't take much expertise to make labels for material locations, or change a sequence of steps to improve the work flow. You will probably be surprised by the resourcefulness in your team. People have all sorts of hobbies that carry over into Lean—woodworking, rebuilding classic cars, even computer programming. When a team doesn't have the right skills, though, the expertise has to come from elsewhere. So, who can help you and what do they offer to the improvement process?

- ***Team members doing the process that is being improved:***
  - Have detailed process knowledge.
  - Understand customer requirements.
  - Have common sense about whether ideas will work.
- ***Team members from other work areas:***
  - Offer best practices and fresh ideas.
  - Expand the team's understanding of the value stream.

- ***Facilities and maintenance:***
  - Change floor plans.
  - Add power sources.
  - Build and remove walls.
  - Fix or modify machines.
  - *Love* tearing stuff down. Demolition! Want to see a facilities worker grin? Ask him to add a door to a wall!
- ***Tooling:***
  - Builds fixtures.
  - Adjusts fixtures to make them faster and easier to use.
  - Builds specialized tools.
- ***Welders:***
  - Build whatever the team thinks of! Really—they can build just about anything. Just ask.
  - Are always in demand on shop floor projects in heavy industry.
- ***Design engineers:***
  - Make product changes to make manufacturing easier.
- ***Manufacturing engineers:***
  - Design and build basic tools. (Tooling handles the precision work; engineers handle the rest.)
  - Design and document processes.
  - Do manufacturing math to figure out how much stuff (machines, materials, tools, etc.) and how many people work areas need.
  - Lay out work areas.
- ***Vendors:***
  - Adjust delivery methods.
  - Confirm capabilities of tools and components.
  - Transmit requests to upstream suppliers.

- ***Information technology:***
  - Makes software changes to support processes.
  - Writes programs.
  - Upgrades hardware.
  - Installs new equipment.
  - Installs or changes telephones.
  - Tends to be more important in office projects than on the shop floor. Offices have computers and programs in a more essential role.
- ***Customers:***
  - Know what they want. Important note: make sure that the ones you talk to are a good sample of all your customers. If not, you might be tailoring your project to a niche.
  - Can participate on projects, but . . . make sure you are ready to air your dirty laundry. If they are on a project they will see *everything*.
- ***Senior leaders:***
  - Have big picture information.
  - Can get things done quickly.
  - Can motivate teams when they (the bigwigs) get their hands dirty.

Do I have to?

Some people do whatever they can to avoid projects. They quickly learn, though, that avoidance doesn't work. Sure, they might be able to stay off project teams for a while. But, as the company gets more and more Lean, the pace of projects will pick up. These people will begin to encounter projects on a regular basis. Trying to avoid projects will be more frustrating than just participating and giving projects a chance. Avoiding projects doesn't prevent change; it just reduces your say in those changes.

In addition, most employees eventually recognize that if they don't participate in Lean, they are affecting the way their bosses look at their performance. It is just common sense. If your boss says that something is important and you don't do it, you won't appear to be a good employee. Think of it this way. If your boss says to show up on time or says to clean up an area and you decide not to, what will happen? At a minimum, you get a bad performance review and you won't get a raise or promotion. At worst, you might get reprimanded or even get fired. Lean is no different than any other everyday assignment.

Trying to stay off projects has another aspect that many people don't consider. It affects your relationships with your coworkers. The company is going to do projects. It is going to need people on the teams. If you don't pull your fair share of the weight, someone else has to stand in for you. After a while, the people you work with will get tired of doing your part of the improvement work. It will affect how they view you. Later, when you need help, you won't be likely to get it. Your work will get harder and your coworkers will like you less. What do you think that will do to your satisfaction?

Since you will almost certainly be involved with projects and teams, it is good to have a plan for how to become successful on them.

Strategies: Adopting a project mentality

Problem: You are not quite sure how to begin your Lean adventure.

How this affects you: Trying something new when it is your own idea can be challenging enough. Trying something new because someone told you to do it might bring you back to the days when your parents tried to get you to eat a new vegetable that didn't look very appetizing. Their opinion that it was good for you didn't really make you more excited to eat it.

Action to take: Volunteer for projects early and often.

Why this works: You have heard a lot of things about Lean, not all of them good. Since you haven't yet experienced the benefits of Lean first hand, you have a one-sided view of what Lean is. You won't really get a full understanding of Lean, however, until you start trying to use its principles to make improvements to your job. Learning about Lean is a hands-on task. Do a project. That will give you a great chance to gain new skills and immediately apply what you learned to your situation. The more you are exposed to something and the better you understand it, the less overwhelming it is. The faster you can get familiar with the ins and outs of Lean, the less it will diminish your job satisfaction.

Problem: Lean is difficult because your boss gives you open-ended instructions.

How this affects you: Ambiguity is hard for some people. Instructions like "5S your area" or "build a rack for your parts" can make Lean rookies break out in a sweat. Most people are used to very clear instructions that specify exactly what to do next. They might struggle when they start having to choose their own paths. They won't have the foggiest idea of how to get started on a 5S project and won't have a clue where to go to get parts for that rack. Feeling incompetent in a job is a recipe for dissatisfaction.

Action to take: You have to get used to the concept that you will be expected to come up with ideas on your own, to try new things, and to figure out how to get tasks done. Unfortunately, the only cure for this is practice. What you can do, though, is stack the deck in your favor. Talk to your boss about giving you some easy tasks to start out with. Let her know that you are willing to try, but that you want to ease into things. Chances are your willingness to take on simple projects will still stand out in a positive way, since many other people will be pushing back against Lean. Those good impressions can make your life easier down the road.

Why this works: A funny thing starts to happen after just a few projects. After the second or third rack, when you are asked to build something, you *will* know where the parts and the tools are and you might even know a good person to go to for help with the design. It is that repetition that makes Lean more familiar. It is not surprising that as you increase your understanding of a topic, it is less intimidating. You start to know what to expect, and you gain confidence. The uncertainty goes away.

Try not to let too much time pass between projects, especially in the beginning. If you do, you can slip backward and have to go through the painful parts of learning again.

Also, remember, not every project will be a success. You will fail on occasion. Expect it! Take heart, though. You frequently learn more from failures than you do from victories.

Problem: You are stuck with a problem because you can't get your boss to schedule a kaizen to fix it.

How this affects you: If you view *kaizen* events as the only method for making gains, your dissatisfaction is likely to grow. Your manager has set targets, and those aren't going to go away because the *kaizen* teams are busy elsewhere.

Action to take: Don't let *kaizen* weeks be the answer for everything. While *kaizens* are extremely effective, they take a lot of resources and need plenty of planning to pull them off. Waiting for a *kaizen* means that you will be tolerating a problem for longer than you need to. You may find it frustrating to hear about all the benefit that Lean is going to bring, and then never get the resources to back up those claims. Remember that Lean has other methods for making improvements. If you only have a minor problem, use daily improvement or small projects in your area to solve it. Talk to your boss if it appears that a *kaizen* for an important problem is too far off. You may be able to get some time freed up to work on it yourself.

Why this works: Formal *kaizens* have an important role in Lean, but they are not the only way to make improvements. When employees stop relying solely on formal projects, outside assistance, charters, and facilitators, and start actively looking for things to improve on their own, Lean really takes off.

Try this experiment. Every day for a week look for small problems at home. Don't just identify the issues—create solutions and put them in place. You might hang a clipboard near the refrigerator to write down items on a shopping list as you use things up. You might put a hook inside the garage door to hang up your car keys so you are not looking for them each morning. At the end of the week, you will suddenly have seven little projects completed that save you time and maybe a little money. You just took control and made your life a little easier and a little better.

Little improvement projects like that slowly but surely will make your life easier. And, if you keep doing those projects, the effort will start to become a habit. At first, it will probably be hard to find solutions. But, after a few successful attempts, you will start finding more and more opportunities. The projects will start coming to you fast and furious.

Before long, you will start to develop an eye for waste in your home. You will soon have a sense for what will make things easy and what will be fast and cheap to put in place.

Now, imagine that you are able to put those changes in place every day. Fast forward to a year from now. How much more smoothly will your house run with all those improvements? What if you are married and your spouse takes on this challenge as well? That amounts to 730 permanent improvements to your home operations over the next year! What would you do with all the time that those little projects free up?

If you try the same approach at work, making one small improvement each day, the gains will also stack up. They may not be as dramatic as a *kaizen* or be able to address as big of a problem, but they will have a cumulative impact on your daily work experience. The best part is, you are in control. You choose what to work on and what will make your job easier. You will probably benefit from your coworkers' improvements, too. Work with your boss to figure out a way to get time to routinely do these small projects.

In the end, you won't have to wait for your boss to schedule that *kaizen* you thought you needed.

Problem: You seem to be doing everyone else's job, as well as your own production work.

How this affects you: It's one thing when work gets balanced and shuffled around between frontline employees. You realize that sometimes this works in your favor—you get to pass off work to your coworkers. It's quite another thing when people in higher pay grades (engineers and supervisors) seem to be offloading their work onto you. You could easily find yourself bitter and resentful over these changes.

Action to take: Let's assume that the workload is not the problem in this situation. (If it is, there are several other strategies that cover that topic.) Instead, let's look at this issue as one of fairness. Why should you have to do your boss's job, or the work of the other people making the big bucks?

This is a case of reframing your interpretation of what it means to be getting this extra work. First of all, consider why the work might be passed on. If your manager is swamped, he is not likely to be working on solving the problems that are plaguing your area. If an engineer is buried with work, she may never get to a suggestion that you came up with three months ago. It is unlikely that your boss is passing on work just so he can get out earlier to play golf every Wednesday. His plate is full, too. Only, when he has a full plate, more work seems to fall onto yours.

Secondly, look at it from a skills perspective. You are probably receiving work that was traditionally management or engineering work. You are broadening your talents, which increases your value. Consider how the new work you are doing would look on a résumé. If you are doing more problem solving, data collection, documenting work, or other high-level tasks, you are gaining sought-after skills.

Why this works: You, like most people, want to feel valued. Sometimes, the impact of the workload or the sense of unfairness masks other possible interpretations. The fact is, if you are being asked to do increasingly complicated work, it is a signal that your leaders trust you and value your skills. If your boss seems to be holding you in higher regard than your coworkers, take an opportunity to remind her of that fact prior to evaluation time. You should be rewarded if you are doing more advanced work than your peers.

Problem: You never seem to have time to work on continuous improvement projects.

How this affects you: You know that you are supposed to be doing continuous improvement, but you are so busy with your regular work that you just can't get the Lean stuff done. You worry that you are risking your boss's displeasure or a formal reprimand.

Action to take: Get yourself away from the "I don't have time" mentality as fast as possible. It is true that when production (in the office or on the shop floor) is cruising along without problems, you will be pretty busy. Production doesn't always go smoothly, though. Whenever a glitch pops up and slows things down, jump on whatever project you can and get to work. When that happens, you will find you can get little things done throughout the day. Those little odds and ends add up after awhile.

If you really don't have spare time, you might have a team member who does. Work out an arrangement where she can cover your work on occasion so you can get a project done and vice versa.

Another option is to talk to your boss. See if she can help you prioritize. It will help her to know that you *want* to participate in Lean and that you are not just refusing it outright.

Also, consider talking to your manager about cross-training someone to work in your position. If other people learn your job and can cover for you, it might free up some time for you to work on your list of projects. Remember—when people are out sick or on vacation, work doesn't come to a screeching halt. Why should it be any different whether you are at home with the flu or out working on an improvement project?

Why this works: It takes active commitment to do continuous improvement well. You have to create opportunities to get it done or you will never see its benefits in your job.

Strategies: Selecting projects

Problem: You don't want your coworkers angry at you for making changes to the team's process.

How this affects you: Most people are concerned with their own work area, and they want to work on projects centered on their own team. Unfortunately, they also know how outspoken their coworkers are. They don't want to be the bad guy who causes a bunch of stress and conflict if a project doesn't work out perfectly.

Action to take: If this is a problem for you, you probably view relationships with your coworkers as more important than autonomy in your work area. Since you have to get on some projects to learn about Lean and you don't want to be at odds with your neighbors, consider finding a project outside of your own work area. If you prefer to work on your own process, try to get on a project with at least one other person from your regular work team. This way you can share the heat if the rest of your coworkers don't like the changes.

Why this works: You are making an active choice to balance what your boss wants—your Lean development—with what you want—job satisfaction. If you choose to work on projects for other teams instead of your own, you might even score bonus points for being a team player who will help other groups. As you get better at Lean and get more confident suggesting changes, you should be more at ease working on projects in your own backyard.

Problem: You've gotten stuck on a few projects that have bored you to tears.

How this affects you: Not all projects are exciting. In fact, some are downright monotonous. Putting *kanban* systems in place is a prime example of this. Someone has to print the cards, laminate them, cut them up, count parts, and attach the cards to the parts containers. It can take the wind out of your Lean sails to be on too many of these excruciatingly boring projects.

Action to take: You can wait to be recruited for a boring project that needs to be done or you can actively seek out a project that interests you. You might as well volunteer so you can be on one that you like. The best way to do this is to find out who the Lean gurus are in your company, and tell them that you want to get in on an exciting project. Make sure you let your boss know what you are doing.

Remember that your concern about boredom can apply to tasks within a project as well as entire projects. Every *kaizen,* for instance, has numerous tasks and possibly several sub-teams. Get on the ones that look the most fulfilling and enjoyable to you. Volunteering early means you have a better chance of getting your choice.

Why this works: The farther out you plan, the more options you will have. Good, fun projects are like night and day when compared with routine or uninspired ones. The more exciting a project is, the better the lessons will stick with you.

Problem: Your project team just got together for the first time and spent most of the meeting arguing about goals and objectives.

How this affects you: Time passes very quickly on a *kaizen.* You certainly don't want to waste it at the beginning of a project watching teammates bicker about goals and the scope of the project. Doing so will haunt you on Thursday night when you have project tasks left to finish and the production area is still completely torn up. You might also question how successful the project will be if you can't even agree on the team's **charter**—the document that spells out the scope and goals of the team.

Action to take: The first rule of thumb on a project is to always read everything the team leader sends out in advance. Often, this includes the charter. Unfortunately, many people let their homework slide and wait until they get into the team's first meeting before reading about the project.

To help head off disagreement, read any documents you get before the first meeting. If you suspect controversy, comment on the information, or ask the team leader a question about the project. This usually sparks a discussion while plenty of time is still available to do something about the details. An effective method is to send the leader an e-mail, with copies to the rest of the team, voicing your concerns. That typically attracts more attention than just sending it to the leader alone.

Since many shop floor employees don't have e-mail, another effective method is to talk to other team members before the project. Mention the project hours or the goals or where the team is meeting. This discussion will serve as a reminder to the rest of the team to go over their materials.

Why this works: Unprepared team members are frequently stunned by the extent of the goals of a project; others have completely misunderstood the purpose of the *kaizen*. Employees don't bring the necessary safety equipment, they go to the wrong location, or they don't make arrangements for working unusual hours. Dealing with these details before a project starts saves a huge amount of time.

Apart from helping steer the project in a more successful direction, the fact that you are prepared makes you stand out in a positive way. It never hurts to have a team leader tell your boss good things about you. (Obviously, the opposite also holds true. If you aren't prepared, your team leader will probably mention that as well.)

Strategies: Being on a team

Problem: You get discouraged when teams have a rough time at the beginning of a project.

How this affects you: Going into a project, you are excited and have high expectations for what it might accomplish. Instead, you are stuck spending the first day watching several team members fight tooth and nail about what time the breaks should be!

Action to take: In 1965, Dr. Bruce Tuckman came up with a theory on how team development progresses.[46] Teams start out by **forming.** In this stage, team members have little familiarity with each other, and the leader has a big role. This is when team members start to feel each other out. As work progresses, the team enters a **storming** period, during which the team tries to establish its identity. At this point, members do not agree much; the team is trying to find its way. During these early stages, avoid taking disagreements personally—this is a natural part of team development. After a while, the team somehow finds direction and enters the next period, which is called **norming.** This is when ideas and plans start to get ironed out, and the group starts to become a cohesive team. Finally, the team starts **performing** to get work done. Keep a close eye out for backsliding. Sometimes, a team will slip back to an earlier stage if its members are not careful.

The obvious goal of a team is to speed through the first three stages and spend as much time as possible performing. The job of moving things along really falls on the experienced facilitator and the project team leader, but you can assist. Your first job is to not get discouraged. Secondly, you should learn to recognize the stages and gently prod your leadership if they don't seem to be taking any action when the group gets stuck. Sometimes team leaders and facilitators miss signals, and they need help to keep them on track.

---

[46] (Smith, 2005)

Why this works: When people regularly work on teams, they get used to moving through the stages. When employees don't work on projects often, they get stressed out by the team's progression. On top of that, confrontation and lack of early progress may cause team members to get discouraged. Knowing what to expect helps participants tolerate what is going on and maybe even enjoy the process.

Problem: You think that friction from a project is ruining a valuable working relationship.

How this affects you: You have repeatedly read in this book that workplace relationships are one of the biggest sources of job satisfaction. So, it worries you that you might risk losing a friendship over a weeklong project.

Action to take: Projects are only temporary. Relationships with coworkers are more permanent. If you are unkind to someone on a project, you *will* pay for it later—primarily because it is difficult to work effectively with someone who feels wronged by you. Take a step back when your blood pressure starts to boil over some decision the team is making. This doesn't mean that you have to avoid conflict—it just means that you should make sure the conflict does not get personal. Follow these three simple rules (1) no personal attacks, (2) no gossip, and (3) no threats. The relationships don't end when the project does.

Why this works: Friends with good coping skills can battle each other on the basketball court and still hang out over a beer later. Conflict and competition don't have to mean anger and shattered relationships. As long as you are careful about not stepping over the invisible line into a realm where confrontation gets personal or harsh in the heat of the moment, relationships will survive.

Problem: Your friends don't seem to help you much on project teams.

How this affects you: You want to do well on your project. Unfortunately, you are starting to realize that your friend from the next cubicle might not have been the best person to partner with. You just don't seem to be getting much done.

Action to take: Select your project partners wisely. You could choose to spend your time with the people you like, but they probably come from your department and have skills that are similar to yours. Instead, team up with people from other areas who have skills that complement yours. If you are part of the way through a project before you realize that you made a poor choice, partner with a different person during the next task. Sub-teams are not set in stone.

Why this works: Several things happen if you choose partners well. First, when you break into sub-teams to do tasks, you will be more effective. Instead of being frustrated at not having the right mix of skills, your team will have an easier time finishing its assignments. Second, a good choice will provide you with a mentor who might be able to teach you something new. Third, you will hopefully have some fun meeting a new person, and you may develop an ally that might be able to assist you when you need help in the future.

Problem: You keep getting asked to be on project teams outside of your work area.

How this affects you: You can't seem to get any of your own regular work done because you are getting sent away to another team for a five day project every few months. Just when you start to get caught up, you get sent to yet another project.

Action to take: It is worrisome and unsatisfying to fall behind in your work. On the shop floor, this problem is not much of a concern—when someone is missing from a production role, the boss has to make sure the work is covered or no product leaves the building. If, however, you are in a role where you have your own backlog—maintenance, IT, engineering, and many office positions—your work could grow while you are gone. Talk to your boss about a plan to avoid coming back to a mountain on your desk. It is not fair for your manager to expect you to come back to a week's worth of work that didn't get done in your absence.

This problem comes from the fact that frontline employees are reluctant to ask their coworkers to take on extra work. After all, everyone is busy. Good bosses should recognize this hesitation, and step in to help coworkers avoid the chance of conflict over workload issues. After all, managers are the ones who are paid to make these kinds of decisions. If your boss does not come up with a plan on her own, ask her how your work is going to be completed while you are gone.

Managers do have a few options. Overtime, borrowing help from another department, extending some deadlines, reducing assignments prior to the project, and parceling out your work are all options. The trick is to have the conversation with your boss about whether the plan will really work. The more specific the conversation is, the better your work will be covered and the less you will have to do when you return. Remember, the more stressed you are about the work piling up on your desk, the less you can enjoy being on a project team. In all likelihood, you will also be far less effective to the project team if your mind is elsewhere.

One more thing to mull over: if you are one of those sought-after people, consider it a compliment. Being in demand should be rewarded. Make sure that your boss understands you were requested to serve on a team, even if you couldn't actually participate. That tangible accomplishment can set you apart when it comes time for the boss to parcel out annual raises or pick people for promotion. Being in demand adds job security.

Why this works: Leaders try to get team members with a variety of skills because, obviously, they want to set the project up for success. If the team needs some programming, they will try to get an IT person. If it needs fixtures, welders are useful. The old saying goes something like, "If the only tool you have is a hammer, everything looks like a nail." This holds true on teams, as well. Leaders don't want to restrict their options on what they can do because they don't have the right skills on their project teams. When company leaders hear that you are good at something, they will likely start asking for you.

If you have experience or training that is in demand, at some point you will probably be asked to be on another group's project team. The chance increases the more skilled you are. For the frontline employee, solid Lean skills and computer expertise make you more valuable to teams. People in certain roles also frequently tend to find themselves on projects. Manufacturing engineers, maintenance workers, welders, and IT gurus all get requested more often than other workers.

Employees are more likely to be effective participants in projects if their managers arrange for reasonable workload coverage. Overall, it is in the best interest of the business to make sure those requested people are able to contribute in a relatively stress-free way.

Strategies: Using good project etiquette

Problem: You have so much going on that you can't seem to get to project meetings on time.

How this affects you: You have repeatedly read that relationships at work are important to your satisfaction. So, what do you think happens to your coworkers' satisfaction with you when you waste their time?

When someone is late, that person wastes a resource—time. Even after the tardy person arrives, that person needs time to get up to speed with the rest of the team and then has to ask questions that have already been asked and answered—all while the rest of the team continues to wait. To make matters worse, the waste of time is actually multiplied by each and every person on the team. If one person is ten minutes late on a six-person team, that person just wasted an hour of time.

Action to take: This should be common sense, but it is amazing how many people demonstrate disrespect to their coworkers by being late to meetings. Show up on time! Time is a limited resource: don't waste it by making your team wait for you.

A general rule of thumb is that the more senior people are, the more likely they are to be late. They have "just one little thing to check on" back in their office or they have an urgent call they have to take. If you are one of these people and you can't say, "No," you have another choice: don't be on a project team. Otherwise, make other arrangements for your regular responsibilities, or deal with them outside of project time.

Some people just always seem to be running late. If this is you, set an alarm, ask a teammate to steer you back into the meeting, or just don't leave the meeting room on breaks.

One technique to draw attention to the importance of time is to ask everyone to synchronize their watches. (Suggest this to the team leader if you don't want to ask the group to do it yourself.) This can also keep people from being late because a watch is a few minutes off. Use a wall clock in the meeting room as the standard time.

Another trick that has proven effective at getting people back to the meeting room on time is to ask the team leader to put five or ten minutes into a "time bank." The team can use this time to leave early, or for extra break time. When someone is late, the time bank starts to tick down. Suddenly, being late switches to eating up personal time instead of company time. Team members will drag each other to meetings to keep the bank from dwindling.

Why this works: The people that are diligent enough to be on time end up paying the price for other people being late. Sitting around waiting is very aggravating, especially when teams are on tight deadlines. If you are the one who is late, you'll be the target of some resentment and take a noticeable hit on your relationships with the rest of the team. If you are a leader, the rest of the team will assume that you are setting the example to be followed by the team—that tardiness is acceptable. Make the extra effort to be on time.

Problem: You can't concentrate with all the side conversations going on in meetings and classes.

How this affects you: It is hard enough to learn something new or figure out what you have to do without having to struggle to hear.

Action to take: Teams often set their own standards. If side conversations are uncommon, people are less likely to break with the norm and start one. If chitchat is frequent, people don't think twice about whispering to their neighbors. Help set the tone and keep sidebars to a minimum. If you have something important to say, either write it down so you won't forget to contribute it later, or join the group conversation. If you see someone overdoing the talking, mention it to them. If doing that would make you feel uncomfortable, ask one of the more senior people on the team or the team leader to take care of it.

Why this works: Side conversations are common in *kaizens*. Sometimes they are about the weekend or the latest TV episodes. More often, though, they are related to the topic at hand. Either way, it is disrespectful not to give your full attention to the person who has the floor. Demonstrate common courtesy by setting a good example and policing each other—both will help establish a good project environment.

Problem: People on the team are treating each other disrespectfully.

How this affects you: You probably don't respond well when people are rude to you. During projects, though, it is easy for people to get angry and for situations to escalate. When this happens, the team probably gets less done than it could if everyone was getting along.

Action to take: This is just common sense. Be courteous and respectful of others. This means both openly and behind the scenes. If you see something going on, give the culprit a gentle reminder or ask your leaders for some help if confrontation is not your style.

Another, more positive way to change a group's behavior is to start an "interruption jar" or something similar, where team members can drop a quarter whenever they talk out of turn. Most groups follow rules better if enforcement comes across as a game. Plus, you can end up buying some treats with the jar's earnings.

Why this works: When people are in an unusual environment, they often revert to group rule. Sometimes, the group tolerates behaviors that wouldn't fly in normal situations. Emotions can take over and become an excuse for treating people badly, for interrupting and yelling, and for bad-mouthing other team members behind their backs.

If these behaviors are not stopped quickly, they can become the group norm. The person who is treated disrespectfully feels angry or hurt. Negative feelings use up energy that could be put to better use. Obviously, nipping inconsiderate behaviors in the bud sets a team up for success.

Problem: Someone on the team uses sarcasm to be funny, but he is overdoing it.

How this affects you: It is hard to get excited about the progress of a team when someone is ridiculing the team's efforts.

Action to take: If you are the sarcastic one, try to reel it in. Use a trick, like only saying every third comment you think of. That way, you can still express yourself, but you won't be so inclined to step over the line. If the guilty party is someone else, you can help minimize that behavior.

Sarcastic comments are usually made to get attention; the person is also usually looking for acknowledgement and support. Simply ignoring the heckler or giving a blank stare goes a long way toward eliminating the reinforcement that keeps the person going. Responding, either positively or negatively, fuels the sarcastic person.

Why this works: Sarcasm can be funny in small doses. The problem is that sarcasm is a very negative form of humor and often has a personal target to it. Excessive sarcasm turns people off in a way that is similar to other negative behaviors like sulking.

Negativity is contagious and brings people down. This means that employees around a Sarcastic Sam will end up being less enjoyable to be around, adding to the problem of poor job satisfaction. Positive humor, however, is a great way to improve job satisfaction. It is fun to have amusing people on the team, as long as work is still being done and no one is harboring bad feelings because of the jokes.

Problem: Some of the tasks you have to do on a project team aren't that fun.

How this affects you: Some tasks on a project team are fun, while others are not. The tasks that aren't fun are tasks that are just boring, menial, or monotonous. These might include cleaning up project rooms, being the scribe, and running stopwatches.

On a project team, everyone has to do their share of difficult and boring tasks. If others don't pull their weight, you have to do more of the tasks that you don't want to do. If you do not want to get your hands dirty or don't do your fair share of the undesirable tasks, your relationships will suffer. You may even have a facilitator comment to your boss that you are not a team player. On the upside, if your coworkers view you positively, they will go out of their way when you need assistance.

Action to take: First of all, not everyone views tasks the same way. Some people might view bungee jumping as terrifying—they would not enjoy it at all. Others would leap at the chance to do it. Look for volunteers to do the tasks that you don't like, and offer to take one of their tasks in return.

Some tasks are no fun for anyone, such as wiping down tables and picking scraps up off the floor. Leaders can remind everyone to do his or her fair share of the work. Unfortunately, that tack doesn't tend to work for long. Volunteers are harder to find as people start getting tired and busy toward the end of the project. Plus, some tasks are just so unappealing to a team that nobody wants to do them.

A good tool for dealing with lack of volunteers is a duty roster. Put everyone's name up on a poster on the wall, and number the names in sequence. Whenever a job comes up that nobody wants to do, the team leader asks for a volunteer. If someone volunteers, his number gets crossed off, and he gets to go to the back of the line. He then gets a new number—one position higher than the largest number left on the list. (For example, if the highest number is seven, the volunteer gets an eight.) If nobody volunteers, though, the person with the next lowest number gets assigned.

Why this works: The roster is a fair way to make sure everyone is contributing to the team. It also encourages people to volunteer so they don't get stuck with a later task that they *really* don't want to do.

Problem: You have a few people on the team that just won't speak up. (One of those people might even be you!)

How this affects you: Teams work best when everyone participates. People who don't participate in the discussion don't get to have a say in the solution. Not having control in your job reduces your satisfaction. This issue can also damage relationships. Those that feel pressured to speak resent those that are doing the pressuring. Those that don't mind speaking in public might think it is unfair they have to carry the whole burden of the project.

Action to take: Keep an open mind about why people don't speak up on a team. Some may just be shy. They may think that it won't matter what they say. They could just be scared of public speaking, or they could be worried about their idea getting rejected. They might even be angry or upset about something completely outside of work.

Be careful not to jump to a negative conclusion. Don't assume another person has nothing to contribute. Don't think the person has a bad attitude. Also, remember—not speaking doesn't mean a person is not paying attention. The bottom line is that your perception might not match what is really going on.

If you are the one that doesn't want to speak up, what are your concerns? Perhaps you think that the team will laugh at your idea or that your boss will think you are not very smart. Would you be willing to try to speak, just once? Maybe things will go far better than you fear. If you just cannot bring yourself to speak, you do have other options.

Could you approach the team leader during a break and give her some ideas, one on one? Could you use the more outspoken person next to you for support? Could you feed her notes with your ideas on them? That way, she can bring up your ideas for you. You won't get credit for them, but at least you might get some control in the outcome of the project. Could you make a game of speaking up? Set a target to make three comments before lunch. Sometimes just having a goal can inspire you to take action.

If you notice someone else who isn't thrilled about public speaking, try to be supportive. Is someone dominating the conversation, making it hard for shy members to take part? Is the quiet person from another part of the factory (or office) and therefore out of place with a team that knows each other really well? Is the quiet one worried about the growing stack of work on her desk? If you understand the reason for the silence, you might be better able to help with a solution.

A good team leader can often help shy people participate. If your team leader is inexperienced, help him out by offering creative ideas. Suggest brainstorming as a written exercise so everyone can participate.

You can even offer some assistance on your own. Watch for specific body language to see if someone *wants* to contribute but can't quite seem to work up the nerve. Typical signs are shaking heads, crossed arms, fidgeting, or furrowed brows. If you see these signals, ask the person directly for comments. Don't push hard, though—that might reinforce discomfort. Sometimes a little nudge is all it takes to get the person to participate.

Why this works: If you are uncomfortable at the thought of speaking up, ask yourself one question: "Is the consequence of not speaking up to present my idea worse than worrying about speaking up in public?"

When teams help each other out on a personal level, the group will perform better. Job satisfaction tends to rise for everyone involved. One bonus—if you get a reputation as someone who goes out of his way to help others, you'll see big dividends down the road. Don't try to fake concern, though. People always end up seeing through those who are not genuine.

Problem: You are frustrated and worry that you might say something that you will regret.

How this affects you: You know how quickly emotions can take hold and affect your decisions. It is easy to get worked up when you are upset. If this results in an inappropriate comment, you might end up paying for it later.

Action to take: Take a deep breath and count to ten.

Why this works: Remember that the situation is temporary but your relationships at work are long lasting. Sometimes a "time-out" can prevent you from saying or doing something that will be impossible to take back. This lets you mentally regroup and decide if the immediate release of an outburst is worth the long-term cost.

Strategies: Performing on project teams

Problem: You can't seem to get people to address your concerns in meetings.

How this affects you: You have some great ideas that you want to bring up during meetings, but you can't seem to get anyone to discuss the topic.

Action to take: Don't fight the agenda in meetings. It causes disruption and wastes time. Instead, talk to the meeting organizer in advance and get your issue added to the agenda.

Why this works: A lot of people think that meetings waste their time. As a result, good meeting leaders will try to set an agenda and keep on topic. There normally just isn't enough time to adequately address new issues that come up during a meeting. If your concern gets added to the agenda beforehand, you get time allocated to discuss your issue, plus participants come to the meeting prepared to discuss your topic.

Problem: Other people seem to have more of their ideas put into action than you do.

How this affects you: You suddenly notice that many of your coworkers' ideas have been put in place, but very few of yours have.

Action to take: Do you know what the biggest factor is in getting an idea implemented? Let's look at this story for an answer. Two sisters were both down on their luck, and they decided that the lottery was their only way out. Every week they watched the drawing, and every week no numbers matched. Finally, one night, they saw their numbers drawn. They jumped up and down and screamed in excitement. When they finally settled down, one sister said to the other, "We finally won. Go get the ticket!" "Ticket? I thought you bought it!" the other sister exclaimed.

Without a ticket, you can't win a prize. Without submitting ideas—lots of them—you probably won't have any implemented.

Keep a notebook handy. When you have an idea, write it down. Don't filter your ideas, either. Some may seem off the wall, but they just might work out.

Why this works: At each review process, fewer and fewer ideas make it through. The more you submit, though, the better your chance is of having one used.

The catch is you have to get used to having lots of ideas tossed into the trash heap. But, then, the first time you walk past a work area where *your* idea has been put into place, you'll realize submitting so many ideas was worth the effort.

Problem: Lots of projects are happening, but things are staying the same.

How this affects you: You spend a lot of time doing projects and working on continuous improvement, but it seems like the process is the same as always. You think it is all a waste of time and energy.

Action to take: When you work on a project, ask yourself what is different about the new process. Try to find some distinctions between the new and the old. If you have trouble finding differences, the team may actually be repackaging the same old stuff. Pay attention to what project team members from outside your work area have to say. They are less vested in keeping the status quo, so they are quicker to identify if the project is just the same old process in a shiny new wrapper. Be especially careful of this in the office environment, where similarities and differences in old and new methods are less obvious and more difficult to observe.

Why this works: Improvement does not happen without change. Sometimes, it is hard for the team to let go of the old ways of doing things. Outsiders will have a more objective view. Making sure you include a "before and after" reality check lets you have more say in the outcome. Why? Managers are driven by results. If they don't see a return on the time and money they invest in a project you are going to have little (or no!) say the next time around.

Projects are expensive. Apart from the real expenses that are incurred (overtime when people have to catch up on work, or the supplies and equipment that your team bought), there is also an **opportunity cost.** This is the cost of what your company gave up to complete the project. What project did the engineer on the team have to table to participate in the *kaizen?* Did a software project get delayed so a programmer could be on the team? Projects have tremendously high costs to them.

Also, consider this. If a project uses up resources, but doesn't deliver an improvement, the original need for the project hasn't gone away. A manager will have to use up precious resources, *again,* on another project for the same purpose. Only, the next time a manager assigns people to a project, he is likely going to tell them exactly what to change. In most cases, the employees won't like that method nearly as much as if they had made a real change in the first place.

Problem: Your boss won't give you the money you need to buy something for a project.

How this affects you: You are actively participating in Lean and you want to get a project done. You see the perfect tool in a catalog. When your boss won't authorize a purchase order, you believe you are getting mixed messages and your frustration rises.

Action to take: The Lean term **"catalog engineer"** describes a person who shops for answers instead of trying to create original solutions. Generic products only solve generic problems. The tool's inventor faced a different situation than you do now, so an expensive tool might only partly solve your problem.

Spend some time thinking about your specific issue. Then, try to come up with some solutions that might cost less or have more bang for the buck than something available in a catalog. As a rule of thumb, find at least one alternate idea for any off-the-shelf solution. Then, try that idea before going to your boss and asking for money. After all, your boss has a keen eye on the budget, so save yourself some time and aggravation and avoid the inclination to reach for the company's wallet first. Get into the habit of trying to create a solution on your own before reaching for a catalog.

Why this works: How does this increase your satisfaction? It helps you avoid conflict with your manager, who most likely has a pretty tight grip on the purse strings. If you show that you have tried other options first, you will be more likely to get what you need without an argument. Being told "No" takes its toll on people. This is a way to get more "Yes" answers.

It will also save you some frustration later when a catalog solution does not work perfectly. Doing a project right the first time can keep you from having to tackle it again later.

Strategies: Dealing with projects in your area

Problem: Your work area is being kaizened, *but you are not on the team.*

How this affects you: You want to have a say in your future. You might find it hard not to have a voice as you watch a team making changes that will greatly affect one of your processes. Plus, when you are not selected, you might feel slighted, or worried about how your boss views your abilities.

Action to take: Not being on the team does not mean you won't have a chance to give input. Many teams place posters in the area where they are making improvements and ask employees who work there to list ideas and problems. If you don't see such a poster, ask your boss when—not if—it is going to be put up.

In an effort to collect information, the team may also come around early in the project to do interviews with your work group. Use this opportunity to give real, fact-based information on the process. By the way, don't wait until they come by to ponder what you want to say. Be prepared. Read the team charter for the project in advance, and make a list of notes. The more interest you show, and the better questions you ask, the more the team will keep you in the loop as they discuss changes.

Finally, ask *when* the team will be meeting with your work group to give project updates. If they have no plans to do so, talk to your boss. You and your coworkers need to know what is going on in a timely manner.

After offering ideas, follow up with the *kaizen* team. It can be discouraging to give input and then not have it used, but sometimes, an idea gets honestly overlooked. It is also possible the team didn't really understand what you meant. Questions about progress and gentle reminders can help make sure your ideas are recognized, understood, and addressed.

Why this works: When you show interest and create opportunities to give feedback, you put project teams on notice that you want to be included in decisions. They will generally comply because they recognize that your support greatly increases their odds of success.

Problem: You are an independent thinker and don't like being told how to do your job.

How this affects you: You don't want to be forced to do a *kaizen* in your area.

Action to take: If you don't want project teams descending on your area, the best way to keep them away is with healthy doses of daily improvement. Do little projects every day, and you will see the gains accumulate. If your team's metrics show constant gains, there will be no urgent need for a *kaizen*. You will probably need to nudge your coworkers to help out—one person probably won't be able to make significant changes on her own.

Why this works: If your team shows consistent progress without needing a formal team, managers will not be inclined to expend time or money on a *kaizen*. In fact, they will be downright happy to see progress that lets them use their limited resources elsewhere. The benefit for you? Changes are at a reasonable pace, and they are completely controlled by people who work in the area.

Remember though, *kaizens* have a time and place, even if you are hitting all your targets. At some point, your team will identify a big opportunity or a pending problem that will need more work and a bigger solution than what small improvement efforts can deliver. Your experience with making regular improvements, though, will make the big project a snap.

Strategies: Coping with *kaizens*

Problem: The report out is coming up, and you are not looking forward to speaking in front of a crowd.

How this affects you: Sweaty palms. Tightness in your chest. Shallow breathing. Nausea. Fear that you will say the wrong thing.

Action to take: A good team leader will try to be prepared well in advance and do a rehearsal, so team members are more comfortable with the material. Rushing to the report out with slides hot off the press only adds to the anxiety. Offer help to your team leader, or shield her from distractions while she is getting the presentation ready.

Many managers and facilitators like to get every team member to speak at report outs. If you have a real problem with this, let the team leader know *in advance.* You may be able to minimize the amount of time you have to speak—maybe you could just introduce the team. An alternative is to run the computer or to flip slides.

Of course, those suggestions assume that you don't want to develop your public speaking skills. Report outs provide good practice, since they are feel-good events. People are there to congratulate you on your hard work, not to criticize your performance, so the atmosphere is relaxed and upbeat.

Why this works: Nobody, to my knowledge, has ever died as a result of presenting facts during a *kaizen* report out, but many have been left dripping in sweat. As you are aware, public speaking ranks right up there as one of the biggest fears people have. Planning ahead helps avoid the stress that precedes the presentation. Some people actually start worrying about it in the middle of the week. Take charge and keep the stress from sapping your satisfaction.

Problem: It's 2:00 a.m. and you are still at work on the kaizen.

How this affects you: When you signed up for the team, you didn't know there would be so many late nights.

Action to take: Make sure you clearly understand expectations when you volunteer or are recruited for a project. The project's hours might interfere with classes, child care, or other personal commitments you have. Many people unexpectedly find themselves feeling guilty about leaving a team when other members are staying late.

You have a few choices. The most obvious one is to try to find projects that fit your schedule. If this can't be done, a second option is to let people on the team know *beforehand* that you will be unavailable at a certain time. Most people will respect this and respond better to it if they know about it upfront. Don't surprise your teammates by walking out the door as they are placing dinner orders and preparing for the long night ahead. A third option is to make alternate arrangements for your personal commitments. Even if you can't completely clear your calendar, sticking around late for one or two nights shows the team that you are making an effort.

You could even go the extra mile and volunteer for the project tasks that nobody else wants to do. That may help you earn back any "points" you may have lost by your early departure.

One important point: no matter what you do, when you are on the project, make sure you are very productive. If you spend time horsing around during the day and leave early as well, expect your reputation to get tarnished.

Why this works: Kaizens tend to burn the midnight oil, especially in the early stages of a Lean implementation. Leaders have invested a lot of resources into the project and want to show big gains. That being said, everyone has commitments outside of work that can't be changed—even managers. Teams usually will make allowances, especially if you put out a strong effort while you are present.

Problem: You pay a price for kaizens.

How this affects you: You bear a cost for projects, even if you are not on them. If you work on a shop floor, in all likelihood, the line will shut down for at least part of the project. This might mean doing some overtime to build up finished products in advance. If you are in an office, you might find that you have to work some long hours before the project even begins in preparation for being short staffed. Offices usually suffer more than shop floors, since many offices don't have very sophisticated backup plans (unless you help create one!). The usual arrangement is to have one person cover for another. That backup basically has to do her own work as well as all of the work of the employee on the project. The covering employee can seldom keep up with both jobs, so *both* the project team member and the backup will usually accumulate massive piles of work during the project week.

Action to take: What can you do? The name of the game is to share the pain. Over time, you will end up being on both sides of this dilemma. Sometimes you will be on a project team and won't be able to do your work. Sometimes you will be covering for other employees when they join project teams. How you treat others will have a lot to do with how they eventually treat you. If you develop a reputation as a team player, your coworkers will go out of their way to help you. That means you have to go out of your way for them.

You can also help your manager develop backup plans for the office. The best strategy involves splitting one person's workload among *several* people, rather than having the full burden given to just one person. That way, pieces of the pie are smaller and more manageable.

An account manager may have twenty customers. Instead of one backup person handling all twenty, four backup people would each cover five customer accounts. Of course, this can be complicated to set up and will take some coordination and training. But the good news is that the burden of getting this in place is significantly lighter than *not* creating a systematic and coordinated plan.

Why this works: Creating a backup plan works because in a continuous improvement environment, things routinely happen to pull people away from their "regular" jobs. When a solid plan is in place, the shift between project mode—or vacation mode, or sick-day mode—and full production mode becomes more seamless. This results in better processes, lower frustration, a more manageable workload, and more satisfaction for you.

Problem: You think you are getting the short end of the stick when it comes to improvements.

How this affects you: You seem to get extra work whenever someone else goes off to do an improvement project.

Action to take: You might find that you will be asked to do tasks that cost you, but benefit other people. Maybe you are asked to scan your documents instead of just filing them away. It might add a few minutes of work for each of your files—not too much fun for you, but it might save a lot of time for the departments that have to manage those files later on.

No manager will give up those gains for the company, even if it means more work for you. The goal for you should be to come up with a plan to manage those extra tasks.

First, gather data about your workload. Figure out what it is you do and how long it takes. If you already have some form of standardization in place, this step is easy. All you will have to do is confirm the numbers.

Second, do some math. Let's say you add three minutes per file to your workload, but the other department saves ten minutes. If your company processes twenty files daily, someone is gaining more than three hours a day (ten minutes per file times twenty files equals three hours and twenty minutes) because of your extra work—it just isn't you. The choice seems like a no-brainer to a leader looking at the numbers. All this continuous improvement has added an hour of work to your day. Figure out exactly how far this extra work will put you in the hole.

Third, talk to your boss, present the numbers and create a plan to manage the extra work. "Would you like me to scan the documents or do the follow up on the Smith account?" Let her help you prioritize your work.

You both should also be looking for solutions. Perhaps one of your tasks can be given to the department that is benefiting from your work. You might also do a *kaizen* or some daily improvement with your own team to come up with other options to manage the extra work.

Why this works: It is all about the numbers. Your boss tends to focus on the big picture, but she also has to be alerted to something that significantly impacts production in her area. Once she is aware of the problem, you can work together to solve it.

CHAPTER 12

The beginning . . .

MOST BOOKS FINISH WITH A CONCLUSION. This one is a little different. Nothing is probably ending. None of the events that led you to start reading it have gone away. Nothing in your life is different, just because you read a book . . . at least not yet.

My hope is that you don't view these last few paragraphs as the last chapter in this book. I want you to look at them as the beginning of a new chapter in your life, one that you start with optimism and a sense of power. I want you to understand that choosing to think about Lean in a different way is the first step to making your job, and your life, better.

Isn't that what really matters, anyway? Finding satisfaction in your job and in your life. As your career winds down, and you look back on your life and reflect, you will undoubtedly be passing judgment about the countless hours you spent working. Well, the hours weren't exactly countless, there will be 92,120 of them, give or take, if you started working when you got out of high school and retire at sixty-five. And that's without overtime. If you frequently work late, you will probably spend over a hundred thousand hours at work over the course of your career.

So, what could you do in a hundred thousand hours? You could watch about thirty-two thousand pro football games or play somewhere around twenty-two thousand rounds of golf. You could listen to about a million and a half songs on the radio, or drive about six million miles on the highway. You could get over twelve thousand good nights of sleep. You could play a lot of catch with your kids, or take a lot of family vacations, or read a lot of bedtime stories.

You could learn a new language, get a degree, or practice playing your guitar. You could plant an award-winning garden. Or even hike the Appalachian Trail—close to seventy times!

The point is that your time is valuable, not only because you can trade it for a paycheck, but also because of all the opportunities every moment of your life holds. When you go to work each day, you are missing out on those opportunities. The crucial question you should ask yourself is whether you think you are making a fair trade. What you give up to go to work seems like a bigger loss when you are not satisfied with your job.

Of course, even if the NFL® did play anywhere near that many games in the course of your career (they won't), you'd still have to buy the tickets. You'd have to spend the money to buy hundreds of thousands of gallons of gas to log six million miles. And sleep doesn't come easy if you can't afford to keep a roof over your head.

Face it. Work is a necessity. Having a painful job is not.

It just starts with a single choice by you. If you decide to commit yourself to making the most of Lean and doing the best job you can do, job satisfaction becomes much less elusive.

Do you believe you have it in your power to make Lean an opportunity for yourself?

Your answer to that question should be a resounding, "Yes!" You *do* have the ability to make Lean a positive experience. Hopefully, you can benefit from my experience and the knowledge of those that have gone down this path before you.

Before I say farewell, I want to share one last thing—my personal view of Lean. Some look at Lean as a management philosophy. Others think of it as a business system or production system. I see Lean differently. I think of it as a commitment to opportunity. Lean opens up possibilities that simply do not exist in other corporate cultures. It creates the potential to use your talents in new ways—ways that not only benefit the company, but that also help *you* as an individual.

The possibilities in a Lean organization are endless. That is because jobs no longer restrict you. The only thing that really holds you back is your *belief* that you are limited. Lean gives you a blank canvas where you can attempt new things; where you can try solving the problems that have seemed permanent until now; where you can strive to make your job more fun. Lack of imagination becomes the only restraint that holds you back.

To me, that's really what this book is all about. It is intended to encourage you not to settle for chronic stress and frustration—simply because you can't figure out how to make Lean work for you. If you let it, Lean can decrease your satisfaction. But, guess what? You don't *have* to let it! Every choice you make alters your path in life just a little bit. When you make those decisions wisely, you will be choosing your own destination instead of just going along for the ride.

Take some time to decide what your goals are. Most people tolerate long-standing difficulties at work simply because they never stop to think what they really want out of their job. Once you figure out what you value and what will make you more satisfied, you can use this book to help you get it. And when that happens, the enjoyment you find at work will spill over to the rest of your life.

Best wishes on your Lean journey!

Jeff Hajek
WhaddayaMean@Velaction.com

Additional Resources

Do you want **FREE** information that will make your job easier and more rewarding in a Lean environment?

Visit www.Velaction.com and download *The Continuous Improvement Companion*—at no charge!* The '*Companion*' is a practical, easy to read, and incredibly helpful desktop reference that is chock full of Lean terms, explanations, and useful strategies for managers and frontline employees.

It is the perfect Lean guide ***that you can individualize***—print the whole manual, or search the extensive list of topics and choose only those that suit your current interests and needs. Obtain just the information that you need, exactly when you need it. All this value and more—without any cost to you. Go to www.Velaction.com and get your complimentary copy today!

**Content, availability, and price are subject to change without notice.*

Bibliography

Amble, Brian. *Job Satisfaction Keeps Falling.* February 26, 2007. www.management-issues.com.

American Institute of Stress, The. *Job Stress.* http://www.stress.org/job.htm?AIS=647dd2c191206670e01b483e60f8d682 (accessed 2008).

Avildsen, John G., director *The Karate Kid.* 1984.

Blanchard, David. "Census of Manufacturers—What's Working for U. S. Manufacturers." *Industry Week,* October 1, 2006.

Blanchard, David. "Census of U. S. Manufacturers—Lean Green and Low Cost." *Industry Week,* October 1, 2007.

Centre for European Labour Market Research. "Job satisfaction is the most critical factor in life satisfaction." *RxPG News.* July 4, 2006.

Colvin, Geoff. *The 100 Best Companies to Work for 2006.* January 11, 2006. www.money.cnn.com.

Corporate Leadership Council. "Linking Employee Satisfaction with Productivity, Performance, and Customer Satisfaction." 2003.

Covey, Stephen R. *The 7 Habits of Highly Effective People.* New York: Simon & Schuster, Inc., 1989.

Davis, Mark M., Nicholas J. Aquilano, and Richard B. Chase. *Fundamentals of Operations Management.* Boston: The McGraw-Hill Companies, 1999.

DeNoon, Daniel J. "Fear of Public Speaking Hardwired." *WebMD.* April 20, 2006. http://www.webmd.com/anxiety-panic/guide/20061101/fear-public-speaking.

Edmans, Alex. "Does the Stock Market Fully Value Intangibles? Employee Satisfaction and Stock Prices." 2008.

Eli Whitney Museum & Workshop, The. "Eli Whitney." eliwhitney.org. http://www.eliwhitney.org/factory.htm (accessed 2008).

Ferriss, Timothy. "The 4-Hour Workweek. Escape 9-5, Live Anywhere, and Join the New Rich." 308. New York: Crown Publishing Group, 2007.

Goenner, Cullen F., PhD. "Investing in Fortune's 100 Best Companies to Work for in America." *Journal of Economics,* 2008.

Job Satisfaction. www.wikipedia.org.

Kotler, Philip. *Marketing Management.* The Millenium Edition. Upper Saddle River, New Jersey: Prentice Hall, 2000.

Marlin Company, The. *2001 Attitudes in the American Workplace VII.* The Marlin Company, 2001.

Marshall, Penny, director *A League of Their Own.* 1992.

McKinsey & Company. "Lean Retailing: Achieving Breakthroughs in Store Profitability." *McKinsey & Company.* http://www.mckinsey.com/practices/retail/knowledge/articles/Leanretailingstoreprofitability.pdf (accessed 2008).

Moore, Steven, and Phil Kerpen. "Historically, Gasoline Prices Are Not Expensive." cato.org. September 6, 2003.

National Institute on Drug Abuse. *Stress and Substance Abuse: A Special Report.* September 12, 2005. http://www.drugabuse.gov/stressanddrugabuse.html (accessed November 16, 2008).

Ohno, Taiichi. *Toyota Production System: Beyond Large-Scale Production.* New York: Productivity Press, 1988.

Sahadi, Jeanne. "You may be paid more (or less) than you think." CNNMoney.com. March 29, 2006.

Salary.com. *Mind the Job Satisfaction Gap: HR Professionals Underestimate Intensity of Employee Job Searches and Employees Fall Victim to "Grass is Greener" Syndrome.* February 22, 2007.

Schwartz, John. "Always on the Job, Employees Pay With Health." *The New York Times,* September 4, 2004.

Scott, Elizabeth. *Stress and Weight Gain: How Stress Can Affect Your Weight.* October 3, 2007. http://stress.about.com/od/stresshealth/a/weightgain.htm.

Segala, Nancy L. "Career of Your Dreams, Career of Your Genes." *Psychology Today.* Sep/Oct 1999. http://www.psychologytoday.com/articles/index.php?term=19990901-000038&page=1.

Smith, M. K. "Bruce W. Tuckman—forming, storming, norming and performing in groups." infed.org. 2005. http://www.infed.org/thinkers/tuckman.htm.

Syptak, J. Michael, David W. Marsland, and Deborah Ulmer. "Job Satisfaction: Putting Theory Into Practice." *American Academy of Family Practices.* October 1999. http://www.aafp.org/fpm/991000fm/26.html.

Tapping, Don, and Anne Dunn. *Lean Office Demystified.* Chelsea: MCS Media, Inc., 2006.

Yang, Sarah. *Americans spend more energy and time watching TV than on exercise, finds new study.* March 10, 2004.

Index